Gods and mortals :
808.819 GOD   34267001004741

D1241308

808.819
GOD

BENBROOK PUBLIC LIBRARY

GODS AND MORTALS

GODS
AND
MORTALS

Modern Poems on Classical Myths

EDITED BY

Nina Kossman

OXFORD
UNIVERSITY PRESS
2001

OXFORD
UNIVERSITY PRESS

Oxford New York
Athens Auckland Bangkok Bogotá
Buenos Aires Calcutta Cape Town Chennai Dar es Salaam
Delhi Florence Hong Kong Istanbul Karachi
Kuala Lumpur Madrid Melbourne
Mexico City Mumbai Nairobi Paris São Paolo Shanghai Singapore
Taipei Tokyo Toronto Warsaw
and associated companies in
Berlin Ibadan

Copyright © 2001 by Nina Kossman

Published by Oxford University Press, Inc.
198 Madison Avenue, New York, New York 10016

Oxford is a registered trademark of Oxford University Press

All rights reserved. No part of this publication may be reproduced,
stored in a retrieval system, or transmitted, in any form or by any means,
electronic, mechanical, photocopying, recording, or otherwise,
without the prior permission of Oxford University Press.

Library of Congress Cataloging-in-Publication Data
Gods and mortals: modern poems on classical myths/
[compiled and edited by] Nina Kossman. p. cm.
Includes bibliographical references and index.
ISBN 0-19-513341-2
1. Mythology—Poetry. I. Kossman, Nina, 1959–
PN6110.M8 G63 2000
808.81'915   00-021115

1 3 5 7 9 8 6 4 2

Printed in the United States of America
on acid-free paper

Among the Gods ■ *Stanley Kunitz*

Within the grated dungeon of the eye
The old gods, shaggy with gray lichen, sit
Like fragment of the antique masonry
Of heaven, a patient thunder in their stare.

Huge blocks of language, all my quarried love,
They justify, and not in random poems,
But shapes of things interior to Time,
Hewn out of chaos when the Pure was plain.

Sister, my bride, who were both cloud and bird
When Zeus came down in a shower of sexual gold,
Listen! we make a world! I hear the sound
Of matter pouring through eternal forms.

The Return ■ *Ezra Pound*

See, they return; ah, see the tentative
Movements, and the slow feet,
The trouble in the pace and the uncertain
Wavering!

See, they return, one and by one,
With fear, as half-awakened;
As if snow should hesitate
And murmur in the wind,
        and half turn back;
These were the "Wing'd-with-Awe,"
      Inviolable,

Gods of the wingèd shoe!
With them the silver hounds
      sniffing the trace of air!

Haie! Haie!
   These were the swift to harry;
These the keen-scented;
These were the souls of blood.

Slow on the leash,
      pallid the leash-men!

CONTENTS

DEMETER
25

APOLLO
35

APHRODITE
45

THE WAY
TO THE UNDERWORLD
85

LOVERS
95

TRANSFORMATIONS
131

TRESPASSERS
141

THE CONDEMNED
163

HEROES
169

CRETE
183

THEBES
193

TROY
203

AFTER TROY
237

THE WANDERINGS
& THE HOMECOMING
OF ODYSSEUS
253

INTRODUCTION

The aim of this anthology is to bring together poems that illuminate Greek myths in the light of modern sensibility, in order to demonstrate the durability of classical mythology and the variety of ways in which it is handled by modern poets. Besides presenting a new picture of Greek myths, the collection offers a wide-ranging catalog of twentieth-century poets. Some of the works are by internationally celebrated poets such as Akhmatova, Auden, Cavafy, Lawrence, Mandelshtam, Rilke, Seferis, Valéry, Yeats, and Walcott, while some are by their lesser-known contemporaries. A few of the poets, such as Hans Magnus Enzenberger, Max Jacob, and Marina Tsvetaeva, are recognized in their own countries although they remain relatively unknown to English-speaking audiences.

The basis for the selection was that a poem be a provocative or unusual treatment of a particular myth. With a few exceptions, I omitted poems that referred to a mythological theme in passing, or poems that referred to mythology in general rather than to a particular myth or mythological character.

The structure of the book is thematic: poems are grouped by particular myths. Although this anthology is not meant to serve as an exhaustive sourcebook on Greek mythology, it does cover a wide spectrum of myths. Some of these stories have inspired more and better poems than others. Among myths whose central characters are mortals, the love-in-death story of Orpheus and Eurydice is by far the most popular, probably as a result of the poets' easy identification with the mythological poet-singer. Among the stories about the Olympians, the ones most popular with modern poets concern rape: the rape of Leda by Zeus, of Persephone by Hades, and Apollo's attempt on Daphne.

I have grouped the Hades and Persephone poems under Demeter, because I see Demeter and her daughter as protagonists of the myth; Hades, the god of the underworld, figures in modern poetry mostly as the abductor of Persephone.

In placing Dionysus among the Olympians, I follow the opinion of some authorities who considered him the youngest of the Olympians, and I part ways with Homer, who barred him from Olympus. A popular notion of Olympus presupposes the presence of the god of wine.

The section "Heroes" covers the major heroes *before* the Trojan War (Perseus, Heracles, Jason). Thus, Achilles and Hector, though certainly heroes, are grouped under "Troy," since it was in the Trojan War that they showed their heroic natures. Theseus is grouped with the characters of the Cretan legends, and not with other heroes, because modern poetry is more concerned with Theseus's Cretan adventure than anything else.

Many Greek myths revolve around love, so I chose to limit the "Lovers" section to those modern poems concerned with characters whose love transcended death in some way: Orpheus who descended into the kingdom of death for the reunion with his beloved; Baucis and Philemon, whose one wish was to be reunited in death; and Alcestis, who chose to die for her husband. Poems based on myths of rape and seduction—for example, the amorous adventures of Zeus or Apollo—are excluded from the "Lovers" section.

Similarly, transformations are so abundant in Greek mythology that the section so entitled contains only those myths where a permanent metamorphosis follows from a mythological character's identity. Narcissus's permanent transformation into a flower is a consequence of his self-love; the metamorphosis of Galatea into a living woman follows from Pygmalion's love for his art; Philomela's transformation into a swallow—a bird that does not sing—is emblematic of her muteness, the result of Tereus's crime. (According to another version of the myth, Philomela was transformed into a nightingale, a bird whose song is thought to express sadness and longing.) However, Zeus's self-transformations into a bull or a swan are temporary; they do not define him.

"Trespassers" covers characters who offend the gods, while "The Condemned" are those who commit crimes by human definition, such as murder or rape. Phaethon, Niobe, Icarus, Marsyas, and Psyche poems are grouped under "Trespassers," and Sisyphus and Tantalus poems under "The Condemned."

* * *

Among many responses to the same myth I found only a few that seem to echo each other, along lines not predetermined by the original story. Here's a striking example. Marina Tsvetaeva, H.D., and Margaret Atwood, three of the women poets in the predominantly male section on Orpheus and Eurydice, speak as Eurydice, reluctant to follow her lover out of the underworld; independently of each other, these three poets make the usually silent female protagonist of the myth express her rejection of the togetherness offered by the lover.

> "... I need the peace
> Of forgetfulness ... For in this shadowy house
> You, living, are a shadow, while I, dead,
> Am real ... What can I say to you except
> "Forget this and leave!""
> (Tsvetaeva)

> "... if you had let me wait
> I had grown from listlessness
> into peace,
> if you had let me rest with the dead,
> I had forgot you
> and the past."
> (H.D.)

> "You would rather have gone on feeling nothing,
> emptiness and silence; this stagnant peace

of the deepest sea, which is easier
than the noise and flesh of the surface."
(ATWOOD)

(Perhaps through her descent into the underworld Eurydice gained awareness of her own unconscious depths. The underworld of Greek myth may be seen as the unconscious itself, the repository of everything not allowed into Apollo's solar domain, daylight consciousness.)

But such similarity in interpretation is rare. More often, poems on the same subject look at it from altogether different angles. "Leda" by D.H. Lawrence and "Leda" by Lucille Clifton provide poignant examples of contrasting attitudes. Clifton's Leda asks Zeus to appear as a man ("You want what a man wants, / next time come as a man / or don't come"), while Lawrence's Leda desires him as the bird, not as the man: "Come not with kisses / not with caresses / of hands and lips and murmurings; / come with a hiss of wings / and sea-touch tip of a beak ..."

There is no shortage of poems that are mere retellings of the myths; of these I chose only the ones that provide an unexpected twist to a familiar story. For example, in Yunna Morits's retelling of the Prometheus myth ("Prometheus"), the eagle that tortures Prometheus is "wound up, like a gramophone box," and although it is "like a real thing," the image belongs to a later, industrial age. In Morits's poem, actually in all Prometheus poems herein, Prometheus exists in a timeless zone which combines the ancients' world and our own, a case in point of a myth that is never dead or "old" as long as there are poets among us who revitalize the old story by entering the mythical dimension and reporting to us from the other side of the myth, or of their own psyche.

The venerable tradition of donning a Greek mask is often used by poets in order to speak of things they would have found difficult to approach otherwise. H.D. is one such poet. She holds the mask so close that at times it is hard to distinguish her own features behind it; the poet becomes the mask. Conversely, the Russian poet Marina Tsvetaeva, a contemporary of H.D., remains resolutely herself, whether she is speaking as Eurydice or the sibyl. Her mythological masks are transparent. By endowing the personae with her own intensity, Tsvetaeva gives us the most impassioned Greek heroines in modern poetry.

Robert Graves, a classicist par excellence, is another poet who makes frequent use of the Greek mask to speak of his own feelings. In such poems, the trappings of the myth become the specifics of his own life. In "Prometheus" the bird that tortures him is jealousy, and the rock on which Prometheus tosses is the poet's own bed. His mask is not as transparent as Tsvetaeva's, yet we are still able to see the man behind it.

Other poets observe the mythic protagonists rather than fuse with them. A case in point is the Welsh poet Barbara Bentley: in "Living Next to Leda" she becomes an eyewitness to the crucial events in Leda's life. Ironically, it is the Greek poet Constantine P. Cavafy who puts the most distance between himself and his mythic protagonists. Cavafy is a whimsical historian of his cultural past, a wise interpreter of the mythological scene from which he himself is removed. The bird's-eye view of the protagonists' emotional extremes offered by Cavafy can also be found in the work of Yannis Ritsos and George Seferis, the other two modern Greeks poets in the anthology. But while Cavafy's speaker is outside the events of the myth, the speaker of Seferis's poems is often present in the mythological sets the poet builds—as Orestes or one of the argonauts. Seferis, like Graves, turns a close-up into a long view, the archaic into the modern, the story into the symbol.

Shifts in perspective make most poems in this anthology resonate far beyond their subject matter. The subject matter—the myths—concerns us more than we may be ready to admit, going about our lives on the brink of the twenty-first century. If we think we now know the answers, it is because the questions were first posed in antiquity. If we now see far, it is because we stand on the shoulders of tradition. Myths belong to us as much or as little as the imagery of our own unconscious: the deeper we dig into our psyches the more likely we are to stumble upon an ancient myth. Our ancestors are us or we are our ancestors: the texture of our bones is passed on, along with the texture of our dreams. And perhaps it is because the myths echo the structure of our unconscious that every new generation of poets finds them an inexhaustible source of inspiration and self-recognition. It is my hope that this book will serve as yet another link between tradition in the classical sense and that shelter which the ancient gods never left: our unconscious.

NINA KOSSMAN

TITANS

Atlas
Prometheus

Atlas

By harsh necessity, Atlas supports the broad sky
on his head and unwearying arms,
at the earth's limits, near the clear-voiced Hesperides,
for this is the doom decreed for him by Zeus the counselor.
—HESIOD, THEOGONY (TR. BY A.N. ATHANASSAKIS)

atlas ■ Lucille Clifton

i am used to the heft of it
sitting against my rib,
used to the ridges of forest,
used to the way my thumb
slips into the sea as i pull
it tight. something is sweet
in the thick odor of flesh
burning and sweating and bearing young.
i have learned to carry it
the way a poor man learns
to carry everything.

Atlas on Grass ■ Vernon Watkins

Atlas on grass, I hold the moving year.
I pull the compass to a point unguessed.
Vast midnight flies to morning in the breast,
All moves to movement, moves and makes a sphere.
Rough Winter loosens leaves long-veined with fear,
Then the seed moves to its unsleeping rest.
Faith springs where beads of longing lie confessed.
Time lost is found; the salmon leaps the weir.
Death stops the mouths of graves, is coverer
Shrouding and hiding what the pulse reveals,
But he, too, moves to his Deliverer;
Judgment will never stop the dancer's heels.
What's gone forever is forever here,
And men are raised by what a myth conceals.

Prometheus

*Prometheus moulded men out of water and earth and gave them also fire, which,
unknown to Zeus, he had hidden in a stalk of fennel. But when Zeus learned of it, he
ordered Hephaestus to nail his body to Mount Caucasus, which is a Scythian mountain.
On it Prometheus was nailed and kept bound for many years. Every day an eagle
swooped on him and devoured the lobes of his liver, which grew by night. That was the
penalty that Prometheus paid for the theft of fire....*
—APOLLODORUS, THE LIBRARY, I.vii (TR. BY J. G. FRAZER)

Prometheus ■ Yunna Morits

Like a cat, the eagle on the roof of the world
is ruffled by wind blowing from the Caucasus.
With both eyes the punished titan is watching
beastly Zeus. This is what the cover of insomnia
must look like. The silver spoon of the moon
stirs the juices of retelling.

Zeus's chest sags from passions,
and his fierce torso is strained—
where people like to gather,
he, like a machine, discharges thunder.
The titan holds onto his liver. He reels,
and the peak of Caucasus sways under him.

The eagle, the issue of Echidna and Typhon
and the brother of Chimera with a goat's head,
is wound up, like a gramophone box,
and feeds on live liver. Meanwhile,
the titan thinks: "I'll learn to take deep
breaths, to preserve my strength."

In the cellar of the valley the fruits of lemon trees
gather the light around a sleeping sheepfold.
A shepherd made of clay and water
pours a boiling broth into a shepherdess' cup.
The eagle, like a real thing, devours the titan
and splutters saliva into the powerful groin.

The titan sees neither the eagle nor his own duress;
he sees, instead, a centaur coming down a slope,
mortally wounded in his knee.
Damnation! An arrow has cut into the noble Chiron,
like an axe into a log,
and he is black with pain, like a crow,

and a luxuriant, cloudy outline of foam
accentuates the length of his body.

4

He begs for death but is immortal—
he curses fate, its bonds of immortality!
There's such pain in him, such torment!
The titan bangs the vaults of heaven—

Zeus comes out: "What do you want, thief?"
The titan dictates: "Destroy the system,
and re-assign my death to my friend,
so his departure is cloudless and sweet:
make sure the Centaur gets the tenderest of graves,
and I—the centrifuge of his deathlessness.

You understand me?" Zeus nods to him unwittingly
and leaves to do as he was bidden.
Buried by Heracles in the shade of a plane tree,
the Centaur no longer suffers pain.
The eagle torments the titan tirelessly,
eating into his liver. But this part of the story
is well known, and enough's been said.

Translated from the Russian BY NINA KOSSMAN AND ANDY NEWCOMB

Prometheus on His Crag (20) ■ Ted Hughes

Prometheus on his crag

Pondered the vulture. Was this bird
His unborn half-self, some hyena
Afterbirth, some lump of his mother?

Or was it his condemned human ballast—
His dying and his death, torn daily
From his immortality?

Or his blowtorch godhead
Puncturing those horrendous holes
In his human limits?

Was it his prophetic familiar?
The Knowledge, pebble-eyed,
Of the fates to be suffered in his image?

Was it the flapping, tattered hole—
The nothing door
Of his entry, draughting through him?

Or was it atomic law—
Was Life his transgression?
Was he the punished criminal aberration?

Was it the fire he had stolen?
Nowhere to go and now his pet,
And only him to feed on?

Or the supernatural spirit itself
That he had stolen from,
Now stealing from him the natural flesh?

Or was it the earth's enlightenment—
Was he an uninitiated infant
Mutilated towards alignment?

Or was it his anti-self—
The him-shaped vacuum
In unbeing, pulling to empty him?

Or was it, after all the Helper
Coming again to pick at the crucial knot
Of all his bonds…?

Image after image. Image after image. As the vulture

Circled

Circled.

Old Prometheus ■ Zbigniew Herbert

He writes his memoirs. He is trying to explain the place of the hero in a system of necessities, to reconcile the notions of existence and fate that contradict each other.

Fire is crackling gaily in the fireplace, in the kitchen his wife bustles about—an exalted girl who did not bear him a son, but is convinced she will pass into history anyway. Preparations for supper: the local parson is coming, and the pharmacist, now the closest friend of Prometheus.

The fire blazes up. On the wall, a stuffed eagle and a letter of gratitude from the tyrant of the Caucasus, who successfully burned down a town in revolt because of Prometheus' discovery.

Prometheus laughs quietly. Now it is the only way of expressing his disagreement with the world.

Translated from the Polish BY JOHN AND BOGDANA CARPENTER

Prometheus ■ Emery George

He fired God and plagiarized the fire,
and published all the flames in the hottest how-to
book of the season. He'd teach people to cook,
make locks and fittings, manufacture armor,
help the consumer if it cost him his game,
cordial relations with Nobodaddy Kronos

up there, and all his foothill-clinging cronies.
He'd had enough of myths. A love-starved groom
will have his bride; a people would not bide
their precious time and live like savages.
Why couldn't they even fry sausages
and eggs for breakfast? What was there left to forbid?
Then Kronos' police and their sadistic humor....
An eagle would be sent to: *de-liver* him,
unless.... It was a nerveless part of a man,
didn't they know? He relaxed with his Homer.

All that took place three thousand years ago.
He had since retired. His "Firehammer School"
prospered at first, but students graduated
to pyrotactics, murderous up-and-go.
Brilliant glass pears, soft-colored tubes at night
lit up; then, over the sea, one afternoon
in August, he felt the stars, sun, and moon
fuse and collapse. He saw a horrible light,
a giant mushroom rising, a tidal-wave-shaped
fortress. Their latest patent.... He recanted, humbled;
in a show of power, two cities were showered
with mushroom fire, and God was reinstated.

Inhabited Liver ■ Marin Sorescu

I feel the wings of the eagle
Stretch wide the lips of my liver;
I feel its talons,
I feel its iron beak,
I feel the enormity of its hunger for life,
Its thirst for flight
With me in its talons.
And I fly.

Whoever said I was chained?
   Translated from the Romanian BY ADAM J. SORKIN AND LIDIA VIANU

New Prometheus ■ Jerzy Ficowski

In the inertia of liberated gestures,
      (not even the shadows will rise)
in the silence of an unlocked scream
      (let the echo sleep in peace),
Prometheus, who no longer has eyes,
      (they didn't last to see the rust)
lies compliant, welded
      (the mountain of doubt holds him)
to the Promethean torture.

He smothers the fire unneeded by the gods
and rips out his own liver,
to die,
in accord with the myth.

Translated from the Polish BY YALA KORWIN

Prometheus ■ Robert Graves

Close bound in a familiar bed
All night I tossed, rolling my head;
Now dawn returns in vain, for still
The vulture squats on her warm hill.

I am in love as giants are
That dote upon the evening star,
And this lank bird is come to prove
The intractability of love.

Yet still, with greedy eye half shut,
Rend the raw liver from its gut:
Feed, jealousy, do not fly away—
If she who fetched you also stay.

PROMETHEUS AND PANDORA
*"…The price for the stolen fire will be a gift of evil
to charm the hearts of all men as they hug their own doom."*
—HESIOD, WORKS AND DAYS (TR. BY A.N. ATHANASSAKIS)

For Pandora, Again ■ Sidhveswar Sen

I was stunned
when you held open
that lid

The whirl of wind
twisted us around, plague-ridden
tornado—greed-grief-lament

For repressed urges, sustenance

When blood-strife-dread
human defeat

Stunned by venomous fumes
I
kept standing

In that lored penumbra—
wordless

Until, again, you
shut it close, with startled hands

That gaping, gaping mouth
of primal horror

By then, they had turned everything
topsy-turvy

Only under the shut lid
fallen—hope

Man staked his all on it
and stood, kept standing
for ever

Translated from the Bengali BY RON D.K. BANERJEE

ZEUS

Zeus and Hera/Zeus in Love

Zeus & Hera/Zeus in Love

"Surely,"
He murmured, "Wife will never learn of this,
My latest masquearade, and if she does,
The girl is worth the threat of Juno's anger."
—OVID, THE METAMORPHOSES, II (TR. BY HORACE GREGORY)

Jupiter on Juno ■ A.D. Hope

Tantaene animis caelestibus irae?

So that's her latest feat of espionage!
There she goes off in an immortal huff;
Slams out with a last shriek of heavenly rage:
'When, when,' she wants to know, 'will you leave off
Chasing mortal girls and learn to be your age?
Are not the pleasures of my bed enough?'
She knows too much, I tell her. Even so
I am tempted to tell her what she does not know.

She does not know how tedious they become,
These goddesses, for ever young and fair,
Flaunting their regal charms of bust and bum,
Queening their way with that Olympian air
Of effortless, nonchalant equilibrium,
Untouched by doubt, by weakness or despair,
Complacent virgins and self-righteous wives
Who never took a risk in all their lives.

She cannot conceive the wonder, the mere bliss
Of loving a woman who, at her peak and prime
Senses her beauty doomed to the abyss;
Who, in the inexorable lapse of time,
Must take her chance, knowing how frail it is,
Yet, daring the unknown, achieves sublime
Ardours she could not know me capable of
And reaches raptures past her hope of love.

She cannot imagine how humanity flowers
From aspirations, of which gods have no need,
To be caught up in this divine of ours;
How ecstasy when laced with terror can breed
Spasms of vision and vision lend them powers
Of divination; how, pregnant with my seed,
Their bodies, grown strange, crave metamorphoses
To other natures: beasts, stones, stars or trees.

What prompts them, in such shapes, to welcome *me*?
What goddess, visited by bull or swan,
Would not just laugh or turn in scorn and flee?
They know me far too well. With women alone
I tap the human springs of fantasy
And in their arms, as never in heaven, have known
That sense of undiscovered light which broods
In mortal poetry's similitudes.

Woman is half a living metaphor
That reaches towards its unknown counterpart.
No goddess needs apotheosis nor
Any fulfilment of the mind and heart;
Nothing that she may think worth wishing for
Demands imagination, knowledge or art.
All things being in her power to attain,
What she enjoys she may enjoy again.

So what words could I find that would convey
The pleasure of sensing worlds beyond my reach
In mortal minds where mine must beat its way
From dim surmise to final lucid speech;
I, threading their labyrinths of doubt, while they
Dazzle through aether, probing each to each;
I, towards her tender, dark mortality
And, groping to discern my numen, she?

In that embrace how exquisite, how brief
The mind's exchange, the body's precarious joy,
Transfigurations of spirit beyond belief
For those whom easy, unending pleasures cloy!
For once to know and share the urge, the grief
Heightening one hour the next hour must destroy;
Yet how explain to an immortal wife
That single hour might be the crown of life?

What good, of course would explanation do?
When all that counts with her has just been said,
What past resentments must it not renew?
What tears of jealous fury would she shed?
Omnipotence leaves so little to pursue,
Omniscience less to talk about in bed
And I, no conversationalist, I admit,
Shine more in love's performance than its wit.

Still she's a heavenly creature, bountiful
And splendid even in anger; what is more,
How can I blame her, godhead being so dull?
Her immortality must prove a chore

Did not some screaming rage restore the full
—Now, why have I not thought of this before?—
The full immediacy, that zest of strife
And plural of spouse which is the spice of life.

Jove o■ Frank O'Hara

He was used to guises and masks
and moonlight, he accepted the fear
to be avoided by an oblique descent,
not to fool himself, but her to reassure.

Whether as bull or swan eluctable
he moved with vigor and cruel light
to possess the deep fount where, downy,
impoverished, the penetrable night

seemed no longer Olympic or vague.
And he loved his victory as beast
as much. Was not his true nature,
but the horns set free what lost

in him the godhead did abuse.
That diadem put off, his thighs
how easily in love pressed being
from mere mythical praise,

the elevation of his brow gave way
to tangled smelly curls. There came
the day when he no longer could
repress his lava from that home:

the ambiguity of his parted crown
fell upon clouds and golden showered.
Fell upon his sweating torso
and to earth. He plunged and flowered.

ZEUS AND LEDA

"...people tell a story about Zeus...
how he once feathered himself into the likeness of a swan,
feigned flight from a pursuing eagle,
lit upon my mother Leda,
and won his way with her."

—EURIPIDES, HELEN (TR. BY ROBERT EMMET MEAGHER)

Leda ■ Rainer Maria Rilke

When the god, yearning, entered the swan,
swan splendor shattered him. He let himself
vanish within its flesh, completely entangled.
Trying to fool her, though, he was drawn to the act

before he could probe what it meant to be and to feel
in this strange way. And what gaped wide in her
already sensed that advent in the swan
and knew: he asked for the one thing that she,

tangled in resisting him, could no longer
withhold. He came at her harder,
and thrusting his neck through her hand growing weaker and weaker

he let his godhead disperse into what he loved.
Only then did he realize feathers were glory
and fully became swan in her womb.

    Translated from the German BY JOHN PECK

Leda ■ Robert Graves

Heart, with what lonely fears you ached,
    How lecherously mused upon
That horror with which Leda quaked
    Under the spread wings of the swan.

Then soon your mad religious smile
    Made taut the belly, arched the breast,
And there beneath your god awhile
    You strained and gulped your beastliest.

Pregnant you are, as Leda was,
    Of bawdry, murder and deceit;
Perpetuating night because
    The after-languors hang so sweet.

Leda ■ D.H. Lawrence

Come not with kisses
not with caresses

of hands and lips and murmurings;
come with a hiss of wings
and sea-touch tip of a beak
and treading of wet, webbed, wave-working feet
into the marsh-soft belly.

Leda and the Swan ■ William Butler Yeats

A sudden blow: the great wings beating still
Above the staggering girl, her thighs caressed
By the dark webs, her nape caught in his bill,
He holds her helpless breast upon his breast.

How can those terrified vague fingers push
The feathered glory from her loosening thighs?
And how can body, laid in that white rush,
But feel the strange heart beating where it lies?

A shudder in the loins engenders there
The broken wall, the burning roof and tower
And Agamemnon dead.
                        Being so caught up,
So mastered by the brute blood of the air,
Did she put on his knowledge with his power
Before the indifferent beak could let her drop?

Leda ■ Mona Van Duyn

> *"Did she put on his knowledge with his power*
> *Before the indifferent beak could let her drop?"*

Not even for a moment. He knew, for one thing, what he was.
When he saw the swan in her eyes he could let her drop.
In the first look of love men find their great disguise,
and collecting these rare pictures of himself was his life.

Her body became the consequence of his juice,
while her mind closed on a bird and went to sleep.
Later, with the children in school, she opened her eyes
and saw her own openness, and felt relief.

In men's stories her life ended with his loss.
She stiffened under the storm of his wings to a glassy shape,
stricken and mysterious and immortal. But the fact is,
she was not, for such an ending, abstract enough.

She tried for a while to understand what it was
that had happened, and then decided to let it drop.
She married a smaller man with a beaky nose,
and melted away in the storm of everyday life.

Leda 3 ■ Lucille Clifton

a personal note (re: visitation)
always pyrotechnics;
stars spinning into phalluses
of light, serpents promising
sweetness, their forked tongues
thick and erect, patriarchs of bird
exposing themselves in the air.
this skin is sick with loneliness.
You want what a man wants,
next time come as a man
or don't come.

Leda ■ Nina Kossman

She recalled the fear that had overwhelmed her soul,
something had seized her throat so she couldn't cry
out to them, white birds, wild, light, drifting
in the sky which had turned the most remote black.
White birds in black sky, white scream in her throat,
hair splashing the shoulders chased by the awesome bird

hung in lulled air like an ancestor's soul, heavy,
languid, and waiting for an infusion of flesh—
another fill of forgetfulness, heaving,
not hiding her—like a mirror refusing a look
at herself from behind her startled shoulder;
the familiar landscape fleeing from her cry for help,

perhaps at the behest of a god, with his sad immortality,
knowing the images to be thus seized and begotten
from this shivering flesh—wild birds, flying,
no, words, healing ... white and fleeting, up in the lightened sky.

She recalled that alone, she of all women, she,
the mother of the nation of mythmakers, the generation of
myth transforming itself into memory—man
of fire, taking her moistened lips; his voice,
chasing her, has become her children's; light,
gentler than her memory still not in her full command,

lighter, with gentler movements, more tact, less mythology,
the singing without the myth within; in the time
allotted for myth-making—her children singing
in the space allotted for healing music; sounds
that she remembered as the very same ...
One last time they have seized her throat: wild black birds, fly ...

Living Next to Leda ■ Barbara Bentley

i
Leda swore she could hear a swan. I ask you. A swan.
They're supposed to be mute. But she insisted
the noise came across as white sound.
Leda had a nervous tic triggered by
sparrows that twitched in her garden.
She said they flitted about like bits of grit
granted flight. When she got jittery,
she tuned into white sound, more calming
than a tranquilizer. At dusk, she strolled to the park
and watched swans nuzzling in lint-soft wings.
According to Leda, swans have poise.

Not like sparrows. Once, one bashed against Leda's pane.
There were feathers and beads unstrung on glass
like the stuff which sticks to free range eggs.
She couldn't touch it. She cringed. So I put the kettle on
and cleaned it up, while she rocked and focussed
on white sound. For weeks she was calm,
until a sparrow flew in. She had to brace herself
to cup the moth-cased heart. A choke of fluff
and the tickle of spindly legs was still on her palms,
she said, days later, on her way to the park.
Her pockets bulged with bread.

ii
They took her in. Crazy Leda who heard swans
and sat by the lake in the dark
was found in her Hygena-white bedroom,
smothering bruises in an eiderdown quilt
and pillows stuffed with real curled feathers.

I went to visit. She asked for slices of bread
which she crammed in her locker. On bad days
she flew from room to room, chasing something.
Swansong, she said. Poor Leda. A bundle of nerves.
When she crashed into walls, they had to restrain her.

I don't breathe a word of Leda's version:
how a cygnet approached, not in fury
but as an emissary. She stroked angel wings,
and drawn by the flame that tipped the bill,
she entered the jet eye and was transformed.

Whatever happened, it was all hushed up.
She's stabilised now. Soon, there'll be twins.
I imagine her weaning two scrawny fledglings,

open-mouthed and insistent for more, more,
while the bastard that did this flies free.

ZEUS AND IO

...Io ran,
Steering her way across the shady groves of Lyrcea,
And there, cloaked by a sudden thundercloud,
Jove overcame her scruples and her flight.
* * *

      But thoughtful Jove felt the arrival
of Juno's spirit in the air, and changed the girl
into a white-milk cow....
—OVID, THE METAMORPHOSES, I (TR. BY HORACE GREGORY)

To Io, Afterwards ■ Laurie Sheck

I suppose you are weary now of remembering,
that being mortal you want to convince yourself you belong
to this earth, and are anchored to the earth by love.

You lie by the river. The sky is still.
If you could you would watch the roots of the grasses,
the roots of the wildflowers hunger through the soil,
how they would cleave, as if forever,
to what they cannot finally hold.
The river's skin is cold and smooth.
When the birds fly up, a sudden panic of black wings,
you turn from the strange dream of their going.

I think of your wandering.
White skin, white hooves, how you passed without touching
what formerly you'd stopped to touch.
The children picking flowers by the river
seemed far away as stars. Allowed no rest,
you moved within the stark cage of exile
while you longed more than anything for hands.
Did the earth grow beautiful then—

the lambs sleeping on the hillsides, the olive trees
swaying where they stood?
The world uttered its unstoppable fullness.
And for the first time you saw it. You who watched it
with longing from a distance unbridgeable as death.

Io Remembers ■ Larissa Szporluk

There is no sound at all on this wild upland.
The horses have stopped falling

in their great arc through the air.
The panic that carried their necks over the crag
became, early on, in their legs, regret.
The dark knowing that spoils the morning
enters them now, showing them how,
like a difference in contour, they weren't the real
power of the field. How their bearing was minor,
their bones meaning more to the earth
than what each aloof mane in the wind had been.
Their eyes, which before were clear, crowd
with the fleas madness brings, as she notes
in the noonday heat how each part lies,
spread across rock, like her own in that scene,
half-girl, half-cow, the cloud half off.

ZEUS AND EUROPA

...the Father
Of all Gods whose right hand held a three-pronged
Thunderbolt, whose slightest nod was earthquake
Up to heaven, dropped his royal sceptre and
Became a bull.
* * *
The princess, innocent on whom she sat,
Climbed to his back; slowly the god stepped out
Into the shallows of the beach and with
False-footed softness took to sea, swimming
Against full tide, the girl his captured prize....
—OVID, THE METAMORPHOSES, II (TR. BY HORACE GREGORY)

■ Osip Mandelshtam

Pink foam of exhaustion round his soft lips,
The bull violently digs at the green billows,
Not in love with rowing, he snorts—a ladies' man,
The burden is new to his spine, the labor is hard.

Once in a while a dolphin leaps out, arcing,
Or a prickly sea-urchin appears.
Tender hands of Europa, take it all,
Where could a bull find a more desirable yoke.

Bitterly Europa listens to the powerful splashing.
The heavy sea around her is boiling.
Frightened of the water's oily shine,
She would like to slide off these rough slopes.

Ah, how much dearer to her the creak of rowlocks,
The lap of a wide deck, a flock of sheep,

And flickers of fish behind a high stern—
But the oarless oarsman swims further with her!

Translated from the Russian BY NINA KOSSMAN

Europa ■ Derek Walcott

The full moon is so fierce that I can count the
coconuts' cross-hatched shade on bungalows,
their white walls raging with insomnia.
The stars leak drop by drop on the tin plates
of the sea almonds, and the jeering clouds
are luminously rumpled as the sheets.
The surf, insatiably promiscuous,
groans through the walls; I feel my mind
whiten to moonlight, altering that form
which daylight unambiguously designed,
from a tree to a girl's body bent in foam;
then, treading close, the black hump of a hill,
its nostrils softly snorting, nearing the
naked girl splashing her breasts with silver.
Both would have kept their proper distance still,
if the chaste moon hadn't swiftly drawn the drapes
of a dark cloud, coupling their shapes.

She teases with those flashes, yes, but once
you yield to human horniness, you see
through all that moonshine what they really were,
those gods as seed-bulls, gods as rutting swans—
an overheated farmhand's literature.
Who ever saw her pale arms hook his horns,
her thighs clamped tight in their deep-plunging ride,
watched, in the hiss of the exhausted foam,
her white flesh constellate to phosphorus
as in salt darkness beast and woman come?
Nothing is there, just as it always was,
but the foam's wedge to the horizon-light,
then, wire-thin, the studded armature,
like drops still quivering on his matted hide,
the hooves and horn-points anagrammed in stars.

■ Boris Filipoff

After abducting Europa,
the bull became sad;
the fight with the sea
had weakened him.

The bull landed at Hellas,
lowered his horns,

and, bored and annoyed,
nibbled on some hay.

"Why did I bother with that girl,
so naked and weak …"
The young moon gave the bull
a mocking look:

"You poor devil, first you kidnap her,
then you grow sad;
you'd trade all your Olympian blessings
for a bit of quiet …"

Translated from the Russian BY NINA KOSSMAN

ZEUS AND ALCMENE

…Alcméné,
wife of Amphitryon. After she lay
in mighty Zeus's arms, she bore a son:
the dauntless, lionhearted Heracles.
—THE ODYSSEY OF HOMER, XI (TR. BY ALLEN MANDELBAUM)

Alcmene ▨ Yannis Ritsos

She who, that first night, slept with a god, not knowing it
—only because of his worldly odor and his broad hairy chest,
almost the same as her husband's yet so very different, did she
seem to have guessed and sensed something—how was she now to sleep
with a mortal? And what did she care about Amphitryon's presents or even
her child's twelve labors and his immortality, or for that matter, hers? She
reminisces about one night only, waits for one night only again, late, the moment
when outside in the garden the Big Dipper dips and near it Orion
shows his silver shoulders (O God, how sweet the roses smell)—
she, ready as she can be, when her husband is away hunting, always ready, bathed,
naked, puts on her earrings again, her bracelets, and lingers in front of the mirror
combing her long hair, still thick, even if lifeless and dyed.

Translated from the Greek BY EDMUND KEELEY

ZEUS AND GANYMEDE

One day the very king of all the gods
Took fire when he looked at Ganymede.
Then, O, he wished himself less masculine—
Yet he became a flashing, warlike eagle
Who swooped upon the boy with one swift blow
And clipped him, wing and claw, to Mount Olympus
Where much to Juno's obvious distate,
The Trojan boy serves drinks to Father Jove.
—OVID, THE METAMORPHOSES, X (TR. BY HORACE GREGORY)

Ganymede ■ W.H. Auden

He looked in all His wisdom from the throne
Down on that humble boy who kept the sheep,
And sent a dove; the dove returned alone:
Youth liked the music, but soon fell asleep.

But he had planned such future for the youth:
Surely, His duty now was to compel.
For later he would come to love the truth,
And own his gratitude. His eagle fell.

It did not work. His conversation bored
The boy who yawned and whistled and made faces,
And wriggled free from fatherly embraces;

But with the eagle he was always willing
To go where it suggested, and adored
And learnt from it so many ways of killing.

The Rape of Ganymede ■ Umberto Saba

It was a day like any other. Mount Ida
stood serene, the goats grazing placidly,
tended by their adoloscent guardian.
Only the dog ran to and fro, uneasy.
Shadows fell over the young boy's face.
Perhaps his father, the king, was severe.
Perhaps he yearned for his companions
                              —many
on Ida were the same age as he,

all enamoured of the same games, where
for a laurel's kiss they used to clutch
each other fiercely to a chorus of shouts—
The clouds raced white across the sky.

The dog still sniffed about warily,
the flock pressed more tightly together.
Unmindful of the omens, forgetful of
his duties, the goatherd boy was dreaming.
From the heavens flashed the sullen eagle.
The flocks dispersed, the dog barked
and barked.
         But the boy was of the sky already
and sprinkled the earth for the last time.

Translated from the Italian BY STEPHEN SARTARELLI

DEMETER

Demeter's Grief
The Abduction of Persephone by Hades

Demeter's Grief

... the anxious frightened mother
Looked for her daughter up and down the world;
Neither Aurora with dew-wet raining hair
Nor evening Hesperus saw her stop for rest.
—OVID, THE METAMORPHOSES, V (TR. BY HORACE GREGORY)

Demeter ■ Valentine Penrose

If it is a stone of sadness there am I seated
There where the swaddlings fall oblique to the plain
Blanched veils. This is fleeting.
Where the goddess huge-eyed tempers the child of the others in fire.

The tree rejects its orientation. The emerald
Keeps its fist clenched. If it is
A stone of sadness there am I seated.
>   *Translated from the French* BY ROY EDWARDS

The Search ■ Rita Dove

Blown apart by loss, she let herself go—
wandered the neighborhood hatless, breasts
swinging under a ratty sweater, crusted
mascara blackening her gaze. It was a shame,
the wives whispered, to carry on so.
To them, wearing foam curlers arraigned
like piglets to market was almost debonair,
but an uncombed head?—not to be trusted.

The men watched more closely, tantalized
by so much indifference. Winter came early and still
she frequented the path by the river until
one with murmurous eyes pulled her down to size.
Sniffed Mrs. Franklin, ruling matron, to the rest:
Serves her right, the old mare.

Demeter's Prayer to Hades ■ Rita Dove

This alone is what I wish for you: knowledge.
To understand each desire has an edge,
to know we are responsible for the lives
we change. No faith comes without cost,
no one believes without dying.
Now for the first time
I see clearly the trail you planted,
what ground opened to waste,
though you dreamed a wealth
of flowers.

There are no curses—only mirrors
held up to the souls of gods and mortals.
And so I give up this fate, too.
Believe in yourself,
go ahead—see where it gets you.

Persephone ■ D.M. Thomas

I have seen you wiping tables in the chilly
silent cafeteria of the almost-deserted
railway terminus; and I have seen you in the dim
city street waiting for stranded revellers;
and I have seen you in a nurse's cap
writing letters under a night-light
waiting for disturbed men to cry out for tablets.

And sometimes, when I have lain awake in the dead
of night, it has been enough to imagine you
in these places, knowing that a light still burns
somewhere and that you are awake,
however tired, however slowly you move, however
alone; and that, through you, day runs into day
without a break, the light uninterrupted.

So I am glad you opened your legs to Hades
and agreed to go with him into his dark kingdom,
solid and beautiful amidst the shadows,
our representative presence, childishly fretful,
demanding pomegranate seeds because you are pregnant,
your thoughts rooted in the living,
a white aspen among the black poplars.

The Abduction of Persephone by Hades

This was the place where Proserpina played;
She plucked white lily and the violet ...
* * *

        ... As if at one glance, Death
Had caught her up, delighted at his choice,
Had ravished her, so quick was his desire,
While she in terror called to friends and mother,
A prayer to mother echoing through her cries.
    —OVID, THE METAMORPHOSES, V (TR. BY HORACE GREGORY)

Persephone ■ Peter Huchel

The unfathomable came,
rose from the earth,
flaring up in moonlight.
She wore the old shard in her hair,
her hip leaned on night.

No smoke of sacrifice, the universe
entered the fragrance of the rose.
    Translated from the German BY MICHAEL HAMBURGER

Persephone ■ Adam Zagajewski

Persephone goes underground again
in a summer dress, with a Jewish
child's big eyes.

Kites fly, and yellow leaves, autumn dust,
a white plane, black crow wings.
Someone runs down the path clutching an overdue letter.

She'll be cold underground in cork
sandals and her hair won't shield
her from the blind wind, from oblivion—

she disappears into the chestnut trees
and only the ribbon on her braid
shines with resignation's rosy glow.
    Translated from the Polish BY CLARE CAVANAGH

Hymn to Proserpine ■ Charles Olson

Each red seed bursts
with a liquid nested

as they are as rooms
of the honey-comb break

in the whole mouth as
a sea
   a halo
of fecundation and around his head
there did spring

clothed in a sac
born in drear December
just after the dead sun
               lingered
a moment to be born

all creation watched
as she put her hand out
for the single flower

and in the moment he
in his chariot spun
as a gore
      tore her
with him into
the shades

and off in the night
on the other side
of the earth
one woman
heard
her caw, "A rape!
A rape!"

but only she
and no one else
not even
the girl's
mother who wandered
thereafter
looking
for her daughter
who was lost
below

Bavarian Gentians ■ D.H. Lawrence

Not every man has gentians in his house
in soft September, at slow, sad Michaelmas.

Bavarian gentians, big and dark, only dark
darkening the day-time, torch-like with the smoking blueness of Pluto's gloom,

ribbed and torch-like, with their blaze of darkness spread blue
down flattening into points, flattened under the sweep of white day
torch-flower of the blue-smoking darkness, Pluto's dark-blue daze,
black lamps from the halls of Dis, burning dark-blue,
giving off darkness, blue darkness, as Demeter's pale lamps give off light,
lead me then, lead the way.

Reach me a gentian, give me a torch!
let me guide myself with the blue, forked torch of this flower
down the darker and darker stairs, where blue is darkened on blueness
even where Persephone goes, just now, from the frosted September
to the sightless realm where darkness is awake upon the dark
and Persephone herself is but a voice
or a darkness invisible enfolded in the deeper dark
of the arms Plutonic, and pierced with the passion of dense gloom,
among the splendour of torches of darkness, shedding darkness on the lost bride
and her groom.

Purple Anemones ■ D.H. Lawrence

Who gave us flowers?
Heaven? The white God?

Nonsense!
Up out of hell,
From Hades;
Infernal Dis!

Jesus the god of flowers—?
Not he.
Or sun-bright Apollo, him so musical?
Him neither.

Who then?
Say who.
Say it—and it is Pluto,
Dis,
The dark one.
Proserpine's master.

Who contradicts—?

When she broke forth from below,
Flowers came, hell-hounds on her heels.
Dis, the dark, the jealous god, the husband,
Flower-sumptuous-blooded.

Go then, he said.
And in Sicily, on the meadows of Enna,

She thought she had left him;
But opened around her purple anemones,

Caverns,
Little hells of colour, caves of darkness,
Hell, risen in pursuit of her; royal, sumptuous
Pit-falls.

All at her feet
Hell opening;
At her white ankles
Hell rearing its husband-splendid, serpent heads,
Hell-purple, to get at her—
Why did he let her go?
So he could track her down again, white victim.

Ah mastery!
Hell's husband-blossoms
Out on earth again.

Look out, Persephone!
You, Madame Ceres, mind yourself, the enemy is upon you.
About your feet spontaneous aconite,
Hell-glamorous, and purple husband-tyranny
Enveloping your late-enfranchised plains.
You thought your daughter had escaped?
No more stockings to darn for the flower-roots, down in hell?
But ah, my dear!
Aha, the stripe-cheeked whelps, whippet-slim crocuses,
At 'em boys, at 'em!
Ho, golden-spaniel, sweet alert narcissus,
Smell 'em, smell 'em out!

Those two enfranchised women.

Somebody is coming!
Oho there!
Dark blue anemones!
Hell is up!
Hell on earth, and Dis within the depths!

Run, Persephone, he is after you already.

Why did he let her go?
To track her down;
All the sport of summer and spring and flowers snapping
    at her ankles and catching her by the hair!
Poor Persephone and her rights for women.

Husband-snared hell-queen,
It is spring.

It is spring,
And pomp of husband-strategy on earth.

Ceres, kiss your girl, you think you've got her back.
The bit of husband-tilth she is,
Persephone!

Poor mothers-in-law!
They are always sold.

It is spring.

Pomegranate ■ D.M. Thomas

Each year more clearly you can see her dark flowers wither
to the sick light, or crush to our tighter embrace,
as she picks up her bag and her coat, drifts out to face
the statutory six-months with her mother.

She turns to my heart's cog; rounded, no longer the child
the courts shared between us, as a pomegranate cleft:
small need any more for the fury who would have left
me nothing … though God knows I have never reviled

her. "Be good to her," I say, this morning; "give her
my—"(I cannot finish). "And—forget me while you're there."
"You both say that!" She flicks her eyes … "Father, must I go?"

My green shoot, Kore, dawdles now at the brightening river's
ferry—waves once—head bent, March uncabling her hair—
then shoulders her bag, full of books I'll expect her to know.

APOLLO

The Nature of Apollo
Apollo's Loves

The Nature of Apollo

...He was the very image
Of the artist, all poise and pose....
—OVID, THE METAMORPHOSES, XI (TR. BY HORACE GREGORY)

Apollo of the Physiologists ■ Robert Graves

Despite this learned cult's official
And seemingly sincere denial
That they either reject or postulate
God, or God's scientific surrogate,
Prints of a deity occur *passim*
Throughout their extant literature. They make him
A dumb, dead-pan Apollo with a profile
Drawn in Victorian-Hellenistic style—
The pallid, bald, partitioned head suggesting
Wholly abstract cerebral functioning;
Or nude and at full length, this deity
Displays digestive, venous, respiratory
And nervous systems painted in bold colour
On his immaculate exterior.
Sometimes, *in verso*, a bald, naked Muse
His consort, flaunts her arteries and sinews,
While, upside-down, crouched in her chaste abdomen,
Adored by men and wondered at by women,
Hangs a Victorian-Hellenistic foetus—
Fruit of her academic god's afflatus.

Linear A ■ Daryl Hine

Δ (*Bassai*)
Apollo, turns [his back upon] the world.
Faced with the uncomely mountainside,
No wonder he's so beautifully preserved,
Ageless [mythological] and blind.
The other mortals, who are More Than Kind,
Say it was no less than he deserved
Because of the anthropo[morphic pride
Naturally incarnate in the word.]

E
"Mind of Apollo"—whatever that may be!
Glazed, hermetic as a casserole.
Know [*thyself,*] *Nothing* [*in excess*], a whole
Treatise on the single letter E:
E[very e[mpty-day] e[piphany].
Inspiration signifies the sole
Undisputed world authority,
Inventor of cosmetics and the soul.

<u>*APOLLO AND DAPHNE*</u>
The god by grace of hope, the girl, despair,
Still kept their increasing pace until his lips
Breathed at her shoulder; and almost spent,
The girl saw waves of a familiar river,
Her father's home, and in a trembling voice
Called, "Father, if your waters still hold charms
To save your daughter, cover with green earth
This body I wear too well," and as she spoke
A soaring drowsiness possessed her; growing
In earth she stood, white thighs embraced by climbing
Bark, her white arms branches, her fair head swaying
In a cloud of leaves; all that was Daphne bowed
In the stirring of the wind, the glittering green
Leaf twined within her hair and she was laurel.
—OVID, THE METAMORPHOSES, I (TR. BY HORACE GREGORY)

Daphne with Her Thighs in Bark ■ Eavan Boland

I have written this

so that,
in the next myth,
my sister will be wiser.

Let her learn from me:

the opposite of passion
is not virtue
but routine.

Look at me.

I can be cooking,
making coffee,
scrubbing wood, perhaps,
and back it comes:
the crystalline, the otherwhere,
the wood

where I was
when he began the chase.
And how I ran from him!

Pan-thighed,
satyr-faced he was.

The trees reached out to me.
I silvered and
I quivered. I shook out
my foil of quick leaves.

He snouted past.
What a fool I was!

I shall be here forever,
setting out the tea,
among the coppers and the branching alloys and
the tin shine of this kitchen;
laying saucers on the pine table.

Save face, sister.
Fall. Stumble.
Rut with him.
His rough heat will keep you warm and

you will be better off than me,
with your memories
down the garden,
at the start of March,

unable to keep your eyes
off the chestnut tree—

just the way
it thrusts and hardens.

Where I Live in This Honorable House of the Laurel Tree ■ Anne Sexton

I live in my wooden legs and O
my green green hands.
Too late
to wish I had not run from you, Apollo,
blood moves still in my bark bound veins.
I, who ran nymph foot to root in flight,
have only this late desire to arm the trees
I lie within. The measure that I have lost
silks my pulse. Each century the trickeries
of need pain me everywhere.
Frost taps my skin and I stay glossed
in honor for you are gone in time. The air
rings for you, for that astonishing rite
of my breathing tent undone within your light.
I only know how this untimely lust has tossed
flesh at the wind forever and moved my fears
toward the intimate Rome of the myth we crossed.

I am a fist of my unease
as I spill toward the stars in the empty years.
I build the air with the crown of honor; it keys
my out of time and luckless appetite.
You gave me honor too soon, Apollo.
There is no one left who understands
how I wait
here in my wooden legs and O
my green green hands.

Daphne Herself ■ Nina Kossman

I will grow myself quiet leaves
in the difficult silence of chastity.

I will hide in the immense namelessness
though each tree murmurs to him my name.

I am the bed of leaves he can never scorch,
not even with his eyes of fire.

I am the naked face of the flower; a cross.
He cannot escape by reaching me.

The god and the goal; the lover and the loved;
the pursuit and the flight, entwined.

Though a god, he will die in the depths of my bark.
I will glisten his face on my leaves.

Every eagle will have his eyelids.
Every event—his speed.

Each one of the thousand suns
will pursue me as he has chased.

Each one of the symbols of silence
will learn his name I refuse to bear.

I am he: the sun, its immense bowl
pouring out selves as from a fount of chastity.

He is I: the ever-green song in flight,
the sun forever pursuing me.

Daphne ■ Edna St. Vincent Millay

Why do you follow me?—
Any moment I can be
Nothing but a laurel-tree.

Any moment of the chase
I can leave you in my place
A pink bough for your embrace.

Yet if over hill and hollow
Still it is your will to follow,
I am off; —to heel, Apollo!

A Footnote to Ovid ▨ John Fuller

Arbor eris certe mea (Metamorphoses, I)
Run slowly now. And I won't follow faster.
Let me without pursuit catch up with you.
Or if my question fails, go on, go on.
But slower now. For see, it puzzles you,
You put down roots into my patient ground.
The tree stirs, seems to be saying yes:
Art is appeased. The slim girl running still.

Daphne After ▨ Kathleen Raine

In the absence of a heart grown
stemwise, silent, slow Daphne drinks
unremembering and unknown,
in the manner of a laurel thinks

in branches, sometimes blossoms. Real
forgetting is her secret, long
detachment, no split sense to heal.
Only sentiment and song

remember how she suffered, ran
in terror, turning tree, and past
to present. Where the myth began,
the laurel is the light's at last.

Apollo and Daphne ▨ Yvor Winters

Deep in the leafy fierceness of the wood,
Sunlight, the cellular and creeping pyre,
Increased more slowly than aetherial fire:
But it increased and touched her where she stood.
The god had seized her, but the powers of good
Struck deep into her veins; with rending flesh
She fled all ways into the grasses' mesh
And burned more quickly than the sunlight could.

And all her heart broke stiff in leafy flame
That neither rose nor fell, but stood aghast;

And she, rooted in Time's slow agony,
Stirred dully, hard-edged laurel, in the past;
And, like a cloud of silence or a name,
The god withdrew into Eternity.

Daphne on Woodbrook Drive ■ Ann Deagon

Brushing my hair at a window into spring
across the budding woodlot I can see
the blasted treetrunk where once lightning knifed
a palate of smooth fleshtoned wood now weathered grey.

Winter and summer I watched an image form
a human face emerging from the trunk
the ragged bark encircling it like hair
its features still distorted by the pang of birth.

Today I walked across to see it close.
Deep eye thin nose and twisted mouth dissolved
into a labyrinth of hollow trails
where some unseen untiring minister devours
his destiny.

Elaborate the minute passageways
construct destruction build their world's collapse
yet down the intersecting corridors
miniscule clustered eggs project the race into
infinity.

Brushing my hair at this mirror into time
I see the tracks of countless smiles and sorrows
wrinkle my image honeycomb my face.

My hair has weathered grey and the patterned bark
encircling first my throat benumbs my senses
spreading around my mouth around my eyes.

Is this Prometheus' secret that I should
see now my face imprisoned in the wood
caught in a myth I had not understood?

Apollo to Daphne ■ Michael Graves

Virgin encased in bark,
You will wither to your roots
More quickly than these trees
I pursued you through,
Imploring daughter of a rival god.
Your lovely curves are in

The smooth bole's rise,
Branching upflung arms,
And fluttering leaves.
Feel my heat
That would melt you back to flesh.

Waking ▪ Margaret Kaufman

Morning light over the sill.
She extends one wooden arm,
pushes her hair back,
bends her neck—from her breasts
the scent of bay leaves.

Finally it is happening—
she lifts the hem of her gown,
steps out of their bed,
over the carpet
down the stairs,
and lifts the latch.

Outside, in stronger light,
she examines her hands,
regards her bare feet: green everywhere.
Your imagination, he'd say.

No! in every step,
she breaks into a run holding her hands
before her, flexing the fingers,
opening, closing, opening.

APOLLO AND MARPESSA

… Idas came to Messene, and Apollo, falling in with him, would have robbed him of the damsel. As they fought for the girl's hand, Zeus parted them and allowed the maiden herself to choose which of the two she would marry; and she, because she feared that Apollo might desert her in her old age, chose Idas for her husband.

—APOLLODORUS, THE LIBRARY, I. VII (TR. BY J.G. FRAZER)

Marpessa's Choice ▪ Yannis Ritsos

It wasn't by chance that Marpessa preferred Idas over Apollo,
despite her passion for the god, despite his incomparable beauty—
the kind that made myrtle tremble into blossom as he went by. She
never dared raise her eyes above his knees.
Between his toenails and his knees, what an inexhaustible world,
what exquisite journeys and discoveries between his toenails and his knees. Still,
at the ultimate moment of choice, Marpessa lost her nerve: What would she do
with a bequest as grand as that? A mortal, she would grow old one day.

She suddenly imagined her comb with a tuft of white hair in it
left on a chair beside the bed where the immortal one would rest shimmering;
she thought also of time's fingerprints on her thighs, her fallen breasts
in front of the black metal mirror. Oh no—and she leaned as though dead
against Idas's mortal shoulder. And he lifted her up in his arms like a flag
and turned his back on Apollo. But as he was leaving, almost arrogantly,
one could hear something like the sound of cloth ripping (a strange sound):
a corner of the flag was held back, trapped by the god's foot.

Translated from the Greek BY EDMUND KEELEY

APHRODITE

As soon as Kronos had lopped off the genitals with the sickle
he tossed them from the land into the stormy sea.
      And as they were carried by the sea a long time, all around them
white foam rose from the god's flesh, and in this foam a maiden
was nurtured.

* * *

And here is the power she had from the start
and her share in the lives of men and deathless gods:
from her come young girls' whispers and smiles and deception
and honey-sweet love and its joyful pleasures.

—HESIOD, THEOGONY (TR. BY A.N. ATHANASSAKIS)

Birth of Eventually Venus ■ Archibald MacLeish

Cast up by the sea
By the seventh wave
Beyond the sea reach
In the rubble of weed and
Wet twig
The not yet amphibious
Animalcula
Gasps and wiggles on the beach
Gathering her long gold hair about her
And gazing with pure eyes
Upon the unknown world.

Episode with Aphrodite ■ Yunna Morits

This woman came out of sea-foam,
Covered her nakedness with her hand,
And got lost in a mortal crowd.

A sweaty baker was breathing over his bags of flour,
A sweaty carpenter was fitting a board to a board,
Two barbers were looking out their window sadly.
This woman came out of sea-foam
And got lost in the crowd.

Behind the city walls flies were devouring dung.
An old woman with a crutch was running away from death.
An infant was keeping porridge behind his cheek.
This woman came out of sea-foam
And got lost in the crowd.

On the way back from the fields, people recognized her,
Bowed to her and invited her in
And, pressing their cheeks to their infants, whispered:
"This woman came out of sea-foam,
And she is filled with a will
That brings ease wherever she goes."

Translated from the Russian BY NINA KOSSMAN AND ANDY NEWCOMB

Aphrodite ■ Olga Broumas

The one with the stone cups

and the stone face, and the grinding
stone settled
between her knees, the one with stone

in her bosom, with stones

in her kidneys, a heart of pure
stone, the one with the stony lips, the one

with the thighs of marble, with
genitals, the one whose glance
turns to stone

this idol, stones
through her ears, stones round her neck, her
wrists, round her fingers, a stone

in her navel, stones in her shoes, this
woman so like a stone
statue, herself

a stone, stands
in the stone square, midway
between the stone-high steeple, the stone—

round well, a stone
in her stone-still hand, and a stony will
waiting

for what will land, stiff
as a long stone, on the grinding
stone, on

her lap.

Praise to Aphrodite ■ Marina Tsvetaeva

How many, how many of them feed off your hands,
White doves and gray doves!
Entire kingdoms coo and dance
Round your lips, Baseness!

Still, the deadly sweat overflows
Your golden bowl.
Even the crested warrior clings
Like a white she-dove.

On an evil day each cloud
Grows as round as breasts.
Every innocent flower
Bears your face, Temptress!

Mortal whitewater, salt of the sea ...
In whitewater and torture,
How long are we to heed your call,
O armless sculpture?

Translated from the Russian BY NINA KOSSMAN

Aphrodite at Solstice ▪ Samn Stockwell

A bird in the tower of sky
and the exile
finds sea rocket growing.
The moonflower blooms;
one on the first night,
two on the second.

She returned through the water.
Just like Athena, miserably screeching
out of her father's head, this was torture.
There is no other home
for the body's longings.
The breast and the sea
are one ocean.

The Re-birth of Venus ▪ Geoffrey Hill

(*Metamorphoses III*)
And now the sea-scoured temptress, having failed
To scoop out of horizons what birds herald:
Tufts of fresh soil: shakes off an entire sea,
Though not as the dove, harried. Rather, she,

A shark hurricaned to estuary-water,
(The lesser hunter almost by a greater
Devoured) but unflurried, lies, approaches all
Stayers, and searchers of the fanged pool.

Venus over the Desert ▪ William Carlos Williams

If I do not sin, she said, you shall not
walk in long gowns down stone corridors.
There is no reprieve where there is no fall—
ing off. I lie in your beds all night, from
me you wake and go about your tasks. My flesh
clings to your bones. What use is holiness
unless it affirm my perfections, my breasts,
my thighs which you part, shaking, and my lips
the door to my pleasure? Sin, you call it,
but there cannot be cold unless the heat
has bred it, how can you know otherwise? Love
comfort me in the face of my defeats! Poor
monks, you think you are gentle but I tell you
you kill as sure as shot kills a bird flying.

The Death of Venus ■ Robert Creeley

I dreamt her sensual proportions
had suffered sea-change,

that she was a porpoise, a
sea-beast rising lucid from the mist.

The sound of waves killed speech
but there were gestures—

of my own, it was to call her closer,
of hers, she snorted and filled her lungs with water,

then sank, to the bottom,
and looking down, clear it was, like crystal,

there I saw her.

OTHER OLYMPIANS

Athene
Hermes
Ares
Artemis
Hephaestus
Dionysus

Athene

I begin to sing of Pallas Athena, the glorious goddess,
gray-eyed, resourceful, of implacable heart.
This bashful maiden is a mighty defender of cities,
the Tritogeneia, whom Zeus the counselor himself
bore from his august head, clad with golden and resplendent
warlike armor, as awe lay hold of all the immortal
onlookers.

—THE HOMERIC HYMNS, 28, TO ATHENA (TR. BY A.N. ATHANASSAKIS)

Athene's Song ■ Eavan Boland

From my father's head I sprung
Goddess of the war, created
Partisan and soldiers' physic,
My symbols boast and brazen gong,
Until I made in Athens wood
Upon my knees a new music.

When I played my pipe of bone,
Robbed and whittled from a stag,
Every bird became a lover,
Every lover to its tone
Found the truth of song and brag.
Fish sprung in the full river.

Peace became the toy of power
When other noises broke my sleep.
Like dreams I saw the hot ranks
And heroes in another flower
Than any there. I dropped my pipe
Remembering their shouts, their thanks.

Beside the water, lost and mute,
Lies my pipe, like my mind,
Remains unknown, remains unknown.
And in some hollow, taking part
With my heart against my hand,
Holds its peace and holds its own.

Athena's Vote ■ Constantine P. Cavafy

When no resolution in justice can be attained,
when the judgment of men is perplexed
and requires help and light from above,
the judges go silent, queasy, small,
and the compassion of the Gods decides things.

Pallas spoke to the citizens of Athens:
"I established your court. Not Greece,
not any other city could want to acquire
a more glorious one. Brave judges,
show yourselves worthy of it. Renounce
unbecoming passions. Have clemency
accompany justice. If your judgement
is austere, let it be clean
as well—immaculate as a diamond, pure.
Your work should show the way
for good and noble deeds, and moderate
command. Never follies of vengeance."

The men of the city answered, moved:
"O Lady, our thought is all unable
to find a tribute in gratitude sufficient
to the shining benefit you have conferred."

                    The grey-eyed
goddess answered them: "Mortals,
Divinity requires from you no wages.
Be virtuous and impartial:
this suffices me. In any case, brave judges,
I have the privilege of a single vote reserved."

The judges said: "Living
in the starry firmament, Goddess,
how do you cast your vote here with us?"

                    "Do not let
this question weary you. I am restrained
in the use of my vote. But if a moment comes
when you are divided into two factions,
one for, the other against, without my leaving
the rooms of heaven you will use
this vote of mine yourselves. Men of the city,
I wish you always to show mercy
to the accused. In the soul
of your Athena dwells forgiveness,
vast, limitless,
and instinctive from Metis,
the crown of wisdom exalted in heaven."

Translated from the Greek BY THEOHARIS C. THEOHARIS

Hermes

Then she bore a child who was a shrewd and coaxing schemer,
a cattle-rustling robber, and a bringer of dreams,
a watcher by night and a gate-keeper, soon destined
to show forth glorious deeds among the immortal gods.
—THE HOMERIC HYMNS, 4, TO HERMES (TR. BY A. N. ATHANASSAKIS)

Hermes ■ Ronald Bottrall

Protector of sheep, goats and cattle,
Pillar of strength, personified phallus,
Herald of gods, arrant pilferer,
Patron of travellers, indefatigable runner,
Flyer like a breath of wind
Over the watery sea and the vast earth,
Leader of the souls of Penelope's slain suitors
As they flew rustling like bats
To the welcoming fields of asphodel,
Where the ghosts of those who are no longer dwell,
What can you do to help us in this hell
Of perpetual wars that we inhabit?
Teach us with your cunning, bit by bit,
To learn to live as ghosts with ghosts
On the world's unbearably barren coasts.

■ Charles Simic

In the fourth year of the war, Hermes showed up. He was not much to look at.
His mailman's coat was in tatters; mice ran in and out of its pockets.
The broad-brimmed hat he was wearing had bullet holes. He still carried the
famous stick that closes the eyes of the dying, but it looked gnawed. Did he let the
dying bite on it? Whatever the case, he had no letters for us. "God of thieves!" we
shouted behind his back when he could no longer hear us.

Hermes, Dog, and Star ■ Zbigniew Herbert

Hermes goes through the world. He meets a dog.
   —I am a god, Hermes introduces himself politely.
   The dog sniffs at his feet.
   —I feel lonely. Humans betray gods; but unknowing, mortal animals, we crave
them. In the evening, after a whole day wandering, we will sit down under an oak. I
will tell you then that I feel old and want to die. It will be a necessary lie, so you
will lick my hands.
   —All right, the dog carelessly replies, I will lick your hands. They are cool, and
have a strange smell.
   They walk, they walk. They meet a star.
   —I am Hermes, the god says, and produces one of his very best faces. Would
you like to go with us to the end of the world? I will make it frightening there, so

you will have to lean your head on my shoulder.

—Good, the star replies with a glassy voice. It's all the same to me where I go; but the end of the world, that is naive. Unfortunately there is no end of the world.

They go. They go. The dog, Hermes, and the star. They hold hands. Hermes thinks that if he sets out to find friends another time, he won't be so frank.

Translated from the Polish BY JOHN CARPENTER AND BOGDANA CARPENTER

Ares

Mighty Ares, golden-helmeted rider of chariots,
stout-hearted, shield-carrying and bronze-geared savior of cities,
strong-handed and unwearying lord of the spear, bulwark of Olympos,
father of fair Victory....
—THE HOMERIC HYMNS, 8, TO ARES (TR. BY A.N. ATHANASSAKIS)

Expiation ■ Yannis Ritsos

The Greeks had little love for wild Ares. His
temples and statues were few. Athena always came out
the victor in battles between the two of them. His hair filled with dirt
as he fell to cover seven acres with his body. The artisans
accepted him only in naked form; they denied him his helmet;
his spear off to one side, abandoned on a chair, diagonally placed,
no longer a symbol—more a bit of decoration. In that posture
we saw him one night when the moon was full, on the pediment of the Parthenon,
beautiful, mild-mannered—we admired him. We even acknowledged
the good memories of our return from Troy, our valuable experiences
our joy in getting through so many dangers (of course the few of us
who survived. As for the others, who knows?)
                                                    Later
we again depicted him nude, a daydreaming young man gazing
into the distance, sex playing between his robust legs.
Would that we could get along this time the way we did then. But now,
coming to our end, we won't give a damn about Ares
dressed or undressed—even though we'd already begun,
in the midst of the gunfire and the smoke, to make productive use of our new
    experiences,
secretly scratching on marble old known allegories
(his spear no longer at an angle now—better horizontal; and perched up there,
a bird: a sparrow or thrush or even that pigeon, the common variety.)
    Translated from the Greek BY EDMUND KEELEY

Mars ■ Alfred Gong

September—the beech trees wrote.
In the park the teacher a-b-c'ed
when suddenly the stranger appeared,
clanking.
Because the teacher grew pale,
the children shrieked.

Mars walked through the city
multiplying the flags;
he accepted the toast.
(He especially liked the little word "just")
A barber trimmed him for nothing,
for nothing a smith shod him.

Mars took quarters in the city hall,
he was enthusiastic about towers
and above all, he appreciated card indexes.
He collected ragpickers and bums,
and made them knight and adviser.
Hidden in a fold of his garment
the locust lurked.

"Strictest blackout!" he commanded
and gnashed his teeth at the moon
when she followed his order
only now and then.

Translated from the German BY GERTRUDE C. SCHWEBELL

Artemis

I sing of Artemis of the golden shafts, the modest maiden
who loves the din of the hunt and shoots volleys of arrows at stags.
She is the twin sister of Apollon of the golden sword,
and through shady mountains and windy peaks
she delights in the chase as she stretches her golden bow
to shoot the bitter arrows.
—THE HOMERIC HYMNS, 27, TO ARTEMIS (TR. BY A. N. ATHANASSAKIS)

Cretan Artemis ■ Rainer Maria Rilke

Wind from the foothills:
didn't her brow flash a mineral gleam?
The seamless oncoming wind
of swift beasts: was it you who formed her,

molding the chiton to her unconscious breasts
the way a premonition swells with change?
Meanwhile, as if all-knowing,
fixed on distances, skirted, cool,

she stormed with nymphs and hounds
putting her bow to the test,
her belt cinched high and tight;

only, at times, from remote settlements,
tugged at, then conquered in a kind of fury,
by cries for birth.

Translated from the German BY JOHN PECK

Diana—or the Objects ■ Günter Grass

When with her right hand she reaches
over her right shoulder into the quiver,
she puts forward her left leg.

When she hit me,
her object hit my soul
which is to her like an object.

Mostly it is objects resting
against which on Mondays
my knee smashes.

But she, with her hunting permit,
may be photographed only
running and among hounds.

When she says yes and hits,
she hits the objects in nature,
but also stuffed ones.

I have always refused
to let my shadow-casting body
be hurt by a shadowless idea.

But you, Diana,
with your bow,
are to me objective and answerable.
   Translated from the German BY CHRISTOPHER MIDDLETON

> *... and you, O Hecate,*
> *Who know untold desires that work our will*
> *And art the mistress of our secret spells....*
> —OVID, THE METAMORPHOSES, VII (TR. BY HORACE GREGORY)

Hecate* ■ Claribel Alegría

I am the virgin
the woman
the prostitute
I am the salt
the mercury
the sulphur
I am heaven
and hell
I am the earth
you see me illuminated
maternal
Don't trust me
I can consign you
to darkness.
   Translated from the Spanish BY D.J. FLAKOLL

* Hecate, goddess of witchcraft and the underworld, was often identified with Artemis.

ARTEMIS AND ACTAEON

Surrounded by good fortune Cadmus had
A grandson, Actaeon, who was first grief,
Whose forehead wore a most peculiar dress,
A brace of antlers, and whose dogs drank deep
Of his own blood. And these disasters
Were fortune's errors and not his—for how can
Error without intention be called a crime?

—OVID, THE METAMORPHOSES, III (TR. BY HORACE GREGORY)

The Fate of Actaeon ■ James Laughlin

"Bathing the body of nymphs, and Diana,
Nymphs white-gathered about her, and the air, air,
Shaking, air alight with the goddess …

The dogs leap on Actaeon,
            'Hither, hither, Actaeon,'
Spotted stag of the wood;
Gold, gold, a sheaf of hair,
            Thick like a wheat swath,
Blaze, blaze in the sun,
            The dogs leap on Actaeon."
            —Pound: Canto IV

Shall I be punished more severely
than Actaeon   he only gazed on the

Goddess from afar in the wood hic
dea silvarum venatu fessa solebat

virgineos artus liquido perfundere
rore her maiden limbs in the crys-

tal water while I in my ardor pur-
sued her into the shower laving

with impious (and soapy) hands
the breasts of the celestial as the

warm rain upon them   circumfus—
aeque Dianam corporibus texere su-

is the nymphs thronging about her
weaving a screen with their bodies

Actaeon was torn to pieces by his
own dogs what fate now awaits me?

ARTEMIS AND ENDYMION

Calyce and Aethlius had a son Endymion who led Aeolians from Thessaly and founded Elis. But some say that he was a son of Zeus. As he was of surpassing beauty, the Moon fell in love with him, and Zeus allowed him to choose what he would, and he chose to sleep for ever, remaining deathless and ageless.

—APOLLODORUS, THE LIBRARY, I. vii (TR. BY J. G. FRAZER)

Endymion ▄ Thomas Kinsella

At first there was nothing. Then a closed space.
Such light as there was showed him sleeping.
I stole nearer and bent down; the light grew brighter,
and I saw it came from the interplay of our two beings.
It blazed in silence as I kissed his eyelids.
I straightened up and it faded, from his pallor
and the ruddy walls with their fleshy thickenings
—great raw wings, curled—a huge owlet-stare—
as a single drop echoed in the depths.

Hephaestus

Hera wrangled with her husband and because of anger,
untouched by him, she bore glorious Hephaistos
who surpasses all the other gods in craftsmanship.
—HESIOD, THEOGONY (TR. BY A.N. ATHANASSAKIS)

■ Osip Mandelshtam

Zeus fired Hephaestus from the job
Saying he didn't know a thing
About blacksmithing ...
But, Thunderer, you knew that all along!

Translated from the Russian BY NINA KOSSMAN

Hephaestus ■ Peter Russell

Halt God with the clubfoot, stop mocking our weal
With the steel of your heart always forging woe

You know what we want is ploughshares
Why encourage that stupid rival of yours
—Ares of rifle and sword—

Prometheus is chained on the peak
Foothills of Caucasus swarming
With Scythian tanks and guns

All you do is to chuckle
And go on shaping new weapons

It is no use listening to you
And our hireling rulers...

Vulcan ■ George Oppen

The householder issuing to the street
Is adrift a moment in that ice stiff
Exterior. 'Peninsula
Low lying in the bay
And wooded—' Native now
Are the welder and the welder's arc
In the subway's iron circuits:
We have not escaped each other,
Not in the forest, not here. The crippled girl hobbles
Painfully in the new depths
Of the subway, and painfully
We shift our eyes. The bare rails
And black walls contain

Labor before her birth, her twisted
Precarious birth and the men
Laborious, burly— She sits
Quiet, her eyes still. Slowly,
Deliberately she sees
An anchor's blunt fluke sink
Thru coins and coin machines,
The ancient iron and the voltage
In the iron beneath us in the child's deep
Harbors into harbor sand.

Dionysus

... *woman-maddener, be propitious to us singers
who start and finish our song with you; there is no way
for the one who forgets you to remember his song.*
—THE HOMERIC HYMNS, I, FRAGMENTS OF THE HYMN TO DIONYSUS
(TR. BY A.N. ATHANASSAKIS)

Once and For All ■ Delmore Schwartz

Once, when I was a boy,
Apollo summoned me
To be apprenticed to the endless summer of light and consciousness,
And thus to become and be what poets often have been,
A shepherd of being, a riding master of being, holding the sun-god's horses,
    leading his sheep, training his eagles
Directing the constellations to their stations, and to each grace of place.
But the goat-god, piping and dancing, speaking an unknown tongue or the lan-
    guage of the magician,
Sang from the darkness or rose from the underground, whence arise
Love and love's drunkenness, love and birth, love and death, death and rebirth
Which are the beginning of the phoenix festivals, the tragic plays in celebration of
    Dionysus,
And in mourning for his drunken and fallen princes, the singers and sinners,fallen
    because they are, in the end,
Drunken with pride, blinded by joy.

And I followed Dionysus, forgetting Apollo. I followed him far too long until I was
    wrong and chanted:
"One cannot serve both gods. One must choose to win and lose."
But I was wrong and when I knew how I was wrong I knew
What, in a way, I had known all along:
This was the new world, here I belonged, here I was wrong because
Here every tragedy has a happy ending, and any error may be
A fabulous discovery of America, of the opulence hidden in the dark depths and
    glittering heights of reality.

Playing Dionysos in *The Bacchae* ■ Kathleen Raine

I moved him, and he moved in me by power,
knowing the pulse and the refrain of blood
that pumped a spring into the veins of dance
along the water's edge and in its hour.
The rhythm in a sparrow and a bud
left everything to art, to art and chance.

DIONYSUS AND PENTHEUS

"He shall see the Bacchae and shall pay the price
With death.
Now, Dionysus, it is for you
To take up the action. You are not far away.
Punish this man. Steal away his reason,
And plant fantastic madness in its stead."

—EURIPIDES, THE BACCHAE (TR. BY NEIL CURRY)

Go Loudly, Pentheus ■ Kathleen Raine

(Dionysos speaks)
Behind the time when dogwood starts to flower
I work and dance inside long changing days
to find the taste, the marrow of the hour
and twist it like a snake into a phrase
that stings with all the passion of a kiss
and smiles with anger in a lying mask
behind your back and turning in your wrist:
I give you back in blood the thing you ask.

And while you climb the mountain like a child,
expecting pleasures and a pretty dance,
I'll screw your trouble into a spring wild
and deadly in the hidden trap of chance.
Under your well-laid palace stones I've cracked
and wriggled like a rooting lightning-gale
and gently, sweetly in bright birds of fact
I'll wind fat songs of fancy up your trail.

Go loudly, grin behind your mask as dead
as I will make you in a ringing glade.
I take joy in the sour blood I've said
into your ignorant ears. Now fade
and take my phosphor in your vein
as suddenly as it has ripped your sky.
Hear as you die the innocent refrain
of birds inside your blue unseeing eye.

Pentheus ■ George Seferis

Sleep filled him with dreams of fruit and leaves;
wakefulness kept him from picking even a mulberry.
And the two together divided his limbs among the Bacchae.

Translated from the Greek BY EDMUND KEELEY AND PHILIP SHERRARD

LESSER IMMORTALS & NEAR-IMMORTALS

Eros

Pan

Satyrs

Centaurs

Dryads

Proteus

Sibyl

Eros

Eros (Love), fairest among the deathless gods,
he unstrings the limbs and subdues both mind
and sensible thought in the breasts of all gods and all men.
—HESIOD, THEOGONY (TR. BY A.N. ATHANASSAKIS)

Eros ■ Denise Levertov

The flowerlike
animal perfume
in the god's curly
hair—

don't assume
that like a flower's
his attributes
are there to tempt

you or
direct the moth's
hunger—
simply he is
the temple of himself,

hair and hide
a sacrifice of blood and flowers
on his altar

if any worshipper
kneel or not.

Hymn to Eros ■ Denise Levertov

O Eros, silently smiling one, hear me.
Let the shadow of thy wings
brush me.
Let thy presence
enfold me, as if darkness
were swandown.
Let me see that darkness
lamp in hand,
this country become
the other country
sacred to desire.

Drowsy god,
slow the wheels of my thought
so that I listen only

to the snowfall hush of
thy circling.
Close my beloved with me
in the smoke ring of thy power,
that we may be, each to the other,
figures of flame,
figures of smoke,
figures of flesh
newly seen in the dusk.

Cupid's Chant ■ Delmore Schwartz

Cupid is
    The king of flutes.
Cupid's kiss
    Wakes winter's roots.
Cupid touches
    A color's curve.
Cupid reaches
    Apples, peaches,
    Eye and nerve.

A tutor of Venus
    In the dark of the sun,
He knows and he teaches
    That the clever are stupid
    For the stupid to discover
How sleep and love are warm and one.

2
Cupid is
A student of leaves,
A scholar of Eros,
A savant of consciousness,
And of sleep's wine-dark seas;
Of the heights of the birds
And the insides of words,
The seed within Adam,
The birth, the death, and the rebirth
Which breathes in Eve
—All that is seedy, loamy, rising, fickle, growing, seeking, flowing,
    flowering, and unknowable, all that we hope and hardly dare to believe.

Pan

*... the goat-footed, two-horned din-loving one, who roams
over wooded glades together with dance-loving nymphs;
they tread on the peaks of sheer cliffs,
calling upon Pan, the splendid-haired and unkempt
god of shepherds, to whose domain all the snowy hills
and mountain peaks and rocky paths fall.*
—THE HOMERIC HYMNS, 19, TO PAN (TR. BY A.N. ATHANASSAKIS)

Pan with Us ■ Robert Frost

Pan came out of the woods one day,—
His skin and his hair and his eyes were gray,
The gray of the moss of walls were they,—
    And stood in the sun and looked his fill
    At wooded valley and wooded hill.

He stood in the zephyr, pipes in hand,
On a height of naked pasture land;
In all the country he did command
    He saw no smoke and he saw no roof.
    That was well! and he stamped a hoof.

His heart knew peace, for none came here
To this lean feeding save once a year
Someone to salt the half-wild steer,
    Or homespun children with clicking pails
    Who see so little they tell no tales.

He tossed his pipes, too hard to teach
A new-world song, far out of reach,
For a sylvan sign that the blue jay's screech
    And the whimper of hawks beside the sun
    Were music enough for him, for one.

Times were changed from what they were:
Such pipes kept less of power to stir
The fruited bough of the juniper
    And the fragile bluets clustered there
    Than the merest aimless breath of air.

They were pipes of pagan mirth,
And the world had found new terms of worth.
He laid him down on the sun-burned earth
    And raveled a flower and looked away—
    Play? Play?—What should he play?

Pan Is Dead ■ Ezra Pound

Pan is dead. Great Pan is dead.
Ah! bow your heads, ye maidens all,
And weave ye him his coronal.

There is no summer in the leaves,
And withered are the sedges;
How shall we weave a coronal,
Or gather floral pledges?

That I may not say, Ladies.
Death was ever a churl.
That I may not say, Ladies.
How should he show a reason,
That he has taken our Lord away
Upon such hollow season?

Satyrs

... the tribe of worthless, helpless Satyrs ...
—HESIOD, FRAGMENTS OF UNKNOWN POSITION, 6 (TR. BY H.G. EVELYN-WHITE)

The Clown's Report on Satyrs ■ Ramon Guthrie

On the hoof or dead, a satyr weighs
about the single same. They mingle
with goddesses and singe themselves in flame
that they ignite with steady gaze
while they recite the name of One
who in the olden days
slept on Naxos' shingle,
and they are golden ruddy in the sun
and hold themselves aloof.
A satyr on the hoof is fleet.
Slaughtered, their dark red meat is strong.

The Satyr ■ Frank O'Hara

The trees toss and plunge in a skyblue surf!
an automobile comes whizzing, falls by
as the floor of the lake against my thigh
flings and leaves like a kiss or scarf

The bend of the shore where my armpits laugh
runs after the cars that drop from my eye
I'll recapture them all before I die
without losing my limbs in the thick turf

Without fearing the bluejays and pine cones
that rob the sun and torment my cold face
I'll become the Lover of the quick world

For those trees waves and thieves I'm eager! whirled
and drowned in maelstroms of rhodondendrons!
full flowers! round eyes! rush upward! rapture! space!

Centaurs

... shaggy Centaurs, wild things of the mountains....
—HOMER, THE ILIAD, I (TR. BY ROBERT FAGLES)

The Centaur ■ Theodore Roethke

The Centaur does not need a Horse;
He's part of one, as a matter of course.
'Twixt animal and man divided,
His sex-life never is one-sided.
He does what Doves and Sparrows do—
What else he does is up to you.

Centaur ■ Max Jacob

It's true. I met the Centaur. It was on a Breton road, round trees scattered over the slopes. The Centaur's coloring? very light coffee; concupiscent eyes—and his rump! more a snake's tail than a horse. I couldn't speak to him, felt so weak, and my family kept just staring from a distance, more scared than me. O sun how you do light up what's mysterious around you.

Translated from the French BY ARMAND SCHWERNER

The Last Centaur ■ Ion Barbu

... from sun which clasps cloud ...

Fitfully, he squeezed himself to the last,
his head ringing ... then smash, over stones gone green
the whole crown cup at one stroke splattering
all that thinking lofted within the beast.

Vaults have melted and poured the contrary whole ...
Flesh went off in freezing jags of mist,
in foggy coils, slowly, though a stripped heart
arrowed by fire winnows itself from night.

Plodding executioner, vast sleeve
with its trains, shadow dragged at the embers, axes
slicing into the glowing clod. And earth

tumbles to slumber. Nevermore centaur: the wild.
Yet under scorching trots at the stud farms, ringing
deep within piled strata, veins of gold.

Translated from the Romanian BY JOHN PECK

Epitaph for a Centaur ■ Joseph Brodsky

To say that he was unhappy is either to say too much
or too little: depending on who's the audience.

Still, the smell he'd give off was a bit too odious,
and his canter was also quite hard to match.
He said, They meant just a monument, but something went astray:
the womb? the assembly line? the economy?
Or else, the war never happened, they befriended the enemy,
and he was left as it is, presumably to portray
Intransigence, Incompatibility—that sort of thing which proves
not so much one's uniqueness or virtue, but probability.
For years, resembling a cloud, he wandered in olive groves,
marveling at one-leggedness, the mother of immobility.
Learned to lie to himself, and turned it into an art
for want of a better company, also to check his sanity.
And he died fairly young—because his animal part
turned out to be less durable than his humanity.

CHIRON

Meanwhile Chiron was happily engaged
In rearing a young demigod....
—OVID, THE METAMORPHOSES, II (TR. BY HORACE GREGORY)

Chiron ■ Yvor Winters

I, who taught Achilles, saw
Leap beyond me by its law,
By intrinsic law destroyed,
Genius in itself alloyed.

Dying scholar, dim with fact,
By the stallion body racked,
Studying my long defeat,
I have mastered Jove's deceit.

Now my head is bald and dried,
Past divisions simplified:
On the edge of naught I wait,
Magnitude inviolate.

When they are born, firs and towering oaks
spring up on the man-nourishing earth
and grow into lush beauty on the high mountains.
* * *
But whenever fated death is near at hand,
first these beautiful trees wither on their ground,
the bark all around them shrivels up, the branches fall away,
and their souls and those of the nymphs leave the light of the sun together.
—THE HOMERIC HYMNS, 5, TO APHRODITE (TR. BY A.N. ATHANASSAKIS)

Then as he hacked the vitals of the oak
A voice came from the centers of its body:
"I who was once a nymph...."
—OVID, THE METAMORPHOSES, VIII (TR. BY HORACE GREGORY)

Dryad ■ Johannes Bobrowski

Birch, cool
with sap, tree, your breath
in my hands, tense
bark, a yielding glass,
but to feel deeper
stirrings, the stretching
in the trunk,
towards the branches.

Let
your hair fall,
fall in your neck, I hear
through the coolness, I hear a fluttering,
hear the current lift,
the rising flood,
hear ecstasy
sing in my ear.

Translated from the German BY RUTH AND MATTHEW MEAD

Virgin in a Tree ■ Sylvia Plath

How this tart fable instructs
And mocks! Here's the parody of that moral mousetrap
Set in the proverbs stitched on samplers
Approving chased girls who get them to a tree
And put on a bark's nun-black

Habit which deflects
All amorous arrows. For to sheathe the virgin shape
In a scabbard of wood baffles pursuers,

Whether goat-thighed or god-haloed. Ever since that first Daphne
Switched her incomparable back

For a bay-tree hide, respect's
Twined to her hard limbs like ivy: the puritan lip
Cries: 'Celebrate the Syrinx whose demurs
Won her the frog-colored skin, pale pith and watery
Bed of a reed. Look:

Pine-needle armor protects
Pitys from Pan's assault! And though age drop
Their leafy crowns, their fame soars,
Eclipsing Eva, Cleo and Helen of Troy:
For which of those would speak

For a fashion that constricts
White bodies in a wooden girdle, root to top
Unfaced, unformed, the nipple-flowers
Shrouded to suckle darkness? Only they
Who keep cool and holy make

A sanctum to attract
Green virgins, consecrating limb and lip
To chastity's service: like prophets, like preachers,
They descant on the serene and seraphic beauty
Of virgins for virginity's sake.'

Be certain some such pact's
Been struck to keep all glory in the grip
Of ugly spinsters and barren sirs
As you etch on the inner window of your eye
This virgin on her rack:

She, ripe and unplucked, 's
Lain splayed too long in the tortuous boughs: overripe
Now, dour-faced, her fingers
Stiff as twigs, her body woodenly
Askew, she'll ache and wake

Though doomsday bud. Neglect's
Given her lips that lemon-tasting drop:
Untongued, all beauty's bright juice sours.
Tree-twist will ape this gross anatomy
Till irony's bough break.

Wooded Forms ■ Joyce Carol Oates

a leafbeat
an interior vertigo
springs to us from the ring-
upon-ring of their spine
their memories engraved in pulp
wooden flesh fragrant at the core
the soul fluid in perfect
poised surrender
to chain-saw
or sun

perfect in possession
of a form
grown of earth in leaps
straining to its farthest tendrils'
possession of dirt and air
measurable cubic yards

their kind of flesh leaps
through history
in one place
singular
multiplied endlessly

     ours strains to see
     our invention is to see
     imagining our own forms
     of blood and air
     across the continent
     wild and tame and back again
     ring upon ring of our memories
     in newer rhythms
     unsingular
     unknown

Proteus

O Proteus, how many times your image
Comes to us as a young man from the sea,
Then as a lion, then a raving boar,
Or as a snake whom many fear to touch!
Horns change you to a bull, or you might be
A sleeping stone, a tree, or water flowing,
Or fire that quarrels with water everywhere.
—OVID, THE METAMORPHOSES, VIII (TR. BY HORACE GREGORY)

Proteus ■ Jorge Luis Borges

Before the oarsmen of Odysseus
would leave their mark upon the wine-dark sea,
I can divine the indefinable forms
of that old god whose name was Proteus.
Shepherd of the wave-flocks of the waters
and wielder of the gift of prophecy,
he liked to make a secret of his knowledge
and weave a pattern of ambiguous signs.
At the demand of people, he took on
the substance of a lion or a bonfire
or a tree, spreading shade on the river bank
or water which would disappear in water.
Proteus the Egyptian should not surprise you,
you, who are one, but also many others.

Translated from the Spanish BY ALASTAIR REID

Proteus ■ Sándor Weöres

Proteus dissimulates by the shore:
now he is almost a god, now an impossibility;
now he flies away, turns into icy pearls,
now he becomes stone; now again, water.

He dives along the sand and ocean's chain of border
but lives between heaven and abyss: he is the sea,
rocking mud on his chest, but in love he
becomes a man, the lord of mud.

He is a council member, a banker, a judge,
weighing his needle-tipped fate while it's spinning;
now he's thrown back into the free-flowing flood;

now, crackling on his fin, he is a human hamstring;
and from each of his cells the sea is dilating:
not in vain did he live in a dust-bitten hut.

Translated from the Hungarian BY GÁBOR G. GYUKICS AND MICHAEL CASTRO

Proteus's Tale ■ Maura Stanton

Water touched water through my heart.
I fell into a white tangle of octopus,
fluttering for air, one molecule, one second ...
something ghosted across my brain, fiber
or seeds rising on the black negative.
Then I fled into whales, into thread-fine
fish where I ate muscle from my own bones,
into the conch, believing I was a sea.
As a sea anemone, prehensile, I waved
tentacles in the dark; crept with snails,
frightened of the impulse snapping
whatever-I-was into eels, minnows, bones,
into coins stamped with bees, into memory.
The membranes weren't sealed. I escaped—
light or energy—through mysterious windows.
Rents appeared in my insane fabric,
I'd tumble out of shape into other edges,
the cliff of my own dreams looming blue
in the shark's thrust for the swimmer.

Proteus ■ W.S. Merwin

By the splashed cave I found him. Not
(As I had expected) patently delusive
In a shape sea-monstrous, terrible through sleeping,
To scare all comers, nor as that bronze-thewed
Old king of Pharos with staring locks,
But under a gray rock, resting his eyes
From futurity, from the blinding crystal
Of that morning sea, his face flicked with a wisp
Of senile beard, a frail somnolent old man.

Who would harness the sea-beast
To the extravagant burden of his question
Must find him thus dreaming of his daughters,
Of porpoises and horses; thus pitiless
Of an old man's complaints, unawed
At what fierce beasts are roused under his grasp,
Between the brutal ignorance of his hands
Must seize and hold him till the beast stands again
Manlike but docile, the neck bowed to answer.

I had heard in seven wise cities
Of the last shape of his wisdom: when he,
Giver of winds, father as some said
Of the triple nightmare, from the mouth of a man
Would loose the much-whistled wind of prophecy.

The nothing into which a man leans forward
Is mother of all restiveness, drawing
The body prone to falling into no
Repose at last but the repose of falling.

Wherefore I had brought foot to his island
In the dead of dawn, had picked my way
Among the creaking cypresses, the anonymous
Granite sepulchres; wherefore, beyond these,
I seized him now by sleeping throat and heel.
What were my life, unless I might be stone
To grasp him like the grave, though wisdom change
From supposition to savage supposition;
Unless the rigor of mortal hands seemed deathly?

I was a sepulchre to his pleadings,
Stone to his arguments, to his threats;
When he leapt in a bull's rage
By horn and tail I held him; I became
A mad bull's shadow, and would not leave him;
As a battling ram he rose in my hands;
My arms were locked horns that would not leave his horns;
I was the cleft and the claws of birds
When he was a serpent between my fingers.

Wild as heaven erupting into a child
He burst under my fists into a lion;
By mane and foot I grappled him;
Closer to him than his own strength I strained
And held him longer. The sun had fought
Almost to noon when I felt the beast's sinews
Fail, the beast's bristles fall smooth
Again to the skin of a man. I loosed him then.
The head he turned toward me wore a face of mine.

Here was no wisdom but my own silence
Echoed as from a mirror; no marine
Oracular stare but my own eyes
Blinded and drowned in their reflections;
No voice came but a voice we shared, saying,
"You prevail always, but, deathly, I am with you
Always." I am he, by grace of no wisdom,
Who to no end battles the foolish shapes
Of his own death by the insatiate sea.

Sibyl

"When on your way you reach the town of Cumae,
the sacred lakes, the loud wood of Avernus,
there you will see the frenzied prophetess.
Deep in her cave of rick she charts the fates,
consigning to the leaves her words and symbols.
* * *
But visit her, the prophetess, with prayers,
that she reveal the oracles herself
and willingly unlock her voice and lips."

—THE AENEID OF VIRGIL, III (TR. BY ALLEN MANDELBAUM)

The Sibyl ■ Marina Tsvetaeva

The sibyl: burned out; the sibyl: charred.
All the birds are dead but the god is alive.

The sibyl: emptied out; the sibyl: a drought.
All veins have withered: the jealous groom.

The sibyl: dropped out; the sibyl: the crater
Of fate and destruction—the tree among maids.

Like a regal tree in the naked woods—
At first, the fire howled just like a tree.

Then, from under its lids—taking off, unaware,
Like rivers gone dry, the god took flight.

He sensed the waste of an outside search,
And his voice and his heart fell into me.

The sibyl: the oracle; the sibyl: the vault.
Thus, the Word came true in that exact

Unaging hour; thus, in gray-haired grass
Her mortal maidenhood became the cave

For the marvelous voice …
                              thus, becoming a starstorm—
The sibyl: dropped out of life.

Translated from the Russian BY NINA KOSSMAN

A Sibyl ■ Rainer Maria Rilke

Ages ago they called her old.
But there she was, walking the same street
each day. So they changed the time-scale,
calculating her age as with forests,

in centuries. Yet she stood
in the same spot each evening,
black as a citadel
towering, cavernous, charred,

and out of it the words that teemed in her
against her will, unwatched,
endlessly flapped and screamed,
while those that returned already
perched beneath her brows
shadowy, set for the night.

Translated from the German BY JOHN PECK

The Sibyl ■ Vernon Watkins

While kings rode forth to conquest I stayed here.
The shadows of their laurels crossed my wall.
While heroes came to terms with their own fear,
They did not know I should outlast them all.
Whether men called me wanton or austere,
My cave became their common port of call:
How many left me, chastened by the tear
Which knew their destiny, but would not fall.

And still my vision behind the bone
To separate their lives and set them free.
I hold from heaven the power to see what's gone
So clearly, that what is or is to be
Hinders no whit the noblest I have known,
His passion rooted, singing like a tree.

THE WAY
TO THE
UNDERWORLD

The Styx; Charon
Cerberus
Lethe

The Styx; Charon

... The journey they began can now continue.
They near the riverbank. Even the boatman,
while floating on the Styx, had seen them coming
across the silent grove and toward the shore.
He does not wait for greeting but attacks,
insulting with these words: "Enough! Stop there!
Whoever you may be who make your way,
so armed, down to our waters, tell me now
why you have come. This is the land of shadows,
of sleep and drowsy Night; no living bodies
can take their passage in the ship of Styx....
—THE AENEID OF VIRGIL, VI (TR. BY ALLEN MANDELBAUM)

On the Banks of the Styx ■ Wislawa Szymborska

Dear individual soul, this is the Styx.
The Styx, that's right: Why are you so perplexed?
As soon as Charon reads the prepared text
over the speakers, let the nymphs affix
your name badge and transport you to the banks.
(The nymphs? They fled your woods and joined the ranks
of personnel here.) Floodlights will reveal
piers built of reinforced concrete and steel,
and hovercrafts whose beelike buzz resounds
where Charon used to ply his wooden oar.
Mankind has multiplied, has burst its bounds:
nothing, sweet soul, is as it was before.
Skyscrapers, solid waste, and dirty air:
the scenery's been harmed beyond repair.
Safe and efficient transportation (millions
of souls served here, all races, creeds, and sexes)
requires urban planning: hence pavilions,
warehouses, dry docks, and office complexes.
Among the gods it's Hermes, my dear soul,
who makes all prophecies and estimations
when revolutions and wars take their toll—
our boats, of course, require reservations.
A one-way trip across the Styx is free:
the meters saying, "No Canadian dimes,
no tokens" are left standing, as you see,
but only to remind us of old times.
From Section Tau Four of the Alpha Pier
you're boarding hovercraft Sigma Sixteen—
it's packed with sweating souls, but in the rear
you'll find a seat (I've got it on my screen).
Now Tartarus (let me pull up the file)
is overbooked, too—no way we could stretch it.

Cramped, crumpled souls all dying to get out,
one last half drop of Lethe in my phial …
Not faith in the beyond, but only doubt
can make you, sorry soul, a bit less wretched.

Translated from the Polish BY STANISLAW BARANCZAK AND CLARE CAVANAGH

Charon's Cosmology ■ Charles Simic

With only his dim lantern
To tell him where he is
And every time a mountain
Of fresh corpses to load up

Take them to the other side
Where there are plenty more
I'd say by now he must be confused
As to which side is which

I'd say it doesn't matter
No one complains he's got
Their pockets to go through
In one a crust of bread in another a sausage

Once in a long while a mirror
Or a book which he throws
Overboard into the dark river
Swift and cold and deep

Shore ■ Zbigniew Herbert

It waits at the shore of a large and slow river
on the other side is Charon the sky shines turbidly
(besides it is not sky at all) Charon
is already here he only throws a rope around a branch
it (the soul) takes out the obol
which isn't sour yet under the tongue
it sits in the back of the empty boat
all this without a word

if there were at least the moon
or the howling of a dog

Translated from the Polish BY JOHN CARPENTER AND BOGDANA CARPENTER

Canto 26 ■ Lars Forssell

All darkness is not equally dark. When he stepped
down into the boat he made us snuff the whole
row of smoldering torches and brands we'd kept.
I drew my mantle round me. It was cold.

"It's in pitch-darkness that I forebode land."
And the boat-hook guided the ferry into black.
Around the stem, Acheron's waters lapped.
"There still remains some thirteen heartbeats' sand

in the hourglass by the tiller. So I won't be late."
Where we saw night's dárk side and coal on coal
he steered by the rocky islets' shadow play,

and by the stone-pines' contours, toward his goal.
In the dark the scrape of keel on gravel bank.
"Here's my arm. Good night. The fare's one obol, thanks."

Translated from the Swedish BY ROGER GREENWALD

Charon ■ Louis MacNeice

The conductor's hands were black with money:
Hold on to your ticket, he said, the inspector's
Mind is black with suspicion, and hold on to
That dissolving map. We moved through London,
We could see the pigeons through the glass but failed
To hear their rumours of wars, we could see
The lost dog barking but never knew
That his bark was as shrill as a cock crowing,
We just jogged on, at each request
Stop there was a crowd of aggressively vacant
Faces, we just jogged on, eternity
Gave itself airs in revolving lights
And then we came to the Thames and all
The bridges were down, the further shore
Was lost in fog, so we asked the conductor
What we should do. He said: Take the ferry
Faute de mieux. We flicked the flashlight
And there was the ferryman just as Virgil
And Dante had seen him. He looked at us coldly
And his eyes were dead and his hands on the oar
Marbled his calves and he said to us coldly:
If you want to die you will have to pay for it.

Cerberus

*These regions echo with the triple-throated
bark of the giant Cerberus, who crouches,
enormous, in a cavern facing them.*
— THE AENEID OF VIRGIL, VI (TR. BY ALLEN MANDELBAUM)

Cerberus ■ Stephen Mitchell

His three fierce mastiff-heads bloodcurdlingly bark. No spirit may enter the Elysian Fields until he is satisfied that it is truly at peace. Some have tried to bribe him, but he is incorruptible. Some have tried to sneak past, but he tore the memory of their bodies to agonized shreds. Pain outlasts its vehicle.

Even he, though, was a puppy once. He sometimes looks out at the vast crowd milling desperately by the gates of horn (or is it the gates of ivory?—he can never keep his classical references straight), and feels a twinge of pity for them, like a minor third. How impatient they are. How they would love to be able to pet him on each of his heads, say "Nice doggy," and move on. But they are no longer living in the trivial, safe universe of their desires. Everything here is real.

Lethe

... But—look—the god
now shakes a bough that drips with Lethe's dew
* * *
*   ... as he struggles,*
his swimming eyes relax. That sudden rest
had just began to let his limbs fall slack....
—THE AENEID OF VIRGIL, V (TR. BY ALLEN MANDELBAUM)

Lethe ■ H.D. (Hilda Doolittle)

Nor skin nor hide nor fleece
    Shall cover you,
Nor curtain of crimson nor fine
Shelter of cedar-wood be over you,
    Nor the fir-tree
    Nor the pine.

Nor sight of whin nor gorse
    Nor river-yew,
Nor fragrance of flowering bush,
Nor wailing of reed-bird to waken you,
    Nor of linnet,
    Nor of thrush.

Nor word nor touch nor sight
  Of lover, you
Shall long through the night but for this:
The roll of the full tide to cover you
    Without question,
    Without kiss.

Lethe ■ Edna St. Vincent Millay

Ah, drink again
This river that is the taker-away of pain,
And the giver-back of beauty!

In these cool waves
What can be lost?—
Only the sorry cost
Of the lovely thing, ah, never the thing itself!

The level flood that laves
The hot brow
And the stiff shoulder
Is at our temples now.

Gone is the fever,
But not into the river;
Melted the frozen pride,
But the tranquil tide
Runs never the warmer for this,
Never the colder.

I immerse the dream.
Drench the kiss.
Dip the song in the stream.

There Is No River Which Is Called Lethe ■ Charles Olson

There is no river which is called Lethe
by the ancients. To forget
is to neglect
or to refuse to
hold on to, to fail
to get ... they should put out to sea
without being discovered by them ... he protected
the murderer unawares

    it is not unknown to me
    that some god led thee

What remains hidden
is also forgetfulness
means, the unnoticed, that which hasn't
been seen yet, *lateo* the Latin what lies
concealed ... lest he perish having known ...

    lest he perish
    having not accomplished his end

II
Thou thoughtest
to escape the gods' notice
in ... to let a thing escape, to forget?

    That she might bear
    unknown?

to forget purposely, to pass over? He chose
to forget?
        Caught by the leg
        he went head first
        through the hole
        into the darkness
        where the waters
        roar

& when he came out
he needed
those who could bathe
him back into
his memory and
his forgetfulness: his wits
were sharp enough
when he was on
sugar & didn't remember
all that had happened
in the year and a half
since he had come in barefoot

III
not to hold
not to remember
not to come by
anything got

LOVERS

Orpheus and Eurydice
Philemon and Baucis
Alcestis

Orpheus & Eurydice

The bride stepped on a snake; pierced by his venom,
The girl tripped, falling, stumbled into Death.
Her bridegroom, Orpheus, poet of the hour,
And pride of Rhadope, sang loud his loss
To everyone on earth. When this was done,
His wailing voice, his lyre, and himself
Came weaving through the tall gates of Taenarus
Down to the world of Death and flowing Darkness
To tell the story of his grief again.

—OVID, THE METAMORPHOSES, X (TR. BY HORACE GREGORY)

Orpheus. Eurydice. Hermes. ■ Rainer Maria Rilke

It was the souls' strange mine:
like silver ore they went, silent
as veins through its darkness. Between roots
sprang the blood that goes on to humans,
and heavy as porphyry it looked in the dark.
There was no other redness.

There were rocks
and spectral forests. Bridges over emptiness
and that great, gray, unreflecting pool
that hung over its distant bed
like rainclouds over a landscape.
And between meadows, soft and long-suffering,
showed the one pale path,
like a long strip of linen, bleaching.

And on this one path they came.

First, the slender man in the blue mantle,
who stared, mute and impatient, straight ahead.
In great bites his stride
devoured the path; his fists hung
heavy in the fall of folds
and forgot entirely the weightless lyre
that had grown into his left hand
like roses twining with the olive branch.
It was as if his senses were divided:
While sight ran before him like a dog,
turned back, again and again stood
distant and waiting at the path's next turn—
hearing lagged behind him, like a scent.
Sometimes it seemed to him as if it reached
just to the movement of those other two,
who should be following this whole ascent.

97

Then again came only faint echoes of his climbing
and the wind in his mantle behind him.
He kept telling himself, they would still come;
said it aloud and heard his own words fade.
They would still come, only there would be two
who walked so terribly softly. Suppose he
turned just once (if only looking back
did not dissolve this whole task,
still incomplete), he had to see them,
the two soft ones who followed him in silence:

The god of journeys, of the distant message,
the petasos over his brilliant eyes,
bearing the slender staff before his body
and the wings beating at his ankles;
and given to his left hand: *she*.

So beloved
that from one lyre
more mourning came
than ever from threneteriai,
that a world grew out of mourning
in which everything existed all over again:
woods and a valley, and a path
and a village, field, stream, animals;
and around this world of mourning,
just as around the other earth,
a sun, and a silent, starry sky,
a mourning sky with stars displaced—:
So beloved.

But she walked on, at the god's hand,
her steps hobbled by the long shrouds,
uncertain, gentle, and without impatience.
Within herself
like a woman hopeful, heavy with child,
and thought not of the man who walked ahead,
nor of the path ascending into life.
Within herself. And having died
fulfilled her like an abundance.
Like a fruit of sweetness and of darkness,
she was so full of her great death,
which was so new, that she understood nothing.

She was again a virgin, again
untouchable; her sex, closed,
like a young flower toward evening,
and her hands were so broken
of being given, that even the gentle god's

infinitely soft and guiding touch
offended her, like a liberty taken.

Now she was no longer that blonde woman
sometimes remembered in the poet's songs,
no longer the broad bed's odor and island
and no longer that man's property.

She was already loosened like long hair
and scattered and absorbed like fallen rain
and meted out like hundredfold provision.

She was already root.

And when suddenly
the god restrained her,
and pronounced the doom: He has turned—,
she understood nothing and said softly: *Who?*

But distant, dark, before the bright opening
stood someone or other whose face
was not to be recognized. He stood and saw,
how on that strip of path between the meadows,
the god of message, silent, sorrowing, turned
to follow the shape
already going back that same way,
her steps hobbled by the long shrouds,
uncertain, gentle and without impatience.

> *Translated from the German* BY RIKA LESSER

Eurydice to Orpheus ▪ Marina Tsvetaeva

For those who have unmarried the last shreds
Of a shroud (no lips, no cheeks!...)
Oh, isn't it a breach of the rules—
An Orpheus descending into Hades?

For those who have thrown off the last earthly
Bonds; those who, on the bed of beds,
Have laid aside the great lie of beholding,
For those who see inside—the rendezvous is a knife.

Paid for—with all the roses of blood—
This spacious garment
Of immortality ...
                    You who loved farther than Lethe's
Riverhead—I need the peace

Of forgetfulness ... For in this shadowy house
You, living, are a shadow, while I, dead,

Am real ... What can I say to you except:
"Forget this and leave!"

I cannot be stirred! I cannot follow!
I have no arms! No lips to press to lips!
With the snakebite of immortality
Female passion ends.

Paid for—remember my shouts!—
This final plain.
Orpheus must not descend to Eurydice
And brothers must not disturb their sisters.

Translated from the Russian BY NINA KOSSMAN

Eurydice ■ H.D. (Hilda Doolittle)

I

So you have swept me back,
I who could have walked with the live souls
above the earth,
I who could have slept among the live flowers
at last;

so for your arrogance
and your ruthlessness
I am swept back
where dead lichens drip
dead cinders upon moss of ash;

so for your arrogance
I am broken at last,
I who had lived unconscious,
who was almost forgot;

if you had let me wait
I had grown from listlessness
into peace,
if you had let me rest with the dead,
I had forgot you
and the past.

v

So for your arrogance
and your ruthlessness
I have lost the earth
and the flowers of the earth,
and the live souls above the earth,
and you who had passed across the light
and reached

ruthless;
you who have your own light,
who are to yourself a presence,
who need no presence;

yet for all your arrogance
and your glance,
I tell you this:

such loss is no loss,
such terror, such coils and strands and pitfalls
of blackness,
such terror
is no loss;

hell is no worse than your earth
above the earth,
hell is no worse,
no, nor your flowers
nor your veins of light
nor your presence,
a loss;

my hell is no worse than yours
though you pass among the flowers and speak
with the spirits above earth.

VI
Against the black
I have more fervour
than you in all the splendour of that place,
against the blackness
and the stark grey
I have more light;

and the flowers,
if I should tell you,
you would turn from your own fit paths
toward hell,
turn again and glance back
and I would sink into a place
even more terrible than this.

VII
At least I have the flowers of myself,
and my thoughts, no god
can take that;
I have the fervour of myself for a presence
and my own spirit for light;

and my spirit with its loss
knows this;
though small against the black,
small against the formless rocks,
hell must break before I am lost;

before I am lost,
hell must open like a red rose
for the dead to pass.

Eurydice ■ Margaret Atwood

He is here, come down to look for you.
It is the song that calls you back,
a song of joy and suffering
equally: a promise:
that things will be different up there
than they were last time.

You would rather have gone on feeling nothing,
emptiness and silence; this stagnant peace
of the deepest sea, which is easier
than the noise and flesh of the surface.

You are used to these blanched dim corridors,
you are used to the king
who passes you without speaking.

The other one is different
and you almost remember him.
He says he is singing to you
because he loves you,

not as you are now,
so chilled and minimal: moving and still
both, like a white curtain blowing
in the draft from a half-opened window
beside a chair on which nobody sits.

Descent ■ Yannis Ritsos

"Eurydice!" he shouted. He descended the stairway hastily.
The caretaker's quarters were without light.
He probed the mirror with his hands.
In the depths, the woman with the yellow umbrella was departing.
The second woman shouted back to him from the basement: "She is dead."
The three airmen came out of the elevator with a suitcase—
in it were her two severed hands and my manuscript.

   Translated from the Greek BY MINAS SAVVAS

Orpheus in Hell ■ D.M. Thomas

Perhaps if he praised Death?…
They might spare her.
But what came to him was a flight of starlings.

He had never known such torture.
He dragged in a writing-desk,
He sharpened a pencil, laid out a sheet

Of white paper, and made himself sit.
But before he could find a line about Death
He was up and pacing the close and lightless

Room and his lips were moving
Joyfully, his image of her
As the earth's menstruation

Had started up an image of poppy-fields
Blowing red in the clean wind.
He ground his teeth

And made himself sit down again
At the hideous blank paper
And she tried to help him concentrate

By pretending to be asleep
Since it was impossible for her to walk out
And leave his lips free to compose.

He tried to praise her death,
But he was up and pacing on his worn shoes
With a lyric of how her warm lips couldn't

Hide their wakefullness, and she opened her eyes
And smiled, and, smiling, he groaned,
Sat down at the desk and scrawled something.

And in time his Ode to Death saved her.
They were content to keep him only.
She rose to life with a whole notebook of poems

That had seeped like immortal living gum
Out of the dead wood of his death ode,
And every morning she ran it through

In her memory, and every night,
So that the trees and rocks still moved with it.

Orpheus and Eurydice ■ Jorie Graham

Up ahead, I know, he felt it stirring in himself already, the glance,
the darting thing in the pile of rocks,

already in him, there, shiny in the rubble, hissing Did you want to remain
completely unharmed?—

the point-of-view darting in him, shiny head in the ash-heap,

hissing Once upon a time, and then Turn now darling give me that look,

that perfect shot, give me that place where I'm erased ...

The thing, he must have wondered, could it be put to rest, there, in the glance,
could it lie back down into the dustiness, giving its outline up?

When we turn to them—limbs, fields, expanses of dust called meadow and avenue—
will they be freed then to slip back in?

Because you see he could not be married to it anymore, this field with minutes in it
called woman, its presence in him the thing called

future—could not be married to it anymore, expanse tugging his mind out into it,
tugging the wanting-to-finish out.

What he dreamed of was this road (as he walked on it), this dustiness,
but without their steps on it, their prints, without song—

What she dreamed, as she watched him turning with the bend in the road (can you
understand this?)—what she dreamed

was of disappearing into the unseen

not of disappearing, lord, into the real—

And yes she could feel it in him already, up ahead, that wanting-to-turn-and-cast-
the-outline-over-her

by his glance,

sealing the edges down,

saying I know you from somewhere darling, don't I,
saying You're the kind of woman who etcetera—

(Now the cypresses are swaying) (Now the lake in the distance)
(Now the view-from-above, the aerial attack of *do you remember?*)—

now the glance reaching her shoreline wanting only to be recalled,
now the glance reaching her shoreline wanting only to be taken in,

(somewhere the castle above the river)

(somewhere you holding this piece of paper)

(what will you do next? (—feel it beginning?)

now she's raising her eyes, as if pulled from above,

now she's looking back into it, into the poison the beginning,

giving herself to it, looking back into the eyes,

feeling the dry soft grass beneath her feet for the first time now the mind

looking into that which sets the _____ in motion and seeing in there

a doorway open nothing on either side
(a slight wind now around them, three notes from up the hill)

through which morning creeps and the first true notes—

For they were deep in the earth and what is possible swiftly took hold.

The Look Back ■ William Bronk

When Orpheus and his Eurydice
walked up from the underworld, they thought
of the light up there, how beautiful it was,
how much they longed for, needed it;
but even so, they'd been a long time
in the dark, too long. They'd learned it needed them.

Eurydice ■ Thomas Merton

Eurydice is impossible
If Orpheus looks away
Eurydice doubts and weeps
If Orpheus looks at her
Eurydice dies

Orpheus ■ Rod Wooden

They had almost reached light.
And as he walked, a space
was left behind in the air
like a keyhole in a door
but him-shaped.
And the door of the air
was opening, opening so wide
he had to turn to close it.

Orpheus ■ Stephen Mitchell

Pluto sits on his ebony throne enchanted. "Beautiful," he sighs. "Ah, beautiful."
Iron tears trickle down his cheeks. He puts his hand on Persephone's arm. "My
dear," he says, "we must grant
this young man's request."

The young queen thinks for a moment. She has ripened since her first, unwill-
ing, visit to the underworld, when all the forms were shadowy, and behind each
shadow lurked a fear. Now she can see clearly in the dreamlight. She is on a first-
name basis with all the inhabitants, from the gentlest to the most savage. She has
learned never to look back.

But this poor boy, this exquisite singer, will have a hard time ahead of him; she
can tell by looking at his eyes. It is one thing to charm animals, trees, and rocks,
and quite another to be in harmony with a woman. She recognizes his attitude, she
has seen it before: fear protected by longing. Hence the bridal image, forever unat-
tainable, forever ideal. No wonder Eurydice took the serpent's way out. Girls who
are seen that way grow up to be maenads. If only, she thinks: if only there were
some way to tell him. But, of course, he will have to learn for himself. To lose his
love again and again, precipitously, as if by chance. To be torn in pieces, again and
again.

She turns to the king. "Yes, darling, " she says. "Let them go."

Betrayals / Hades, Eurydice, Orpheus ■ Gregory Orr

She stood before his throne,
her body so beautiful
it made the old king wince.

And we ghosts, gray husks,
gathered close as if
to warm ourselves at embers.

Then *he* entered, his boots
like thunder echoing
in that dark, silent hall.

And what had he brought?
Songs of anguish and desire—
all she had gladly forgot.

His words about the world
were meant to lure her back,
to hurt her into memory.

And they worked. I watched
her brow furrow,
her placid face lose all repose.

I thought we'd lost her then
until our sly king
whispered in the singer's ear:

"Take her. She's yours.
And trust her if you dare,
but be alert.

Do not turn your back on her."

Orpheus in the Underworld ▪ Louis Simpson

Night, dark night, night of my distress—
The moon is glittering with all the tears
Of the long silence and unhappiness
Of those who loved in vain for many years.

And so it glittered on the sleeping town
When Orpheus alone and sadly went
To death, to fetch Eurydice, and down
The fearful road pursued his dark descent.

Here were the walls, the gates where death had set
His warnings—in a city carved in stone
The citizens were busy; farmers whet
Their scythes in meadows never to be mown.

The kings and judges sat in their high places.
Then, at the sound of a loud trumpet blown,
They crowded, with pale terror on their faces,
From Death ascending to his dreadful throne.

Orpheus entered. As the eery light
Dwindled, he grasped his lute, and stumbling bent
His footsteps through the thick, enshrouding night.
Then suddenly, the lute by accident

Was struck—the sound exploded like a star
And shone and faded, and the Echoes woke
And danced, and ran before him. Down the far
Corridors it seemed the silence spoke.

He touched the strings again, began to play
In the same order. Fearfully he went
Toward the Echoes, and they still gave way.
And so he followed his own instrument.

At last to the deep hall of death he came.
And there the King sat, motionless and dread.
The night coiled from his nostrils like a flame;
The eyes lacked luster in the massive head.

And by his icy feet, pale in her shroud,
The beautiful Eurydice was laid.
Orpheus knelt beside her, and he bowed
His head, and touched the lute again, and played.

Night, dark night, night of my distress—
Once by the Mediterranean in May
I heard a nightingale, and the sadness of roses
In the murmuring wind, but this was sadder than they.

Night, dark night, night of my distress—
I too have waked her, seen the heavy shawl
Of night slip from her shoulders, and the darkness
Fly from her open eyes. And through the hall,

Through cities and the country of the dead
With the one I loved, hand in hand, have gone.
The dog of death was quiet as we fled,
And so we passed, as shadows over stone.

Under the hills in their enormous silence
And by the sea where it is always still,
I felt her hand in mine, the fearful sense
Of mortal love. And so we fled, until

I turned toward her. With a cry she vanished.
Goodbye, pale shadow of my happiness!
I to the light have been forever banished
That is the night, the night of my distress.

Then Orpheus pursued his lonely way
Upward into the world, and a strange glory
Shone from his face. The trees, when he would play,
Were moved, and roses wept to hear his story.

It's Orpheus in the wind. His music grieves
The moon. He tells the water of his loss.
And all the birds are silent, and the leaves
Of summer in that music sigh and toss.

Eurydice in Darkness ■ Peter Davison

Here far underground I can hear the trees
Still moving overhead where he, the poet,
Mourns. Let him stir stumps if he chooses.
Soon enough he'll sing his courage up
To penetrate the earth, clinging to that lyre
As though the world depended on it, and unstring
One after the other of my familiars,
(The three-headed lapdog, the boatman at the river,
The gaggle of furies, my Undertaker himself)
With instrument still twangling from the effort.
His fingers will be raw, but I'll be waiting
Dressed to kill and ready with a plan
He'll find acceptable. He'll turn his back
(Its every flabby muscle I have pinched
A thousand times) and clump him to sunlight.
And so I shall—murmuring at times,
Whining that he walks too fast, complaining
That he might at least give me a look
After such absence, brushing my breasts against him.
Not till the sunlight seeps in overhead
Will I tax him: a man and not a poet
Would have kept the country free of snakes
And left off that everlasting mooning and fiddling.
He could have prevented all this! And he might, please,
Give me a hand here, I'll fall with these sandals.
That's it! He turns from the light, his face engorged
With pity and self-pity. He thrusts out his hand,
And I shall dance away, my laughter dancing
Before me every mile of the way back home.

Orpheus and Eurydice ■ Geoffrey Hill

Though there are wild dogs
        Infesting the roads
We have recitals, catalogues
        Of protected birds;

And the rare pale sun
        To water our days.
Men turn to savagery now or turn
        To the laws'

Immutable black and red.
        To be judged for his song,
Traversing the still-moist dead,
        The newly-stung,

Love goes, carrying compassion
        To the rawly-difficult;
His countenance, his hands' motion,
        Serene even to a fault.

Orpheus' Dream ■ Edwin Muir

And she was there. The little boat
Coasting the perilous isles of sleep,
Zones of oblivion and despair,
Stopped, for Eurydice was there.
The foundering skiff could scarcely keep
All that felicity afloat.

As if we had left earth's frontier wood
Long since and from this sea had won
The lost original of the soul,
The moment gave us pure and whole
Each back to each, and swept us on
Past every choice to boundless good.

Forgiveness, truth, atonement, all
Our love at once—till we could dare
At last to turn our heads and see
The poor ghost of Eurydice
Still sitting in her silver chair,
Alone in Hades' empty hall.

Darkness Spoken ■ Ingeborg Bachmann

Like Orpheus I play
death on the strings of life,
and to the beauty of the Earth
and your eyes, which govern heaven,
I can only speak of darkness.

Don't forget that you also, suddenly,
on that morning when your camp
was still damp with dew, and a carnation
slept on your heart,
you saw the dark stream
race past you.

The string of silence
taut on the pulse of blood,
I grasped your beating heart.
Your curls were transformed
into the shadow hair of night,
black flakes of darkness
buried your face.

And I don't belong to you.
Both of us mourn now.
But like Orpheus I know
life on the strings of death,
deepening the blue
of your forever closed eye.

   Translated from the German BY PETER FILKINS

ORPHEUS WITHOUT EURYDICE

… when the poet, great-grandson of the gods,
Sat down to sing and touched his golden lyre,
There the cool grasses waved beneath green shadows,
For trees came crowding where the poet sang,
The silver poplar and the bronze-leaved oak,
The swaying lina, beechnut, maiden-laurel,
Delicate hazel and spear-making ash….

—OVID, THE METAMORPHOSES, X (TR. BY HORACE GREGORY)

Orpheus ■ Veno Taufer

he sings of spring under a cherry tree in bloom
holding the music sheet upside down,
singing with angelic sadness and comically as the devil
women and children watch him without malice

blossoms fall on his forehead, his head echoes
crows are biding their time for the fruit to ripen
the voice in his throat is stopped by saliva
women and children already feel the pips between their teeth

his heart is a bird of prey
it sits on his nose stares him in the eye
cools his death sweat with the fan of its wings

his heart is a bird of prey
it pecks his eyes out inhabits his skull

in airless draught it claws after moisture

   Translated from the Slovenian BY JUDITA MIA DINTINJANA

A Tree Telling of Orpheus ■ Denise Levertov

White dawn. Stillness.   When the rippling began
        I took it for sea-wind, coming to our valley with rumors
        of salt, of treeless horizons. But the white fog
didn't stir; the leaves of my brothers remained outstretched,
unmoving.
        Yet the rippling drew nearer—and then

my own outermost branches began to tingle, almost as if
fire had been lit below them, too close, and their twig-tips
were drying and curling.
                                    Yet I was not afraid, only
                                    deeply alert.
I was the first to see him, for I grew
            out on the pasture slope, beyond the forest.
He was a man, it seemed: the two
moving stems, the short trunk, the two
arm-branches, flexible, each with five leafless
                                                twigs at their ends,
and the head that's crowned by brown or gold grass,
bearing a face not like the beaked face of a bird,
            more like a flower's.
                                    He carried a burden made of
some cut branch bent while it was green,
strands of a vine tight-stretched across it. From this,
when he touched it, and from his voice
which unlike the wind's voice had no need of our
leaves and branches to complete its sound,
                                                came the ripple.
But it was now no longer a ripple (he had come near and
stopped in my first shadow) it was a wave that bathed me
                        as if rain
                                    rose from below and around me
                        instead of falling.
And what I felt was no longer a dry tingling:
            I seemed to be singing as he sang, I seemed to know
            what the lark knows; all my sap
                        was mounting towards the sun that by now
                                    had risen, the mist was rising, the grass
was drying, yet my roots felt music moisten them
deep under earth.

            He came still closer, leaned on my trunk:
            the bark thrilled like a leaf still-folded.
Music! There was no twig of me not
                                    trembling with joy and fear.

Then as he sang
it was no longer sounds only that made the music:
he spoke, and as no tree listens I listened, and language
                        came into my roots
                                    out of the earth,
                        into my bark
                                    out of the air,
                        into the pores of my greenest shoots
                                    gently as dew
and there was no word he sang but I knew its meaning.

He told of journeys,
        of where sun and moon go while we stand in dark,
   of an earth-journey he dreamed he would take some day
deeper than roots …
He told of the dreams of man, wars, passions, griefs,
       and I, a tree, understood words—ah, it seemed
my thick bark would split like a sapling's that
           grew too fast in the spring
when a late frost wounds it.

          Fire he sang,
that trees fear, and I, a tree, rejoiced in its flames.
New buds broke forth from me though it was full summer.
     As though his lyre (now I knew its name)
     were both frost and fire, its chords flamed
up to the crown of me.
         I was seed again.
        I was fern in the swamp.
        I was coal.

And at the heart of my wood
(so close I was to becoming man or a god)
    there was a kind of silence, a kind of sickness,
      something akin to what men call boredom,
                something
(the poem descended a scale, a stream over stones)
      that gives to a candle a coldness
       in the midst of its burning, he said.

It was then,
    when in the blaze of his power that
          reached me and changed me
   I thought I should fall my length,
that the singer began
     to leave me.   Slowly
    moved from my noon shadow
           to open light,
words leaping and dancing over his shoulders
back to me
      rivery sweep of lyre-tones becoming
slowly again
     ripple.
And I
     in terror
       but not in doubt of
         what I must do
in anguish, in haste,
     wrenched from the earth root after root,
the soil heaving and cracking, the moss tearing asunder—

and behind me others: my brothers
forgotten since dawn. In the forest
they too had heard,
and were pulling their roots in pain
out of a thousand years' layers of dead leaves,
        rolling the rocks away,
            breaking themselves
                out of
                their depths.
You would have thought we would lose the sound of the lyre,
           of the singing
so dreadful the storm-sounds were, where there was no storm,
           no wind but the rush of our
        branches moving, our trunks breasting the air.
        But the music!
           The music reached us.

Clumsily,
      stumbling over our own roots,
                rustling our leaves
                in answer,
we moved, we followed.

All day we followed, up hill and down.
                We learned to dance,
for he would stop, where the ground was flat,
              and words he said
taught us to leap and to wind in and out
around one another   in figures   the lyre's measure designed.
The singer
      laughed till he wept to see us, he was so glad.
                At sunset
we came to this place I stand in, this knoll
with its ancient grove that was bare grass then.
      In the last light of that day his song became
farewell.
      He stilled our longing.
      He sang our sun-dried roots back into earth,
watered them: all-night rain of music so quiet
                we could almost
          not hear it in the
             moonless dark.
By dawn he was gone.
        We have stood here since,
in our new life.
      We have waited.
        He does not return.
It is said he made his earth-journey, and lost
what he sought.

It is said they felled him
and cut up his limbs for firewood.
                          And it is said
his head still sang and was swept out to sea singing.
Perhaps he will not return.
                          But what we have lived
comes back to us.
                  We see more.
                          We feel, as our rings increase,
something that lifts our branches, that stretches our furthest
                                          leaf-tips
further.
        The wind, the birds,
                          do not sound poorer but clearer,
recalling our agony, and the way we danced.
The music!

Orpheus Alone ▨ Mark Strand

It was an adventure much could be made of: a walk
On the shores of the darkest known river,
Among the hooded, shoving crowds, by steaming rocks
And rows of ruined huts half-buried in the muck;
Then to the great court with its marble yard
Whose emptiness gave him the creeps, and to sit there
In the sunken silence of the place and speak
Of what he had lost, what he still possessed of his loss,
And, then, pulling out all the stops, describing her eyes,
Her forehead where the golden light of evening spread,
The curve of her neck, the slope of her shoulders, everything
Down to her thighs and calves, letting, letting the words come,
As if lifted from sleep, to drift upstream,
Against the water's will, where all the condemned
And pointless labor, stunned by his voice's cadence,
Would come to a halt, and even the crazed, dishevelled
Furies, for the first time, would weep, and the soot-filled
Air would clear just enough for her, the lost bride,
To step through the image of herself and be seen in the light.
As everyone knows, this was the first great poem,
Which was followed by days of sitting around
In the houses of friends, with his head back, his eyes
Closed, trying to will her return, but finding
Only himself, again and again, trapped
In the chill of his loss, and, finally,
Without a word, taking off to wander the hills
Outside of town, where he stayed until he had shaken
The image of love and put in its place the world
As he wished it would be, urging its shape and measure
Into speech of such newness that the world was swayed,

And trees suddenly appeared in the bare place
Where he spoke and lifted their limbs and swept
The tender grass with the gowns of their shade,
And stones, weightless for once, came and set themselves there,
And small animals lay in the miraculous fields of grain
And aisles of corn, and slept. The voice of light
Had come forth from the body of fire, and each thing
Rose from its depth and shone as it never had.
And that was the second great poem,
Which no one recalls anymore. The third and greatest
Came into the world as the world, out of the unsayable,
Invisible source of all longing to be; it came
As things come that will perish, to be seen or heard
A while, like the coating of frost or the movement
Of wind, and then no more; it came in the middle of sleep
Like a door to the infinite, and, circled by flame,
Came again at the moment of waking, and, sometimes,
Remote and small, it came as a vision with trees
By a weaving streaming, brushing the bank
With their violet shade, with somebody's limbs
Scattered among the matted, mildewed leaves nearby,
With his severed head rolling under the waves,
Breaking the shifting columns of light into a swirl
Of slivers and flecks; it came in a language
Untouched by pity, in lines, lavish and dark,
Where death is reborn and sent into the world as a gift,
So the future, with no voice of its own, nor hope
Of ever becoming more that it will be, might mourn.

from *The Sonnets to Orpheus* ■ Rainer Maria Rilke

II, XIII

Be ahead of all parting, as though it already were
behind you, like the winter that has just gone by.
For among these winters there is one so endlessly winter
that only by wintering through it will your heart survive.

Be forever dead in Eurydice—more gladly arise
into the seamless life proclaimed in your song.
Here, in the realm of decline, among momentary days,
be the crystal cup that shattered even as it rang.

Be—and yet know the great void where all things begin,
the infinite source of your own most intense vibration,
so that, this once, you may give it your perfect assent.

To all that is used-up, and to all the muffled and dumb
creatures in the world's full reserve, the unsayable sums,
joyfully add your*self*, and cancel the count.

Translated from the German BY STEPHEN MITCHELL

Passion ■ Georg Trakl

Third Version
Orpheus strums the lute silverly,
Lamenting the dead in the evening garden.
Who are you, resting under tall trees
Rustling with lament beneath the autumn reeds?
The blue pond
Dies under the blossoming trees
And follows a sister's shadow.
Dark love
Of a wild lineage
Whose time has passed by on the golden wheels of this day.
Still night.

Under the dark firs
Two wolves united their blood
In a stony embrace; a goldness
Vanished from the clouds above the bridge.
Patience and stillness of childhood.
Again, the delicate corpse appears
At the pond of Triton,
Slumbering in his hyacinth hair.
If only his cool head would finally crumble!

And, as always, a blue deer
Keeps watch under the twilit trees
Of these dark paths,
Waking and stirring in the night's melody.
Gentle madness,
Or the sound of strings continuing,
Filled with their obscure rapture
At the cold feet of the repentant
In the stone city.

Translated from the German BY DANIEL SIMKO

Finding Eurydice ■ Jack Gilbert

Orpheus is too old for it now. His famous voice is gone
and his career is past. No profit anymore from the songs
of love and grief. Nobody listens. Still, he goes on
secretly with his ruined alto. But not for Eurydice.
Not even for the pleasure of singing. He sings because
that is what he does. He sings about two elderly
Portuguese men in the hot Sacramento delta country.
How they show up every year or so, feeble and dressed
as well as their poverty allows. The husband is annoyed
each time by their coming to see his seventy-year-old
wife, who, long ago when they were putting through
the first railroads, was the most beautiful of all

the whores. Impatient, but saying nothing, he lets them
take her carefully upstairs to give her a bath. He does not see the sleek,
gleaming beauty of her hidden in the bright water.

Orpheus Opens His Morning Mail ■ Donald Justice

Bills. Bills. From the mapmakers of hell, the repairers of fractured
   lutes, the bribed judges of musical contests, etc.

A note addressed to my wife, marked: *Please Forward.*

A group photograph, signed: Your admirers. In their faces a certain
      sameness, as if "I" might, after all, be raised to some modest
      power; likewise in their costumes, at once transparent and
      identical, like those of young ladies at some debauched
      seminary. Already—such is my weakness—I picture the rooms
      into which they must once have locked themselves to read my
      work: those barren cells, beds ostentatiously unmade; the
      single pinched chrysanthemum, memorializing in a corner
      some withered event; the mullioned panes, high up, through
      which may be spied, far off, the shorn hedge behind which a
      pimply tomorrow crouches, exposing himself. O lassitudes!

Finally, an invitation to attend certain rites to be celebrated, come
      equinox, on the river bank. I am to be guest of honor. As
      always, I rehearse the scene in advance: the dark; the guards,
      tipsy as usual, sonorously snoring; a rustling, suddenly,
      among the reeds; the fitful illumination of ankles, whitely
      flashing … Afterwards, I shall probably be asked to recite
      my poems. But O my visions, my vertigoes! Have I imagined
      it only, the perverse gentility of their shrieks?

THE DEATH OF ORPHEUS
… Maenads came at Orpheus,
Piercing his flesh with sharpened boughs of laurel,
Tearing his body with blood-streaming hands,
He was stoned, beaten, and smeared with hardened clay.
*   *   *
Scattered in blood and tossed in bloody grasses,
Dismembered arm from shoulder, knee from thigh,
The poet's body lay, yet by a miracle the River Hebrus
Caught head and lyre as they dropped and carried them
Midcurrent down the stream. The lyre twanged sad strains,
The dead tongue sang; funereally the river banks and reeds
Echoed their music.
—OVID, THE METAMORPHOSES, XI (TR. BY HORACE GREGORY)

Orpheus (2) ■ Margaret Atwood

Whether he will go on singing
or not, knowing what he knows
of the horror of this world:

He was not wandering among meadows
all this time. He was down there
among the mouthless ones, among
those with no fingers, those
whose names are forbidden,
those washed up eaten into
among the gray stones
of the shore where nobody goes
through fear. Those with silence.

He has been trying to sing
love into existence again
and he has failed.

Yet he will continue
to sing, in the stadium
crowded with the already dead
who raise their eyeless faces
to listen to him; while the red flowers
grow up and splatter open
against the walls.

They have cut off both his hands
and soon they will tear
his head from his body in one burst
of furious refusal.
He foresees this. Yet he will go on
singing, and in praise.
To sing is either praise
or defiance. Praise is defiance.

■ Marina Tsvetaeva

So they drifted: the lyre and the head,
Downstream, towards the endless stretch.
And the lyre sighed: "I will miss ..."
And the lips completed: "the world ..."

Spilling the silver-red trail,
The double trace in red silver,
Along the swooning Hebrus—
My beloved brother! My sister!

At times, in unquenchable longing
The head slowed down.
But the lyre implored: "Float past!.."
And the lips responded: "Alas!"

Bound as with a wedding wreath
By the distant rippling riverhead,
Is it the lyre that sheds its blood?
Or the hair—its silver?

Descending the river's staircase
To the cradle of rippling waves,
To that isle where the nightingale sings
His falsehoods sweater than anywhere ...

Where are these hallowed remains?
Answer to this, salt water!
Did a bare-headed Lesbian
Catch them in her net?

Translated from the Russian BY NINA KOSSMAN

The Poem as a Mask ■ Muriel Rukeyser

Orpheus
When I wrote of the women in their dances and wildness, it was a mask,
on their mountain, gold-hunting, singing, in orgy,
it was a mask; when I wrote of the god,
fragmented, exiled from himself, his life, the love gone down with song,
it was myself, split open, unable to speak, in exile from myself.

There is no mountain, there is no god, there is memory
of my torn life, myself split open in sleep, the rescued child
beside me among the doctors, and a word
of rescue from the great eyes.

No more masks! No more mythologies!

Now, for the first time, the god lifts his hand,
the fragments join in me with their own music.

The Head of Orpheus ■ Robert Kelly

When Orpheus walked beneath the trees
all the leaves were Eurydices

when Orpheus looked into a well
he saw the skies of hell

when Orpheus took up his lyre
he saw his funeral pyre

on which the Maenads tossed
his scattered limbs and hissed

"Everything he did was wrong:
love and theory, wife and song"

yet when they picked up his head
they kissed his mouth and said

"All the lies these lips told
kept us from ever growing old—

now keep them wet eternally."
And Orpheus saw them throw it in the sea.

Orpheus ■ Joel Oppenheimer

therefore to open
mouth, and let
the voice

> flayed, and eaten, piece
> by lean piece, and with what
> savorings, and with what
> shovings of the greasy fingers
> to the mouth, to get
> full flavors

who, also, went
down, and, came
up, a
coming back and,
then, hid

he fell to the
cannibal girls
after this

Orpheus ■ Alan Dugan

Singing, always singing, he was something
of a prig, like Rilke, and as dangerous
to women. They butchered him; but loud
as ever, wanted or not, the bloody head
continued singing as it drifted out to sea.

Always telling, brave in counsel, ruthlessly glib,
he tamed that barbarous drunk, Dionysus,
out of his ecstasy, and taught the Greeks,
once dirt to the gods and damned to hell,
to pray for heaven, godhood, and himself.

O Maenads, who could choke off his revolt?
Shrined as an oracle, the lovely head
went on with its talking, talking, talking,
until the god, the jealous Apollo himself,
came down in a rage and shut it off.

from *The Sonnets to Orpheus* ■ Rainer Maria Rilke

I, XXVI
But you, divine poet, you who sang on till the end
as the swarm of rejected maenads attacked you, shrieking,
you overpowered their noise with harmony, and
from pure destruction arose your transfigured song.

Their hatred could not destroy your head or your lyre,
however they wrestled and raged; and each one of the sharp
stones that they hurled, vengeance-crazed, at your heart
softened while it was in mid-flight, enchanted to hear.

At last they killed you and broke you in pieces while
your sound kept lingering on in lions and boulders,
in trees and in birds. There you are singing still.

Oh you lost god! You inexhaustible trace!
Only because you were torn and scattered through Nature
have *we* become hearers now and a rescuing voice.

   Translated from the German BY STEPHEN MITCHELL

Philemon & Baucis

'I hope I never see my dear wife's grave,
Nor may she see earth cover my remains."

* * *

In frail old age they stood at ease before
The temple's door and spoke of years gone by,
Philemon saw Baucis shake green leaves,
Around their faces branches seemed to tremble,
And as bark climbed their lips as if to close them,
They cried, "Farewell, good-bye, dear wife, dear husband."
In Thrace the natives show their visitors
Two trees so close together that their branches
Seemed to grow upwards from a single trunk.

—OVID, THE METAMORPHOSES, VII (TR. BY HORACE GREGORY)

Philemon and Baucis ■ Thom Gunn

Love without shadows. —w.c.w.

Two trunks like bodies, bodies like twined trunks
Supported by their wooden hug. Leaves shine
In tender habit at the extremities.
Truly each other's, they have embraced so long
Their barks have met and wedded in one flow
Blanketing both. Time lights the handsome bulk.
   The gods were grateful, and for comfort given
Gave comfort multiplied a thousandfold.
Therefore the couple leached into that soil
The differences prolonged through their late vigour
That kept their exchanges salty and abrasive,
And found, with loves balancing equally,
Full peace of mind. They put unease behind them
A long time back, a long time back forgot
How each woke separate through the pale grey night,
A long time back forgot the days when each
—Riding the other's nervous exuberance—
Knew the slow thrill of learning how to love
What, gradually revealed, becomes itself,
Expands, unsheathes, as the keen rays explore:
Invented in the continuous revelation.

They have drifted into a perpetual nap,
The peace of trees that all night whisper nothings.

Powers of Thirteen (#44) ■ John Hollander

This whole business of outliving—it is as if, once,
One mild summer evening we were sitting outside,
Eating a few leftovers, when two great Presences

Came by, tired, and in their gentle way quite ravenous,
And we shared all of what little we had with them, and
Not that the bottle and the few bowls refilled themselves,
But that you and I were emptied of our appetites
That mild summer evening under the slumbering
Green of low trees, and that the departing Presences
Left us with the gift of a common moment of death.
An old story. Yet for all practical purposes,
When I go, you go—whether or not a laurel bush
And a myrtle just then spring up there outside our house.

Alcestis

Admetus, you can see how it is with me. Therefore,
I wish to have some words with you before I die.
I put you first, and at the price of my own life
made certain you would live and see the daylight. So
I die, who did not have to die, because of you.
I could have taken any man in Thessaly
I wished and lived in queenly state here in this house.
—EURIPIDES, ALCESTIS (TR. BY RICHMOND LATTIMORE)

Alcestis ■ Rainer Maria Rilke

Then suddenly the messenger was among them,
thrown into the fermenting wedding banquet
like brewer's yeast.
The drinkers did not notice the secret
entrance of the god, who hugged his godhood
to him like a wet cloak,
and seemed to be one of them, one or another
passing through. But suddenly, in the middle
of speaking, one of the guests saw
the young master at the head of the table,
somehow snatched up, no longer reclining,
and everywhere, his entire being mirroring
a strangeness that spoke terribly to him.
And then all at once, as if mixture settled,
there was stillness; only, with the lees of muddy
din at the bottom, and a precipitate
of falling babble, already rotten, reeking
of musty laughter that had gone flat.
And then they recognized the slender god,
just as he was, inwardly full of mission
and inexorable,—they almost knew.
And yet, when it was uttered, it was
beyond all knowledge, not to be grasped at all.
Admetus must die. When? This very hour.

But he fractured the shell of his fear
and from the chips stuck out his hands
to bargain with the god:
for years, for one year more of youth,
for months, for weeks, for a few days,
O, not days, nights, only one,
One Night, just this one: for this.
The god denied him, and then he cried out,
outwards, let it all out, crying
as his mother cried out in childbirth.

125

And she came to him, an old woman,
and the father came as well, the old father,
and they both stood, old, lost, obsolete,
beside the crier who suddenly, as never before
so closely, saw them, stopped, gulped, and said:
Father,
does this mean much to you, what remains,
this scum that keeps you from swallowing?
Go, pour it off. And you, woman,
old Mother,
what more have you to do here: you have given birth.
And he held them both in one grip
like animals to be sacrificed. And then let them go,
pushed the old folks off, inspired, beaming,
drawing breath and calling: Creon! Creon!
And nothing but this; nothing but this name.
But in his face stood the Other,
waiting for the name he did not speak,
just as he proffered it to the young friend,
the beloved, glowingly across the bewildered table.
The old ones, obviously, are no ransom,
they are used up and wretched and nearly worthless,
but you, you, in your perfect beauty—

But then he no longer saw his friend,
who stayed behind, and what came forth was *she*,
even a little smaller than he knew her
and slight and sad in the pale wedding dress.
All the others are only her street,
down which she comes and comes—: (soon she will be
there in his arms that painfully unfold).

Still as he waits, she speaks; but not to him.
She speaks to the god, and the god hears her,
and now all hear it, as if within the god:

There can be no deputy. There is me.
I am deputy. For no one is at the end as I am.
What remains for me of what I was here?
What matters is my dying.
Did she not tell you, when she gave the order,
that the bed waiting in there
belongs to the underworld? I bade farewell.
Farewell after farewell.
None dying bids more. Oh yes, I went,
so that everything buried beneath Whatever
is now my husband may disperse and dissolve—;
so, lead me off: even now I die for him.

And like the wind on the high seas, veering,
the god strode, almost as to one dead,
and at once was distant from her husband,
to whom he tossed, implied in the gesture,
one hundred lives of earth.
He rushed, reeling toward the pair,
grasping for them as in dream. Already
they approached the entrance crowded
with red-eyed women. But once
more he saw the virgin's face, that turned
with a smile, bright as a hope,
almost a promise: to return grown,
from the deep death,
to him, the living one—

Then he flung
his hands before his face, just as he knelt there,
in order to see nothing more after that smile.

Translated from the German BY RIKA LESSER

Alcestis, or Autumn: A Hymn (IV) ■ Allen Grossman

Of all the women whom I know it is
Alcestis I most passionately admire,
Who died for an unworthy man, being
Sure that love was death
And nothing more. Nothing is pure in
Nature. Not childhood, nor infancy
Nor the moment of begetting with its
Too many images. Uneasy in my
Labor, uneasy in my rest. In love
Distressed; and in my loneliness quite lost—
I walk out in this storm, as in a mind
Deranged but not unclean;
Alcestis is my dream, who died forever
And then rose—for three days mute and strange.

Alcestis ■ Maura Stanton

for STANLEY KUNITZ

She pulled her gown from her shoulders,
kicked off her shoes, then passed a mirror:
Her wan face did not appear.
She left without kissing her husband.

In the boat to hell she discovered
that crowded souls flowed together.
She wept at the casual hands
swarming through her heart, waving

away flies or lighting tiny matches
to view the caverns of dark water.
When she stroked her braid
she could not distinguish it from air.

After the boat docked, she observed
her father on the porch of a hotel
dozing beside the guitar he'd played
at her wedding. She tried to wake him.

Her fingers glided through his jacket.
She could not twang the guitar.
Yet, she thought, a girl once danced
under the stars to its real music.

Would she sleep this soundly? Her father
bowed his head, as if listening:
She sensed the eyes at every window
waiting for her to come inside

where a maid turned down the sheets
on the customary mattress of dirt.
At the door she recalled the candles
flaring on her last birthday cake.

What was it she wished for then?
She glanced back across the river
wishing someone called her name.
The stone floor chilled her foot.

The dogs dreaming by the stairs
lifted their muzzles for affection,
but by then she had no gestures left
within her cold and formal hand.

Alcestis ■ Kate Daniels

To escape him and my traitorous body
made me happy.
The nights he crept into my room
sucking himself to sleep,
great wings I could not beat down
rose in me.
He was only there for himself,
slept afterwards,
while I smoothed the feathers of my heart
afraid to grow frail and hysterical.
I wanted the company of cold people
who would never touch me.

Death, the little I saw of it,
was satisfying. Even if accidentally
they touched each other,
their fingers slid right through
leaving no print.
And their eyes were frozen balls
I could look into and not see myself.

Back here in my husband's house
I can't stop thinking about it—
the huge paw of Hercules
strangling my saviour,
how I tried running farther on
so I could never come back.
Blue veins beat on the hand
that ripped me back to life.
There was nothing cold about the fingers
that wrenched my shoulders
and left their marks,
singe marks of the fire
licking my body
I try and try to quench, but cannot.

TRANSFORMATIONS

Echo & Narcissus
Philomela
Pygmalion & Galatea

… she slipped beyond
The shelter of the trees to throw her arms
Around the boy she would embrace. Yet he
Ran from her, crying, "No, you must not touch—
Go, take your hands away, may I be dead
Before you throw your fearful chains around me."
"O fearful chains around me," Echo said,
And then no more.

—OVID, THE METAMORPHOSES, III (TR. BY HORACE GREGORY)

Narcissus, Echo ■ Clive Wilmer

She seeks him; but he shuns the love
Of all who are phenomenal.

Only reflection sanctifies,
For him, the beauty she holds dear.

All mass is burden; he sinks its power:
Potential drowned, the perfect flower.

He knelt to the one pure idea,
Self-love: the perfect sacrifice.

She calls and calls to him, till all
The vacant world resounds with love.
*
Only reflection sanctifies,
For him, the beauty she holds dear.
He kneels to the one pure idea,
Self-love: the perfect sacrifice.

For he has shunned all forms of love
That are, like hers, phenomenal.
She calls and calls to him, till all
The vacant world resounds with love.
*
Only reflection sanctifies,
For him, the beauty she holds dear.

She calls and calls to him, till all
The vacant world resounds with love.

THE DEATH OF NARCISSUS

Himself the worshipped and the worshipper,
He sought himself and was pursued, wooed, fired
By his own heat of love. Again, again
He tried to kiss the image in the well;
Again, again his arms embraced the silver
Elusive waters where his image shone....

* * *

Then with his last "Good-bye," "Good-bye," said Echo.
At this he placed his head deep in cool grasses
While death shut fast his eyes....

—OVID, THE METAMORPHOSES, III (TR. BY HORACE GREGORY)

Narcissus ■ Stephen Mitchell

It was not the image of his own face that transfixed him as he bent down over the pool. He has seen that face often before: in mirrors, in a thousand photographs, in women's eyes. It was an undistinguished face, but handsome enough, with its long eyelashes, full lips, and stately nose sloping to a curious plateau near the tip.

No, it was something else now that rooted him to the spot. Kneeling there, gazing into the so taken-for-granted form, he grew more and more poignantly aware that it was mere surface. When the water was calm, *it* was calm; when the water rippled at the touch of a leaf or a fish, it too rippled; or broke apart when he churned the water with his hand. More and more fascinated, he kept staring through the image of his face into the depths beneath, filled with a multitude of other, moving, shadowy forms. He knew that if he stayed there long and patiently enough, he would be able to see through to the bottom. And at that moment, he knew, the image would disappear.

Narcissus ■ May Sarton

His eyes are darker than he knows.
They flash out from a fire so deep
It draws him down to burning shadows.
It draws him further down than sleep.
And there in any quiet room
He faces a peculiar doom.
Within the mirror's empty face
His own eyes dreadfully expose
His solitary self, that place
He cannot leave, he cannot reach.
Whatever mirrors have to teach
He will learn now before he moves,
Lost in himself, but far from love.

It is not love that makes him fall
Deep into perilous reflection,
Not love that holds him there at all,
But rather something glimpsed and gone,

Angels and unicorns he sees
Vanish among the little trees,
Their lives so innocent and wise
That draw him into his own eyes,
Those fleeting selves that come quite near
But never tell him who they are.
He knows that he can never leave
Without the gift they have to give,
Powers that he must catch and tame
Or, drawn into the mirror, drown.

Narcissus (I) ■ Rainer Maria Rilke

Narcissus perished. His being's very closeness
rose from his beauty ceaselessly,
thick as a heliotrope's aroma. Yet
his law was that he see himself.

What went from him he loved back inside again
and folded himself no more in the open wind
and closed the world of forms in his rapture and cancelled
himself out and ceased being able to be.
  Translated from the German BY JOHN PECK

The Rape of Narcissus ■ Mihai Ursachi

But the water would not stay in place.
Invoked, its substance came forth, as if
from the amorphous night of caves,
faithfully to reveal his likeness.
And arriving there, the water
was for an instant his very form,
with which it filled to its depths;
and each of its molecules, for a brief instant,
was Narcissus.
But the water would not stay in place.
Continuously flowing onward, each molecule
bore away a trace of his image,
and the entire brook became him.
And continuously flowing, he turned into a stream,
into broad rivers; and then, in the vast Ocean,
his icon dissolved, exactly like grains of salt.

In the meadow, by the side of the brook,
there remained a drift of flowers.
But the water would not stay in place.
  Translated from the Romanian BY ADAM J. SORKIN

Narcissus at 60 ■ Linda Pastan

If love hadn't made him clumsy,
if he hadn't fallen forward,
had never drowned
in his own perfection,

what would he have thought
about his aging face
as it altered, year after year
season by season?

In the old conspiracy
between the eye
and its reflection, love casts
a primal shadow.

Perhaps he would blame
the wrinkling surface of the pool
for what he saw
or think the blemishes

on his once smooth cheek
were simply small fish
just beneath the lethal skin
of the water.

Narcissus in the Desert ■ William Carlos Williams

Three faces in a single one

Too much sand for the sun
Sets madness afire
Its liquid shadow sprawls out

A new break asserts itself

The mirror is too keen
At its contact the eyes die of thirst
And turn their looks away
The paper keeps it neutral white as dry as space is
To weld the prop to life
To follow the trail
To make a poem violent as a mirage
With love to drink three faces as one
Plunge thine hair under
And Narcissus will have lived.

Philomela

Pandion married Zeuxippe, his mother's sister, and begat two daughters, Procne and Philomela, and twin sons, Erechtheus and Butes. But war having broken out with Labdacus on a question of boundaries, he called in the help of Tereus, son of Ares, from Thrace, and having with his help brought the war to a successful close, he gave Tereus his own daughter Procne in marriage. Tereus had by her a son Itys, and having fallen in love with Philomela, he seduced her also saying that Procne was dead, for he concealed her in the country. Afterwards he married Philomela and bedded with her, and cut out her tongue. But by weaving characters in a robe she revealed thereby to Procne her own sorrows. And having sought out her sister, Procne killed her son Itys, boiled him, served him up for supper to the unwitting Tereus, and fled with her sister in haste.... Tereus snatched up an axe and pursued them. And being overtaken at Daulia in Phocis, they prayed the gods to be turned into birds, and Procne became a nightingale, and Philomela a swallow.

—APOLLODORUS, THE LIBRARY III. xiv (TR. BY J. G. FRAZER)

Philomela ■ Mikhail Kreps

Once a year Philomela flies into the house
Where she lost her innocence and her tongue.
A juniper-tree, now spread out, covers the window
From which she used to watch the red sunset.

Grey snow covers the furniture and the mirrors;
Dresses she left behind in a rush are reduced to dust.
And here is the thread with which she sowed the words
Which brought death to everyone yet survived the ages.

Revenge, your reward is terrible and beyond the strength
Of the fragile woman with a swallow's tail.
I'm neither a queen, nor a bird, and where could I fly,
Where can I lose my memory, like a feather, beyond what bridge?

Translated from the Russian BY NINA KOSSMAN

Philomela ■ Yannis Ritsos

So, even with a severed tongue, Philomela recounted her tribulations,
weaving them one by one into her robe with patience and faith,
with modest colors—violet, ash, white and black—and as is always true
with works of art, there's an excess of black. All the rest—
Procne, Tereus with his axe, their pursuit in Daulis,
even the cutting out of the tongue—we consider insignificant, things we forget.
That robe of hers is enough, secret and precise, and her transformation
at the crucial moment into a nightingale. Still, we say: without all the rest,
those things now contemptible, would this brilliant robe and the nightingale exist?

Translated from the Greek BY EDMUND KEELEY

Philomela with a Melody ■ Erich Fried

He who breaks
Philomela's heart
to save her from
the pain of love
is a liar
a liar.

What is the nightingale's
sweet song
it means
get lost
get lost.

On these trees
I'm
the only
male.

Translated from the German BY LEONID KOSSMAN

Pygmalion & Galatea

> *... He took to art,*
> *Ingenious as he was, and made a creature*
> *More beautiful than any girl on earth,*
> *A miracle of ivory in a statue,*
> *So charming that it made him fall in love.*
>
> * * *
>
> *Pygmalion, half-dazed, lost in his raptures,*
> *And half in doubt, afraid his senses failed him,*
> *Touched her again and felt his hopes come true,*
> *The pulse-beating stirring where he moved his hands.*
>
> —OVID, THE METAMORPHOSES, X (TR. BY HORACE GREGORY)

Pygmalion ■ John Dickson

On the earth in its act of quietly spinning
with its dazed cargo of puzzled people,
half of them sleeping, half of them not,
there can be heard the sound of tapping
from a ground floor window of the Greenwood Inn—
Pygmalion sculpting, fashioning, tapping,
freeing someone or something from the stone,
from the huge rock he's brought into his room.
So far, a rough roundness at the top
and a definite narrowing halfway down.

On a night of flapping catalpa leaves,
a distant guitar strumming its anguish
and ten point seven dogs per hundred
baying at the moon, there is still
the tapping, tapping, tapping
coming from the Greenwood Inn.
Now the rock has a hint of a head with stone hair
almost tumbling onto its possible shoulders.

And on a night of tangible quiet,
of werewolves leaving tracks in the snow
as they hide behind, peek around, various tree trunks,
there is still the sound of tapping ... tapping ...
coming from the Greenwood Inn
where this graceful woman with sturdy arms
and faraway eyes and the hint of a smile
stands up to her waist in stone
while he, bending down, keeps chipping away
at what could become a thigh and a knee.
He is working compulsively, driven as though
he is certain to run out of time.

On a morning of sun chasing clouds from their puddles,
not a sound can be heard from the Greenwood Inn—
not the clatter of catalpa leaves
nor chipping sounds from the open window—
only a now-and-then flap of its shade
that echoes through the empty room.
The only sign of recent life
are two sets of footprints that lead to the door
through a heavy layer of rock dust.

Galatea Encore ■ Joseph Brodsky

As though the mercury's under its tongue, it won't
talk. As though with the mercury in its sphincter,
immobile, by a leaf-coated pond
a statue stands white like a blight of winter.
After such snow, there is nothing indeed: the ins
and outs of centuries, pestered heather.
That's what coming full circle means—
when your countenance starts to resemble weather,
when Pygmalion's vanished. And you are free
to cloud your folds, to bare the navel.
Future at last! That is, bleached debris
of a glacier amid the five-lettered "never."
Hence the routine of a goddess, née
alabaster, that lets roving pupils gorge on
the heart of the color and temperature of the knee.
That's what it looks like inside a virgin.

TRESPASSERS

Phaethon
Niobe
Icarus & Daedalus
Arachne
Marsyas
Psyche/Amor & Psyche

Phaethon

... *Phaethon, fire pouring through fiery hair,*
Sailed earthward through clear skies as though he were
A star that does not fall, yet seems to fall
Through long horizons of the quiet air.
Far from home he fell, across the globe
Where River Eridanus cooled his face.
—OVID, THE METAMORPHOSES, II (TR. BY HORACE GREGORY)

Phaethon's Dream ▥ Nina Kossman

The sky-sized paddock of a magnified dream
was open, was, at last, Phaethon's;
his own, yet no more glowingly alive
than it was when it used to entrap him.
As it was, it was no longer Phaethon who drove
the chariot, but the loosened reigns of his satisfied wish.

The horses flew higher and higher in wild arcs.
The jolts fed a desire for something spectacular,
a final deed in his final dream,
in which he himself was the sun, or
the sun's chariot, or what he could be:
proudly calm, proudly insouciant
of his own death. When the dream disclosed
the globe on fire, he thought the flames looked
almost real, and the distant screams
he mistook for shouts of joy. Surprised,
but not shocked, he was hurled from the chariot.
His dreaming body fell from the sky like a burning log.

Phaeton ▥ Kathleen Raine

I must explore this country of the dawn,
break purple into roses, let the fading stars
collapse beneath my wheels as I come on;
I must, I must discover at the end
my father's love, and bend those golden bars
as wisely as he does; I must suspend

the day in my careening metaphor
and feel the wind of power in my face,
discover after in what comes before.
These Hours and their moments must give way
to me, and in the motion of my grace
must open to me secrets of the day.

O father, give me time, yet give me speed.

Remembering, as I fall slowly, burn,
the morning full of roses and my need
I open to my own dawn and too late
enter the world I ruin to return
the quiet vengeance of my twisted fate.

My sisters drop their slow stone tears into
the river I speak from. Let your hand
drift lifeless in this water and look through
the myth of me. Out of these poplar trees
a young wind shakes like stars into the sand
those ambers: who hears, who in the current sees?

Niobe

Even Niobe with her lustrious hair remembered food,
though she saw a dozen children killed in her own halls,
six daughters and six sons in the pride and prime of youth.
True, lord Apollo killed the sons with his silver bow
and Artemis showering arrows killed the daughters.
—HOMER, THE ILIAD, XXIV (TR. BY ROBERT FAGLES)

Even her entrails had been turned to stone.
Yet eyes still wept, and she was whirled away
In a great wind back, to her native country,
Where on a mountaintop she weeps and even now
Tears fall in rivulets from a statue's face.
—OVID, THE METAMORPHOSES, VI (TR. BY HORACE GREGORY)

"Niobe, Also, of the Beautiful Hair, Thought of Eating" ■ Laurie Sheck

and for one moment
she did not think of her seven sons,
all dead, her seven daughters
ten days dead. The bread
was coarse and warm against her palms,
and she raised it to her lips
not thinking: sword, or blood, or loss,
but tasting the deep sweetness,
the fragrant, simple goodness
of the grain. And as she ate
she raised her eyes
as if for the first time
to the cypresses leaning on the hillside,
sunlight swarming in the streambed,
the neighbors' children playing
in the garden, their bodies
quick and stuttery as birds.
If love is the soul's looking
then she loved the world for that one moment
like one who has no hands
to touch it, like one whose hands
have been removed. And when she was done,
the taste of the good, sweet bread
still branded on her tongue,
her eyes filled with the weaving
shadows of children, the shadows
of the swaying trees,
she knew she could turn from the world
without blasphemy, she knew
she was ready—

and she knelt by her dead children
as her long hair stiffened
into stone, and as evening fell
her grief-palled body hardened also
beyond longing or remembrance,
a white and rain-struck stone.

◼ Hayden Carruth

Niobe, your tears
are your children now. See how
we have multiplied.

Niobe Now ◼ Muriel Rukeyser

Niobe
    wild
        with unbelief
            as all
                her ending
                    turns to stone

Not gentle
    weeping
        and souvenirs
            but hammering
                honking
                  agonies

Forty-nine tragic years
            are done
                and the twentieth century not begun:
All tears,
    all tears,
        all tears.
Water
    from her rock
        is sprung
            and in this water
                lives a seed
That must endure
        and grow
        and shine
            beasts, gardens
                at last rivers
A man
    to be born
        to start again
            to tear

a woman
>> from his side

And wake
> to start
>> the world again

Icarus & Daedalus

... Icarus began to feel the joy
Of beating wings in air and steered his course
Beyond his father's lead: all the wide sky
Was there to tempt him as he steered toward heaven.
Meanwhile the heat of sun struck at his back
And where his wings were joined, sweet-smelling fluid
Ran hot that once was wax. His naked arms
Whirled into wind; his lips, still calling out
His father's name, were gulfed in the dark seas.

—OVID, THE METAMORPHOSES, VIII (TR. BY HORACE GREGORY)

Daedalus: The Dirge ■ George Oppen

The boy accepted them;
His whole childhood in them, his difference
From the others. The wings
Gold,
Gold for credence,
Every feather of them. He believed more in the things
Than I, and less. Familiar as speech,
The family tongue. I remember
New expedients, frauds, ridiculous
In the real withering sun blazing
Still. Who could have said
More, losing the boy anyway, anyway
In the bare field there old man, old potterer ...

Musée des Beaux Arts ■ W.H. Auden

About suffering they were never wrong,
The Old Masters: how well they understood
Its human position; how it takes place
While someone else is eating or opening a window or just walking dully along;
How, when the aged are reverently, passionately waiting
For the miraculous birth, there always must be
Children who did not especially want it to happen, skating
On a pond at the edge of the wood:
They never forgot
That even the dreadful martyrdom must run its course
Anyhow in a corner, some untidy spot
Where the dogs go on with their doggy life and the torturer's horse
Scratches its innocent behind on a tree.

In Brueghel's *Icarus*, for instance: how everything turns away
Quite leisurely from the disaster; the ploughman may
Have heard the splash, the forsaken cry,
But for him it was not an important failure; the sun shone

As it had to on the white legs disappearing into the green
Water; and the expensive delicate ship that must have seen
Something amazing, a boy falling out of the sky,
Had somewhere to get to and sailed calmly on.

Icarus ■ Erik Lindegren

His memories of the labyrinth go numb with sleep.
The single memory: how the calls and the confusion rose
until at last they swung him up from the earth.

And how all cleavings which have cried out always
for their bridges in his breast
slowly shut like eyelids,
and how the birds swept past like shuttles, like arrows,
and finally the last lark brushing his hand,
falling like song.

Then: the wind's labyrinth, with its blind bulls,
cacophonous lights and inclines,
with its dizzying breath which he through arduous
struggle learned how to parry,
until it rose again, his vision and his flight.

Now he is rising alone, in a sky without clouds,
in a space empty of birds in the din of the aircraft …
rising towards a clearer and clearer sun,
turning gradually cooler, turning cold,
and upwards toward the spring of his blood, soul's cataract:
a prisoner in a whistling lift,
a seabubble's journey toward the looming magnetic air:
the bursting of the foetal membrane, transparently near,
and the vortex of signs, born of the springtide, raging of azure,
crumbling walls, and drunkenly the call of the other side:
Reality fallen
      Without reality born!

Translated from the Swedish BY JOHN MATTHIAS AND GÖRAN PRINTZ-PÅHLSON

Icarus to Eve ■ Ramon Guthrie

Madam, I'm Adam
madA m'I, madaM
Madam, I'm Icarus, your son.
The one who flew too near the sun. Remember? No?

The elder Brueghel sees and sums it all:
not even a ripple in the bright small waves.
Steered by the title, the eye looks twice to find
the limp, unwieldy, disappearing legs.

(The headlong carcass outdistanced breath and sense:
sheer velocity makes instant anesthesia.)
Filling the foreground, the plowman goes about
finishing his chore. The contoured furrows and
horse's humble rump spell order and patience.
A man is fishing from the bank. Beyond,
a gawking shepherd seems to let his flock
tend *him*. A dog of sorts sits at his feet.
Nearby a ship, a fresh wind in her sails,
heads down the estuary. Sailors are on deck
and in the rigging. In this tight cosmos, nothing
notes the splash—except perhaps a rod or so away
one straggling sheep that seems to lift its muzzle
a moment from its grazing. A spring day is ending.
A pale smudged sun is setting in the sea.
Madam, I am Icarus, your son.
Wax melted when I flew too near … Remember?
No? There's no wonder. I have so many siblings
that the only wonder is that even
an absent-minded sheep should note our fall.

(Without us, legs would still be fins.
"Johny! Don't you go too near that land.
You want to get all dry!")

Waiting for Icarus ■ Muriel Rukeyser

He said he would be back and we'd drink wine together
He said that everything would be better than before
He said we were on the edge of a new relation
He said he would never again cringe before his father
He said that he was going to invent full-time
He said he loved me that going into me
He said was going into the world and the sky
He said all the buckles were very firm
He said the wax was the best wax
He said Wait for me here on the beach
He said Just don't cry

I remember the gulls and the waves
I remember the islands going dark on the sea
I remember the girls laughing
I remember they said he only wanted to get away from me
I remember mother saying: Inventors are like poets,
                                        a trashy lot
I remember she said those who try out inventions are worse
I remember she added: Women who love such are the worst of all
I have been waiting all day, or perhaps longer.
I would have liked to try those wings myself.
It would have been better than this.

Icarus ▦ Leonid Bulanov

The gift from above
the penalty from above—
threads of the same spool.
If it weren't for his wings
who would have known
that Icarus was a fool?

Translated from the Russian BY NINA KOSSMAN

To a Friend Whose Work Has Come to Triumph ▦ Anne Sexton

Consider Icarus, pasting those sticky wings on,
testing that strange little tug at his shoulder blade,
and think of that first flawless moment over the lawn
of the labyrinth. Think of the difference it made!
There below are the trees, as awkward as camels;
and here are the shocked starlings pumping past
and think of innocent Icarus who is doing quite well:
larger than a sail, over the fog and the blast
of the plushy ocean, he goes. Admire his wings!
Feel the fire at his neck and see how casually
he glances up and is caught, wondrously tunneling
into that hot eye. Who cares that he fell back to the sea?
See him acclaiming the sun and come plunging down
while his sensible daddy goes straight into town.

Icarus Descended ▦ Michael Blumenthal

I was a bird once, and I flew,
high over the clouds. The landscape
was beautiful, beckoning, a rich cornucopia
of women and flowers, and I was a happy raptor,
moral as a condor. Wherever I went
the envy of those who had fallen prey
to their own goodness washed over me,
but I must have felt, somewhere,
the tipped arrows of their envy
entering my happy flesh and lodging there.

Tame, subliminated, psychoanalyzed,
I walk out now among the terrestrial animals
and smiling, moribund creatures,
with their dark pieties
of happiness and sacrifice.
Oh where are the bright galaxies
of yesteryear? I ask,
the rapidly beating hearts
of those who could never have me?

Silly boy, who thought
he could defeat death so easily,
who thought he could live forever
in the moans of abandoned women, look
how you have joined the dark, plaintive race
of your brothers and sisters, just look
at your newly descended world: eight wheels
of cold metal where your wings once were.

Icarus by Night ■ Ann Deagon

From the ascending jet
the cities recede
like a wilderness
of expanding constellations
like the heroic past.
If engines falter
what to fall back on
what underlies us
but universal darkness
pocked with fleeing stars?
We do most fear to fall
into no thing
but falling.

They have blown out
even the flaming sun
by which God candled
this egg shaped earth
saw in its molten yolk
a stir of feathers
set it warm to brood
nested in orbit.
From this dark egg
we all have hatched
we Icarus, at moth
to a doomed star
now free-fall
out of time.

Daedalus ■ Alastair Reid

My son has birds in his head.

I know them now. I catch
the pitch of their calls, their shrill
cacophonies, their chitterings, their coos.
They hover behind his eyes and come to rest
on a branch, on a book, grow still,

claws curled, wings furled.
His is a bird world.

I learn the flutter of his moods,
his moments of swoop and soar.
From the ground I feel him try
the limits of the air—
sudden lift, sudden terror—
and move in time to cradle
his quivering, feathered fear.

At evening, in the tower,
I see him to sleep and see
the hooding-over of eyes,
the slow folding of wings.
I wake to his morning twitterings,
to the *croomb* of his becoming.

He chooses his selves—wren, hawk,
swallow or owl—to explore
the trees and rooftops of his heady wishing.
Tomtit, birdwit.
Am I to call him down, to give him
a grounding, teach him gravity?
Gently, gently.
Time tells us what we weigh, and soon enough
his feet will reach the ground.
Age, like a cage, will enclose him.
So the wise men said.

My son has birds in his head.

Arachne

... And with a twist of rope around her head,
She swung, and Pallas with a twinge of mercy
Lifted her up to say, "So you shall live,
Bad girl, to swing, to live now and forever,
Even to the last hanging creature of your kind."

* * *

Hair, ears, and nose fell off, the head diminished,
The body shrivelled, and her quick long fingers
Grew to its sides with which she crept abroad—
All else was belly, and the girl a spider,
The tenuous weaver of an ancient craft.

—OVID, THE METAMORPHOSES, vi (TR. BY HORACE GREGORY)

Arachne's Story ■ John Hollander

The skill at weaving was itself a web
All right, but not one I was caught in—neither
That, nor my oh-so-celebrated pride in it
Led me to want to show her my stuff.
But rather to show her—

Well, weaving, admittedly, can be the best
Of work: onto the warp of unsignifying strength
Are woven the threads of imaging that
Do their unseen work of structure too,
But can depict even while they draw
The warp together: my images are thus
Truly in and of the fabric, texture itself becoming
Text rather than lying like painting
Lightly upon some canvas or some wall.

It was not to challenge her,
Like some idiot warrior going up against some
Other idiot warrior: say rather
That it was to hear the simultaneous song
Of two harmonious shuttles, nosing in
And out of their warp like dolphins out
Of their one blue and into another.

But they will say that what I so wonderfully wove
Was all those terrible unfunny rapes her father
Changed himself into those shapes—flame,
Gold, swan, bull and all—in order more amusingly
To carry out: he was at least a connoisseur
Of bestialities. And not to speak of Neptune,
Apollo and the rest of them with their dallying below stairs.

No, it was none of that: who needs
Yet more porn, and yet more subtleties
Of formal treatment—legs, arms, and affrighted
Lineaments rhyming with patterns compliant branches make, and
Glittering vague waves and high suggestive clouds?

And then the whole array of nasty vignettes bordered with
Flowers and ivy intertwined—*intertextos*—says
That liar, Ovid, as if I had been reading
Some old book of the floral! No, it was none of that:
Who needs yet more vegetative decoration
Reducing the restless gaze to the blankly satisfied stare?

No: it was she herself I would show, the weaver
Woven into my web, the face of terrifying wisdom
Beyond the knowledge of Apollo and the tricky lore
Of Hermes. And that is what went into my web,
What grew out of my dancing hands and singing
Eyes and seeing heart. Her face emerged from
My sky and my clouds—was it not then something
Of my face, as well? She paused in her own work
And gazed at mine;
And to the Goddess' gray eyes
That image of her seemed, for too long a moment,
To be even more real than she was herself.
Too long, but still
A moment: for then her thread of thought broke as
A sudden wind blew through the chamber
We were working in, and shook the veil
And set the face of wisdom a-trembling,
Which with trembling gaze she coldly noted.

And that was all for weaving and for me.

All the mechanics and the pain—oh oh the pain
Of the transformation will go undescribed.
No, there will be none of that.
Say only that here I am, what I have never
And yet somehow ever been.

Back then when I was not as I am,
Spinning my jail of gossamer,
But wove, in and out, the shuttle working
Almost as—should I say, its own sweet will?
Now I spin instead of weaving, and make
Webs that deceive by no pictorial sleights, but
Trompent l'oeil in another way: not imagining things
That seem to be, but building traps that seem not to.

And it is not that I sit now at the center of the whole
Thing, waiting for its delicate strong threads to trap
The stupidly unwary, or to fascinate the clever
Who trace the pattern of its trusswork
And wonder how much its yielding beauty
In a gentle breeze may in itself be a trope
Of a trap, until they too are trapped in that metaphor of a metaphor,
The thing itself, the very thing. It is not that
I sit there, for that minutely dense center
Is a riddling figure of me: all the rest
May be seen as being drawn out of it, as from myself.

No: I sit tight in an upper corner
Regarding my lovely gossamer garden,
Until someone unwise is caught in the toils of my *toile*.
Then he becomes the center
Of my concern, and I wrap my lines about him,
Preserved if not eternized in the cocoon
Of my sonnet. But in time
He will be gone, and my web will break,
And float to and fro in some breeze or other.

And then? As I start out again to spin
A new tale, another jail of voile, another
Geometric wonder, I remember
The face of the Goddess, as I
Affix my prime filament to the right
Place, and begin
To spin, upward as I move down, hanging
Like life itself, after all, by a thread.

Arachne ■ Rhina Espaillat

Aging, the mind contracts
and learns to do with less:
out of itself exacts
a filament, a tress

to trap the lightest prize,
a joy too fine for sense,
that passion would despise
but for its impotence.

Marsyas

"O I give in, I lose, forgive me now,
No hollow shin-bone's worth this punishment."
In one wound, blood streaming over muscles,
Veins stripped naked, pulse beating, entrails could be
Counted as they moved; even the heart shone red
Within his breast.

—OVID, THE METAMORPHOSES, vi (TRANS. BY HORACE GREGORY)

Marsyas and the Flute ■ Xiaoyun Lin

The rope that cuts deeply into his ankles
was tied to the tree branch by none other
than Apollo himself, source of light, protector of the arts—
arts that are meant only for the Olympian high society.
Gods, deaf to the flute's harmonies, are not blind
to usurpation by a self-proclaimed musician, a satyr.
That slender, fragile pipe, once so humble yet so tantalizing,
now lies in fragments, mixed with threads of his flayed skin.
His skinless body dangles and burns; his lips touch the damp earth
which is indifferent to his fatal attempt to bring it closer to heaven.

Translated from the Chinese BY THE AUTHOR

"... no sooner had I shone my lamp on the bed than I saw a marvellous sight: Venus's divine son, Cupid himself, lying there in tranquil sleep. The joy and relief were too great for me. I quite lost my head and didn't know how to satisfy my longing for him; but then, by a dreadful accident, a drop of burning oil from the lamp spurted on his shoulder. The pain woke him at last. When he saw me holding a lamp and the knife, he shouted: 'Wicked woman, out of this bed at once!'"

—APULEIUS, THE GOLDEN ASS (TR. BY ROBERT GRAVES)

Aftermath ■ Daryl Hine

I

Psychology was Psyche's fault:
The bedside lamp, the burning drop
She let fall upon the flawless
Shoulder of the unconscious god.
For a moment though she saw him
Almost as he was, soft not hard
As she had always known him in the dark,
His nakedness no longer unashamed
But vulnerable as a mortal
Lost in a dream, the midnight black
Of his hair about the secret face
Of love: only for a moment
Before the immortal god
Woke and knew her and flew away.

II

His departure an epiphany,
The work of night, without a word
Of apology he went away
As it was written, by another way
Into his own country. Boy or bird,
There for the time being he will stay.
In valediction what was she to say?
For all her insight Psyche cannot say
Candidly she understood his stay
Although offended by its brevity.
Was her anxiety absurd
In the light of yesterday?
Humiliated and bewildered
She will follow anyway.

III

Above the unintelligible
Pack with human faces,
Wings like parentheses
Stuck upon his back,

He hovered out of reach,
Taunting and afraid,
Abruptly fallible,
Frantic to escape
The trap of consciousness.
What did his flight portend?
Faith might have divined.
Without an informing myth,
Bored beyond belief
Psyche can only guess.

IV

Compared to daily life her other tasks
Were child's play: sorting out the letters
Of the infatuated alphabet
To spell the name of her mistake;
Fetching refreshment from the dead;
The sort of tests that one is set in nightmare,
A bedtime story or an allegory,
Which must be solved before you wake,
Penitences possible except
Her final labour, to forget
The stolen sight of Love in bed
Beside her, naked and asleep,
The moving shadow on his cheek,
His surprised look before he fled.

Psyche Pleads with Cupid ■ Delmore Schwartz

O heart, O dearest heart, dusk again becomes black night
As quickly as the falling of a leave: and I am left
Fondling the formless faceless presence I love, quite lost:
—All that I am is seed, all that I am is morning, waiting to see,
All that I am is flower, forbidden the light and hidden
In sleep's purpose and sleep's patience, power and growth:
So I must ask again, knowing how it angers you
And knowing that you would be more angered if you knew
How much this mostly unasked question obsesses me:
Why is love dark?
Why must your face remain concealed from me?
My sisters taunt and torment me. They say
I have invented a religion, a superstition, a deity
To hide the love of a monster or monstrous usages
Nursed by love's absence, love's unquelled desire.
Must you be hidden from me forever?
My sisters sometimes say that I will never see
The strangeness or the strange face of the deity
To whom I am espoused in reality or in the dark forest of fantasy!

Does your face possess the glitter and radiance
Possessed by your voice? Your voice possesses
A bell clarity, a trumpet brilliance, a harpsichord delicacy.
It is blessed by the gentleness of the first morning, exquisitely!
Sometimes it has a sunset's roaring eloquence and turbulence
… Yet my sisters laugh at me. And think of me
As one who is very strange, as one possessed
By lunacy, or by a dream dispossessed, when in all blessedness
—By joy overcome, beside myself, outside myself, in ecstasy's aftermath—
I come and say to them that God has captured and kidnapped me!
Dearest, is all love dark? Must all love be
Hidden in night from the one who is nearest?
Or is the mystery of divinity an abyss of black?
How then can you come to me? why do you come back?
Why do you desire my love? Is it love, in truth, if I lack
The sight and vision which begins all intimacy?

Psyche with the Candle ■ Archibald MacLeish

Love which is the most difficult mystery
Asking from every young one answers
And most from those most eager and most beautiful—
Love is a bird in a fist:
To hold it hides it, to look at it lets it go.
It will twist loose if you lift so much as a finger.
It will stay if you cover it—stay but unknown and invisible.
Either you keep it forever with fist closed
Or let it fling
Singing in fervor of sun and in song vanish.
There is no answer other to this mystery.

> *… she ran down the road to the Underworld. She passed in silence by the lame man with the lame ass, paid Charon the first coin, stopped her ears to the entreaties of the floating corpse, refused to be taken in by the appeal of the spinning women, pacified the dreadful dog with the first sop and entered Proserpine's palace. There she refused the comfortable chair and the tempting meal, sat humbly at Proserpine's feet, content with a crust of common bread, and finally delivered her message.*

—APULEIUS, THE GOLDEN ASS (TR. BY ROBERT GRAVES)

■ Osip Mandelshtam

When Psyche—life—goes down to the shades,
To search for Persephone in the translucent forest,
A blind swallow flings itself at her feet
With Stygian tenderness and a green twig.

A throng of shades rushes towards the fugitive,
Greeting the new companion with lamentations,
And they wring their weak hands at her
With bewilderment, shyly hopeful.

One holds out a mirror, another a flask of perfume—
The soul is a woman after all, she likes trinkets,
And the leafless forest of transparent voices
Is sprinkled with dry laments like fine rain.

And not knowing where to begin in this tender commotion,
The soul does not recognize the transparent groves;
She breathes on the mirror and delays handing over
The copper lozenge for the foggy ferrying.

Translated from the Russian BY NINA KOSSMAN

THE CONDEMNED

Sisyphus
Tantalus

Sisyphus

And I saw Sisyphus' atrocious pain;
he tried to push a huge stone with his hands.
He'd brace his hands and feet and thrust it up
a slope, but just when he had neared the top,
its weight reversed its course; and once again
that bestial stone rolled back onto the plain.
Sweat drenched his straining limbs: again he thrust,
and dust rose from the head of Sisyphus.

—THE ODYSSEY OF HOMER XI (TR. BY ALLEN MANDELBAUM)

The Myth of Sisyphus ■ Stephen Mitchell

We tend to think of Sisyphus as a tragic hero, condemned by the gods to shoulder his rock sweatily up the mountain, and again up the mountain, forever.

The truth is that Sisyphus is in love with the rock. He cherishes every roughness and every ounce of it. He talks to it, sings to it. It has become the mysterious Other. He even dreams of it as he sleepwalks upward. Life is unimaginable without it, looming always above him like a huge gray moon.

He doesn't realize that at any moment he is permitted to step aside, let the rock hurtle to the bottom, and go home.

Tragedy is the inertial force of the mind.

instructions for sisyphus ■ Hans Magnus Enzensberger

what you are doing is hopeless. all right;
you understand that; admit it
but do not be contented with it,
man with the rock. no one is going
to thank you; chalk-lines,
that a dull rain is licking away,
are marking death. do not rejoice
too early; hopelessness
is no career. only changelings,
scarecrows, augurs are on easy terms
with their own tragedy. be silent,
say a word to the sun,
while the rock is rolling, but
do not relish your impotence,
but increase the wrath of the world
by a hundredweight, by a grain.
there is a lack of men
silently doing what is hopeless,
weeding out hope, rolling
their laughter, the future,
rolling their wrath uphill on the mountains.

Translated from the German BY GERTRUDE C. SCHWEBELL

■ Lucille Clifton

Nothing is told us about Sisyphus in the underworld. —ALBERT CAMUS

nothing is told about the moment
just after the ball fits itself
into the bottom of the hill
and the world is suspended
and i become king of this country
all imps and impostors watching
me,
waiting me, and i decide, i decide
whether or not i will allow
this myth to live. i slide
myself down. demons restoke the
fire.
i push my shoulder into the round
world and taste in my mouth
how sweet power is, the story
gods never tell.

New Sisyphus ■ José Emilio Pacheco

Breathe deep
There
Good
now push
your grain of sand
like a man
with backbone
No staggering

And when you find
at last you're at the summit
and you see it roll downhill
set to searching it out   a thousand and one times
in the multiplicity of this desert

Translated from the Spanish BY GEORGE McWHIRTER

Sisyphus ■ Miguel Torga

Begin anew ...
If you can,
Without distress and without haste,
And the steps that you take
On this harsh road
Of the future,
Take them in freedom.
While never arriving
Never rest.
Don't accept only half of the fruit.

And, never sated,
Harvest illusion upon illusion
From the orchard along the way.
Keep dreaming
And seeing,
Wide awake
The delusion of the task.
You are only a man, don't forget!
The madness where clearly
You recognize yourself
Is yours alone.

Translated from the Portuguese BY IVANA RANGEL CARLSEN

The Maxims of Sisyphus ■ Delmore Schwartz

(*Sisyphus' Success*)
Although I was tenacious, I never learned
    the wisdom and will of tenacity;
Although I was persistent, and praised for persistence,
At first faint falling off of inspiration's desire
    the black hood of despondency covered my face,
    fell over it
To till and toil and delve and dig, dumb in the darkness
    chinning and clutching, darkness and weakened
I never knew … nor knew how the piddling puddling
    persistent will is the perpetual way,
    the royal real route to the richest fulfillment.

    … Persistent, but faint of heart, passionate and
    Yet apathetic,
    How often I turned my face away,
    How often avoided unpleasant imperfection,
    Squeamish and absolute, but ran away and ran back.
How could I perceive how often success was won after
    many repeated Sisyphean failures
    (when I often had been drunken with the romance
    and fortune of spontaneity, when often the more
    the effort, the worse the denial or outcome or …
    When all that I most wanted was near as my hands
    and feet, and had been, ever …

Tantalus

... Above his head,
trees—leafy, high—bore fruit: from pomegranates
to pears, sweet figs, bright apples, and plump olives.
But just as soon as he reached out to touch,
winds blew that fruit up toward the shadowed clouds.
—THE ODYSSEY OF HOMER, XI (TR. BY ALLEN MANDELBAUM)

The Abnegation ■ William Bronk

I want to be that Tantalus, unfed
forever, that my want's agony declare
that such as we want has nothing to say to the world;
if the world wants, it nothing wants for us.
Let me be unsatisfied. Hearing me scream,
spare me compassion, look instead at man,
how he takes handouts, makeshifts, sops
for creature comfort. I refuse. I will not
be less than I am to be more human, or less
than human may be to seem to be more than I am.
I want as the world wants. I am the world.

Tantalus ■ Len Krisak

My fate is cruel? No doubt it makes you think
Of Dante, how I'm in it up to here.
The pool is warm, I tell myself; to drink
It wouldn't cool me anyway, so tears
Are not in order. And to eat the fruit
That hangs above me on that long, lone branch
Would only lead to fouling what I stand
In. No, it's better this way. This way suits
Me fine, thank you. In water free of stench,
I contemplate one perfect apple wind
Would only blow away were I to reach.
Weep not for me, my gentle reader. Each
Man wants some object that will always tease
And taunt. The trick is learning to be pleased.

HEROES

Perseus
Heracles
Jason & the Argonauts

Perseus

He ran through unknown ways, thick-bearded forests
And tearing rocks and stones, until he found
The Gorgon's home. And as he looked about
From left to right, no matter where he turned,
He saw both man and beast turned into stone,
All creatures who had seen Medusa's face.
Yet he himself glanced only at its image—
That fatal stare—reflected in the polished
Bronze of the shield he wore on his left arm.
When darkest sleep took hold of dread Medusa,
Even to the writhing serpents of green hair,
He struck her head clean from her collarbone....
—OVID, THE METAMORPHOSES, IV (TR. BY HORACE GREGORY)

Medusa ■ Vincent O'Sullivan

Sits at the window, waits the threatened steel
as any common housewife waits near dark
for groceries that should have come at four,
when it's too late to phone to hear they're certain,
to know the boy is pedalling up the hill
and not gone home. A boy who's late—
it could be simply that, so still her hands.

Two or three birds. Bare branches.
A thrush taps on the gravel, tilts its head.
Her eyes, she thinks, could hold it if she wanted,
could make it come up close, think this is home.
Sits there, her folded hands, her lips cold,
the expected blade already on her skin.

A piece of wind no bigger than a man
moves the dead leaves, bends the sopping grass.
A blind cord knocks the window like a drum.
'Perseus, stalwart, honest, comes his way,
his footstep nicks the corners of the day,
like something hard against a grey, chipped stone.'
The stone he says she makes with those grey eyes.
Jade in the dusk. Heavier than grey.

And when he comes, how talk moves like a mirror,
a polished shield, in shadows, then in light,
always his care to stay behind its hurt.
Talks of her greatest gift—to deck out men
in stone: stone heart, stone limbs, the lot.
Turns men to stone, turns them to herself.
'The only way to end, for both our good.'

And like a man who shows off coins or gems
he lets his words fall in the room by ones,
and twos, or if in piles, it's when
their rushing sounds and feels a streaming sword.
Edges in close with that, to do his work.
And all her strength, to keep her eyes from his.

Medusa ■ Stephen Stepanchev

A pond of shadow
Widens into a lake.
It's dusk. I am on a raft,
Drifting toward a hardening shore.
I hear bells, bronzing in the gloom.

She is waiting, watering her tulips
With a bronze watering can.
Her smile is full of teeth.
She has sprinkled a spider
Web hanging from the lip
Of a tulip, and diamonds of water
Are beading it.

"Welcome home!" she says.

I freeze. I see beside her,
On the floor,
My head, turned to stone.

Ode: The Medusa Face ■ W.S. Merwin

When did I pass the pole where I deprived
Three hags of their one eye, then, staring, seized
The total of their dark
And took their answer?
For that way I came though the eye forgets:
Now tall over the breathless shore this day
Lifts on one equal glare
The crass and curling face.
I cannot tell if stone is upon me
Healing me, clotting time until I stand
Dead. If the heart yet moves,
What shield were faithful found,
What weapon? I stand as in sloth of stone,
Amazed, for a maimed piece of one's own death,
Should that lithe hair stiffen,
Were the shape of her fall.

Tableau Vivant ◼ Daryl Hine

Perseus on an ornamental charger,
German work, sixteenth century,
Hovering above the slumbering Medusa
Like a buzzing fly or a mosquito
On beaten, golden wings. His head averted
From her agate gaze. In his right hand
A sword, in his left a mirror.

Helmeted by night, slipshod by darkness.
Wondering where to strike. She looks asleep
As if dreaming of petrified forests,
Monumental dryads, stone leaves, stone limbs,
Or of the mate that she will never meet
Who will look into her eyes and live.

Perseus ◼ Louis MacNeice

Borrowed wings on his ankles,
Carrying a stone death,
The hero entered the hall,
All in the hall looked up,
Their breath frozen on them,
And there was no more shuffle or clatter in the hall at all.

So a friend of a man comes in
And leaves a book he is lending or flowers
And goes again but as good as dead,
And you are left alive, no better than dead,
And you dare not turn the leaden pages of the book or touch the flowers, the
    hooded and arrested hours.
Close your eyes,
There are suns beneath your lids,
Or look in the looking-glass in the end room—
You will find it full of eyes,
The ancient smiles of men cut out with scissors and kept in mirrors.

Ever to meet me comes, in sun or dull,
The gay hero swinging the Gorgon's head
And I am left, with the dull drumming of the sun, suspended and dead,
Or the dumb grey-brown of the day is a leper's cloth,
And one feels the earth going round and round the globe of the blackening mantle,
a mad moth.

The Muse as Medusa ■ May Sarton

I saw you once, Medusa; we were alone.
I looked you straight in the cold eye, cold.
I was not punished, was not turned to stone—
How to believe the legends I am told?

I came as naked as any little fish,
Prepared to be hooked, gutted, caught;
But I saw you, Medusa, made my wish,
And when I left you I was clothed in thought ...

Being allowed, perhaps, to swim my way
Through the great deep and on the rising tide,
Flashing wild streams, as free and rich as they,
Though you had power marshaled on your side.

The fish escaped to many a magic reef;
The fish explored many a dangerous sea—
The fish, Medusa, did not come to grief,
But swims still in a fluid mystery.

Forget the image: your silence is my ocean,
And even now it teems with life. You chose
To abdicate by total lack of motion,
But did it work, for nothing really froze?

It is all fluid still, that world of feeling
Where thoughts, those, silent, feed and rove;
And, fluid, it is also full of healing,
For love is healing, even rootless love.

I turn your face around! It is my face.
That frozen rage is what I must explore—
Oh secret, self-enclosed, and ravaged place!
This is the gift I thank Medusa for.

Heracles

Heracles, mighty son of fair-ankled Alkmene,
accomplished his grim labors....

* * *

Blessed is he! His exploits all finished,
he is now among the gods, griefless and ageless forever.
—HESIOD, THEOGONY (TR. BY A.N. ATHANASSAKIS)

Heracles ■ C.K. Williams

A mysterious didactic urgency informs the compelling stories he is obsessively recounted.

Misty, potent creatures, half-human, half-insane with hatred and with lustings for the hearth:

the childhood of the race, with always, as the ground, the urgent implication of a lesson.

Some of it he gets, that there are losses, personal and epic, but bearable, to be withstood,

and that the hero's soul is self-forged, self-conceived, hammered out in outrage, trial, abandon, risk.

The parables elude him, though: he can never quite grasp where the ever-after means to manifest.

Is he supposed to *be* this darkly tempered, dark fanatic of the flesh who'll surely consume himself?

Or should it be the opposite: would all these feats and deeds be not exemplary but cautionary?

The Labours of Hercules (13) ■ John Fuller

For (no one left) pretending not to care
Becomes an academic exercise:
I could as easily hold up the skies
As sit here writing in a summer chair
Or find that voluntary garden where
I can assert my title to the prize
That's mine if I unravel the disguise,
That doubleness we live in as in air.

I do care. Even at the eleventh hour
One has to hope for a miraculous birth,
Though from the golden tree the dragons sigh
Who have the whole of life within their power,
Who will yield nothing. And the widowed earth
Will sit there bravely smiling and not cry.

… the Lion of Nemea,
who was reared by Hera, the glorious wife of Zeus,
and settled on the hills of Nemea as a scourge to mankind.
There was his abode and from there he preyed on the tribes of men
and lorded it over Apesas and Nemean Tretos,
but the strength of mighty Heracles subdued him.
—HESIOD, THEOGONY (TR. BY A. N. ATHANASSAKIS)

Hercules at Nemea ▪ Robert Graves

Muse, you have bitten through my fool's-finger.
Fierce as a lioness you seized it
In your white teeth most amorously;
And I stared back, dauntless and fiery-eyed,
Challenging you to maim me for my pride.

See me a fulvous hero of nine fingers—
Sufficient grasp for bow and arrow.
My beard bristles in exultation:
Let all Nemea look and understand
Why you have set your mark on this right hand.

That country was then ruled by Antaeus, son of Poseidon, who used to
kill strangers by forcing them to wrestlle.
Being forced to wrestle with him, Hercules hugged him, lifted him aloft,
broke and killed him; for when he touched
earth so it was that he waxed stronger, wherefore some said that he was a
son of Earth.
—APOLLODORUS, THE LIBRARY, II.V (TR. BY J.G. FRAZER)

Hercules and Antaeus ▪ Seamus Heaney

Sky-born and royal,
snake-choker, dung-heaver,
his mind big with golden apples,
his future hung with trophies,

Hercules has the measure
of resistance and black powers
feeding off the territory.
Antaeus, the mould-hugger,

is weaned at last:
a fall was a renewal
but now he is raised up—
the challenger's intelligence

is a spur of light,
a blue prong graiping him
out of his element
into a dream of loss

and origins—the cradling dark,
the river-veins, the secret gullies
of his strength,
the hatching grounds

of cave and souterain,
he has bequeathed it all
to elegists. Balor will die
and Byrthnoth and Sitting Bull.

Hercules lifts his arms
in a remorseless V,
his triumph unassailed
by the powers he has shaken,

and lifts and banks Antaeus
high as a profiled ridge,
a sleeping giant,
pap for the dispossessed.

Jason & the Argonauts

Now in a ship that had been built at Pagasae
The Argonauts cut through the restless waves.
And on their way they saw blind Phineus,
His pitiful old age in endless night;
Sons of the North Wind came to drive away
The girl-faced vulturs plucking at his lips.
This was one of the many swift adventures
Shared by the Argonauts, led by bright Captain Jason,
Who steered them safe at last ...

—OVID, THE METAMORPHOSES, VII (TR. BY HORACE GREGORY)

The Argonauts ■ D.H. Lawrence

They are not dead, they are not dead!
Now that the sun, like a lion, licks his paws
and goes slowly down the hill:
now that the moon, who remembers, and only cares
that we should be lovely in the flesh, with bright, crescent feet,
pauses near the crest of the hill, climbing slowly, like a queen
looking down on the lion as he retreats—

Now the sea is the Argonauts' sea, and in the dawn
Odysseus calls the commands, as he steers past those foamy islands;
wait, wait, don't bring me the coffee yet, nor the *pain grillé.*
The dawn is not off the sea, and Odysseus' ships
have not yet passed the islands, I must watch them still.

Mythistorema (4) ■ George Seferis

Argonauts

And a soul
if it is to know itself
must look
into its own soul:
the stranger and enemy, we've seen him in the mirror.

They were good, the companions, they didn't complain
about the work or the thirst or the frost,
they had the bearing of trees and waves
that accept the wind and the rain
accept the night and the sun
without changing in the midst of change.
They were fine, whole days
they sweated at the oars with lowered eyes
breathing in rhythm
and their blood reddened a submissive skin.
Sometimes they sang, with lowered eyes

as we were passing the deserted island with the Barbary figs
to the west, beyond the cape of the dogs
that bark.
If it is to know itself, they said
it must look into its own soul, they said
and the oars struck the sea's gold
in the sunset.
We went past many capes many islands the sea
leading to another sea, gulls and seals.
Sometimes disconsolate women wept
lamenting their lost children
and others frantic sought Alexander the Great
and glories buried in the depths of Asia.
We moored on shores full of night-scents,
the birds singing, with waters that left on the hands
the memory of a great happiness.
But the voyages did not end.
Their souls became one with the oars and the oarlocks
with the solemn face of the prow
with the rudder's wake
with the water that shattered their image.
The companions died one by one,
with lowered eyes. Their oars
mark the place where they sleep on the shore.

No one remembers them. Justice.

Translated from the Greek BY EDMUND KEELEY AND PHILIP SHERRARD

The Decline of the Argo ■ Yannis Ritsos

Tonight, during talk of how all things age, fade, cheapen—
beautiful women, heroic deeds, poems—we suddenly remembered
the legendary ship that they brought to Corinth one spring evening,
now eaten through, the paint gone, oarlocks removed,
all patches, holes, memories. The great procession through the forest,
with torches, wreathes, flutes, athletic games for the young. Truly a grand offering
to Poseidon's temple, that aged *Argo*. The night lovely, and the chanting of the
    priests.
An owl hooted above the temple's pediment, and the dancers leaping with light feet
on the ship, their mimicry of crude action done with unbecoming charm, the
    movement
of nonexistent oars, the sweat and the blood. Then an old sailor
spat at the ground by his feet, moved off to the grove nearby and took a leak.

Translated from the Greek BY EDMUND KEELEY

Jason's Grave in Jerusalem ■ Dan Pagis

Jason, that cunning old sailor,
one of King Yannai's inner circle,
pretends that he was buried
far from the sea,
in an attractive grave in a holy city.
"Room within room he is hidden, adorned by pillars and arches;
peace and perpetual glory were carved for him in this limestone."

The grave is empty.
Only a drawing of a ship
is scratched on the wall.

Overhead, kingdoms have fallen,
new men have descended into Hades.

Not Jason. He slips away
again and again,
out of the blank wall,
in a fast ship
(cuts through the sea of air, maintaining
absolute radio-silence)
and with great profit, as always, smuggles
very expensive merchandise:
sunlight of water,
velvet of sea breeze,
marble of foam.

    Translated from the Hebrew BY STEPHEN MITCHELL

JASON'S MARRIAGE: MEDEA

Jason swore that his hand was hers forever.
She took him at his word....

   * * *

       There Medea found
Jason remarried, and with her deadly spells
She burnt his bride to ashes while two seas
Witnessed the flames that poured from Jason's halls.
Even then her blood-red steel had pierced the bodies
Of their two sons; yet she escaped the edge
of Jason's sword by taking refuge in her
Dragon's car, those flying monsters born
Of Titan's blood.

—OVID, METAMORPHOSES, VII (TR. BY HORACE GREGORY)

Medea ■ Kathleen Raine

Anguish and revenge made visible, her serpents lifted
Medea above pity and horror of the enacted
Crime; murderess to herself most cruel,
Absolute in power of absolute loss,
Invulnerable by human justice or human hate,
Apollo whose ancestral fire seethed in her veins
Snatched among the gods who acknowledge only
The truth of life, fulfilled in her
To the last bitter blood-drop of her being.
On amphora and crater apotheosis
Has raised into the myths of Greece the barbarous
Wronged woman whose outstretched parting hand
Warns that there are furies among the immortals,
That anguish is an avenging frenzy
Of passionate love that slaughters her own children.
What could earth-bound Jason who rated calculation above the gods
Answer Medea departing on the dragon-chariot of her desolation?

CRETE

Pasiphae
Ariadne, Theseus, the Minotaur
Phaedra

Pasiphae

Your wife was more than proper wife to you,
That creature who disguised herself in bark
So she could kneel to let a bull mount on her
And carry in her womb half-man, half-bull.
—OVID, THE METAMORPHOSES, VIII (TR. BY HORACE GREGORY)

Pasiphae ■ A.D. Hope

There stood the mimic cow; the young bull kept
Fast by the nose-ring, trampling in his pride,
Nuzzled her flanks and snuffed her naked side.
She was a queen: to have her will she crept
In that black box; and when her lover leapt
And fell thundering on his wooden bride,
When straight her fierce, frail body crouched inside
Felt the wet pizzle pierce and plunge, she wept.

She wept for terror, for triumph; she wept to know
Her love unable to embrace its bliss
So long imagined, waking and asleep.
But when within she felt the pulse, the blow,
The burst of copius seed, the burning kiss
Fill her with monstrous life, she did not weep.

Lament for Pasiphaë ■ Robert Graves

Dying sun, shine warm a little longer!
My eye, dazzled with tears, shall dazzle yours,
Conjuring you to shine and not to move.
You, sun, and I all afternoon have laboured
Beneath a dewless and oppressive cloud—
A fleece now gilded with our common grief
That this must be a night without a moon.
Dying sun, shine warm a little longer!

Faithless she was not: she was very woman,
Smiling with dire impartiality,
Sovereign, with heart unmatched, adored of men,
Until Spring's cuckoo with bedraggled plumes
Tempted her pity and her truth betrayed.
Then she who shone for all resigned her being,
And this must be a night without a moon.
Dying sun, shine warm a little longer!

Ariadne, Theseus, the Minotaur

You would have died in the twisting halls without
        the string that I gave to be your guide.
You said to me, "I swear by these perils that
        as long as we live, you will be mine."
We are alive, Theseus, but I am not yours;
        though buried by your deceit, I live.
—OVID, HEROIDES, X (TR. BY HAROLD ISBELL)

Within this maze Minos concealed the beast,
And at two seasons placed nine years apart
He fed the creature on Athenian blood;
But when a third nine years had made their round,
The monster faced the season of his doom.
—OVID, THE METAMORPHOSES, VIII (TR. BY HORACE GREGORY)

Ariadne ■ Thomas Merton

All through the blazing afternoon
The hand drums talk together like locusts;
The flute pours out its endless, thin stream,
Threading it in and out the clatter of sticks upon wood-blocks.
Drums and bells exchange handfulls of bright coins,
Drums and bells scatter their music, like pennies, all over the air,
And see, the lutanist's thin hand
Rapidly picks the spangling notes off from his wires
And throws them about like drops of water.

Behind the bamboo blinds,
Behind the palms,
In the green, sundappled apartments of her palace
Redslippered Ariadne, with a tiny yawn,
Tosses a ball upon her roulette wheel.

Suddenly, dead north,
A Greek ship leaps over the horizon, skips like a colt, paws the foam.
The ship courses through the pasture of bright amethysts
And whinnies at the jetty.
The whole city runs to see:
Quick as closing your hand
The racing sail's down.
Then the drums are stunned, and the crowd, exalted, cries:
O Theseus! O Grecian hero!

Like a thought through the mind
Ariadne moves to the window.
Arrows of light, in every direction,
Leap from the armor of the black-eyed captain.

Arrows of light
Resound within her like the strings of a guitar.

Theseus and Ariadne ■ Robert Graves

High on his figured couch beyond the waves
He dreams, in dream recalling her set walk
Down paths of oyster-shell bordered with flowers,
Across the shadowy turf below the vines.
He sighs: "Deep sunk in my erroneous past
She haunts the ruins and the ravaged lawns."

Yet still unharmed it stands, the regal house
Crooked with age and overtopped by pines
Where first he wearied of her constancy.
And with a surer foot she goes than when
Dread of his hate was thunder in the air,
When the pines agonized with flaws of wind
And flowers glared up at her with frantic eyes.
Of him, now all is done, she never dreams
But calls a living blessing down upon
What he supposes rubble and rank grass;
Playing the queen to nobler company.

Ariadne auf Naxos ■ Nicholas Christopher

The windows are curtained.
Tanks of saltwater line the walls
and in their bright blue light
fish dart among the anemones.
Down a hallway a dog is barking,
and upstairs a woman paces
on a polished floor, clicking
out a message of distress.
A man enters the room, sliding
from shadow to shadow, assuming
the shape of successive objects—
chair, bureau, potted palm …
finally merging with the statue
of Bacchus beside a dark screen.
He waits, knowing she will come
to him, despite herself—
her fear of being abandoned again.
At dawn, when the curtains are drawn,
there are no fish in the tanks
and no people in the room;
just a single statue of a woman
with sea-twined hair and a cold smile,
a cluster of grapes in her hand.

Requiem ■ Rosario Ferré

Theseus is finally convinced:
the Minotaur is his destiny.
He rises and buckles up his shield.
As he straps on his sandals
the bracelets of his arms ring out
like lightning.
Legs apart, Cyclopean, he stands over
and resolutely fits the dagger to his waist.
He whispers in her ear one day he'll return
with a rich horn of ivory on a damasked cushion
from across the seas.
Theseus embraces her for the last time
and strides off with a dagger
lighting up the labyrinth with the gleam of his sword.
Ariadne leans against the wall.
A reed of icy bones
has splintered down the length of her back.
She sits
on the stamped-down dust
of nothingness
—no bottom there.
A sudden pain tears at her insides.
She feels the warm wine
as it runs down between her legs.
She's begun to abort the Minotaur.

Translated from the Spanish BY THE AUTHOR

The Minotaur ■ Muriel Rukeyser

Trapped, blinded, led; and in the end betrayed
Daily by new betrayals as he stays
Deep in his labyrinth, shaking and going mad.
Betrayed. Betrayed. Raving, the beaten head
Heavy with madness, he stands, half-dead and proud.
No one again will ever see his pride.
No one will find him walking to him straight
But must be led circuitously about,
Calling to him and close and, losing the subtle thread,
Lose him again; while he waits, brutalized
By loneliness. Later, afraid
Of his own suffering. At last, savage and made
Ravenous, ready to prey upon the race
If it so much as learn the clews of blood
Into his pride his fear his glistening heart.
Now is the patient deserted in his fright
And love carrying salvage round the world
Lost in a crooked city; roundabout,

By the sea, the precipice, all the fantastic ways
Betrayal weaves its trap; loneliness knows the thread,
And the heart is lost, lost, trapped, blinded and led,
Deserted at the middle of the maze.

Minotaur ■ John Frederick Nims

Sweet flesh was shipped the bull-man once to eat.
You think it's changed, you children on the street?
Go home and pack. Tomorrow, off for Crete.

The Labyrinth ■ Jorge Luis Borges

Zeus, Zeus himself could not undo these nets
Of stone encircling me. My mind forgets
The persons I have been along the way,
The hated way of monotonous walls,
Which is my fate. The galleries seem straight
But curve furtively, forming secret circles
At the terminus of years; and the parapets
Have been worn smooth by the passage of days.
Here, in the tepid alabaster dust,
Are tracks that frighten me. The hollow air
Of evening sometimes brings a bellowing,
Or the echo, desolate, of bellowing.
I know that hidden in the shadows there
Lurks another, whose task is to exhaust
The loneliness that braids and weaves this hell,
To crave my blood, and to fatten on my death.
We seek each other. Oh, if only this
Were the last day of our antithesis!
    Translated from the Spanish BY JOHN UPDIKE

Phaedra

Go now, pay your respects to the bed
which your father denies by his wicked deeds.
If I seem a stepmother who would
lie with her husband's son, ignore such silly
words. Such virtue was out of date in
Saturn's reign and it died in the next age when
Jove decreed that virtue was pleasure.

—OVID, HEROIDES, IV (TR. BY HAROLD ISBELL)

Phaedra in the Farm House ■ Thom Gunn

From sleep, before first light,
I hear slow-rolling churns
Clank over flags below.
Aches me. The room returns.
I hurt, I wake, I know
The cold dead end of night.

Here father. And here son.
What trust I live between.
But warmth here on the sheet
Is kin-warmth, slow and clean.
I cook the food two eat,
But oh, I sleep with one.

And you, in from the stable.
You spent last evening
Lost in the chalky blues
Of warm hills, rabbitting.
You frown and spell the news,
With forearms on the table.

Tonight, though, we play cards.
You are not playing well.
I smell the oil-lamp's jet,
The parlour's polished smell,
Then you—soap, ghost of sweat,
Tractor oil, and the yards.

Shirt-sleeved you concentrate.
Your moleskin waistcoat glints
Your quick grin never speaks:
I study you for hints
—Hints from those scrubbed boy-cheeks?

I deal a grown man's fate.

The churns wait on in mud:
Tomorrow's milk will sour.
I leave, but bit by bit,
Sharp through the last whole hour.
The chimney will be split,
And that waistcoat be blood.

THEBES

Oedipus

Oedipus

> Oedipus: *Come, prophet, show your title! When the Sphinx*
> *Chanted her music here, why did not you*
> *Speak out and save the city?*
>
>   * * *
>
> Teiresias: *You have your sight, and yet you cannot see*
> *Where, nor with whom, you live, nor in what horror.*
> *Your parents—do you know them? or that you*
> *Are enemy to your kin, alive or dead?*
> *And that a father's and a mother's curse*
> *Shall join to drive you headlong out of Thebes*
> *And change the light that now you see to darkness?*
>
> —SOPHOCLES, OEDIPUS THE KING (TR. BY H.D.F. KITTO)

Oedipus ■ Constantine P. Cavafy

Written after reading a description of the painting
"Oedipus and the Sphinx" BY GUSTAVE MOREAU

The Sphinx has fallen upon him
with teeth and nails outstretched
and with the full ferocity of life.
Oedipus fell at her first onslaught,
her first appearance horrified him—
until then he had never imagined
such a face or such talk.
But for all the monster's leaning
her two legs on Oedipus' breast,
he recovers quickly—and now
he has no fear of her at all, because he has
the solution ready and will win.
And yet he is not joyful over this victory.
His fully melancholy gaze
is not turned on the Sphinx, beyond
he sees the narrow road that leads to Thebes,
and that finally will end at Colonus.
And his soul is clearly and prophetically aware
that there the Sphinx will speak to him again
with more difficult and with more extensive
riddles that have no answer.

Translated from the Greek BY THEOHARIS C. THEOHARIS

Oedipus and the Riddle ■ Jorge Luis Borges

At dawn four-footed, at midday erect,
And wandering on three legs in the deserted
Spaces of afternoon, thus the eternal
Sphinx had envisioned her changing brother
Man, and with afternoon there came a person

Deciphering, appalled at the monstrous other
Presence in the mirror, the reflection
Of his decay and of his destiny.
We are Oedipus; in some eternal way
We are the long and threefold beast as well—
All that we will be, all that we have been.
It would annihilate us all to see
The huge shape of our being; mercifully
God offers us issue and oblivion.

    Translated from the Spanish BY JOHN HOLLANDER

The Sphinx's Riddle to Oedipus ■ Randall Jarrell

Not to have guessed is better: what is, ends,
But among fellows, with reluctance,
Clasped by the Woman-Breasted, Lion-Pawed.

To have clasped in one's own arms a mother,
To have killed with one's own hands a father
—Is not this, Lame One, to have been alone?

The seer is doomed for seeing; and to understand
Is to pluck out one's own eyes with one's own hands.
But speak: what has a woman's breasts, a lion's paws?

You stand at midday in the marketplace
Before your life: to see is to have spoken.
—Yet to see, Blind One, is to be alone.

The Theban Sphinx ■ John Heath-Stubbs

Her last riddle, the one
Oedipus did not solve was this:
That she herself, winged lion with a pitiless face,
Was also royal Jocasta, who would finish
Hanging from a palace beam, a hempen neckinger
Around her delicate throat.

But it was enough, he had demonstrated
That he was a king, a cunning man,
Clever enough to be the bridegroom
Of Turandot, or Antiochus's daughter.

Myth ■ Muriel Rukeyser

Long afterward, Oedipus, old and blinded, walked the
roads.   He smelled a familiar smell.   It was
the Sphinx.   Oedipus said, "I want to ask one question.
Why didn't I recognize my mother?"   "You gave the

wrong answer," said the Sphinx.   "But that was what
made everything possible," said Oedipus.   "No," she said.
"When I asked, What walks on four legs in the morning,
two at noon, and three in the evening, you answered,
Man.   You didn't say anything about woman."
"When you say Man," said Oedipus, "you include women
too. Everyone knows that."   She said, "That's what
you think."

What Riddle Asked the Sphinx ■ Archibald MacLeish

to the memory of André Gide

In my stone eyes I see
The saint upon his knee
Delve in the desert for eternity.

In my stone ears I hear
The night-lost traveller
Cry *When?* to the earth's shadow: *When? Oh where?*

Stone deaf and blind
I ponder in my mind
The bone that seeks, the flesh that cannot find.

Stone blind I see
The saint's eternity
Deep in the earth he digs in. Cannot he?

Stone deaf I hear
The night say *Then!* say *There!*
Why cries the traveller still to the night air?

The one is not content
With silence, the day spent;
With earth the other. More, they think, was meant.

Stone that I am, can stone
Perceive what flesh and bone
Are blind and deaf to?

    Or has hermit known,
Has traveller divined,
Some question there behind
I cannot come to, being stone and blind?

To all who ken or can
I ask, since time began,
What riddle is it has for answer, Man?

Dialogue with the Sphinx ■ Ramon Guthrie

So I spoke in a chorus of three different voices:
　of a gun-shy banshee,
　　of a landlocked merman,
　　　of Orpheus himself wih a bad case of laryngitis,
and said, Where is this performance getting us?

And the Sphinx—at least I took her for the Sphinx:
according to the sextant,
the fix seemed right for the road to Thebes,
and she had the same firm
hoyden impersonal breasts that Ingres endows her with—
said, "Not much of anywhere as far as I can tell.
Where are you *trying* to get to?"
　　Nowhere that I know of.
"Then you are heading the wrong way,
　　turning your back on it. This is the road
from nowhere that you know of
　　to nowhere that you *don't* know of."
Is there much difference?
　　"How should I know? All that *I've* been to
is the nowhere that *I* know of."

So I scuffed it all out
　　and started over again.

　And that was that: I had spoken with the Sphinx.

Oedipus II ■ Michael Blumenthal

The oracle said: *you will always be alone,*
But he kept falling in love, he kept
meeting lovers whenever the road forked
back into his own solitude.

The oracle said: *you will be childless,*
you will plant your seed only into the wind.
But he kept fathering children, kept squirting his seed
into the darkness of the wrong engenderings.

The oracle said: you must enter the darkness,
you must learn to swim in it, live in it,
pass through it like a burrowing mole. But he
kept yearning for the light, kept flying into it
like a moth lured to its own extinguishment.

Finally, the oracle said: you will spend your whole life
resisting this, you will pass all your days yearning
for love, children, the bright light of your bettering.

Now he was starting to grow tired. *Yes*, he said, *yes*,
looking up at the dimming light, his fleeing love,
his only child calling out to him from across the sea.

Sphinx Ludens ■ Ann Deagon

Thebes of the 7 gates in
to whose maw
generation up
on generation
all potent heroes come
who tread the earth

and at whose out
skirts shrivel the de
tumescent un
entombed fore
fathers of the epi
goni

     in
penetrable city
spread your gates
we two come in to
lay us down with Laius
I your casta
you my swollen son in
cestuous and zestful re
enact
the play of Thebes

The Approach to Thebes ■ Stanley Kunitz

In the zero of the night, in the lipping hour,
Skin-time, knocking-time, when the heart is pearled
And the moon squanders its uranian gold,
She taunted me, who was all music's tongue,
Philosophy's and wilderness's breed,
Of shifting shape, half jungle-cat, half-dancer,
Night's woman-petaled, lion-scented rose,
To whom I gave, out of a hero's need,
The dolor of my thrust, my riddling answer,
Whose force no lesser mortal knows. Dangerous?
Yes, as nervous oracles foretold
Who could not guess the secret taste of her:
Impossible wine! I came into the world
To fill a fate; am punished by my youth
No more. What if dog-faced logic howls
Was it art or magic multiplied my joy?

Nature has reasons beyond true or false.
We played like metaphysic animals
Whose freedom made our knowledge bold
Before the tragic curtain of the day:
I can bear the dishonor now of growing old.

Blinded and old, exiled, diseased, and scorned—
The verdict's bitten on the brazen gates,
For the gods grant each of us his lot, his term.
Hail to the King of Thebes!—my self, ordained
To satisfy the impulse of the worm,
Bemummied in those famous incestuous sheets,
The bloodiest flags of nations of the curse,
To be hung from the balcony outside the room
Where I encounter my most flagrant source.
Children, grandchildren, my long posterity,
To whom I bequeath the spiders of my dust,
Believe me, whatever sordid tales you hear,
Told by physicians or mendacious scribes,
Of beardless folly, consanguineous lust,
Fomenting pestilence, rebellion, war,
I come prepared, unwanting what I see,
But tied to life. On the royal road to Thebes
I had my luck, I met a lovely monster,
And the story's this: I made the monster me.

The Other Oedipus ■ Edwin Muir

Remembered on the Peloponnesian roads,
He and his serving-boy and his concubine,
White-headed and light-hearted, their true wits gone
Past the last stroke of time into a day
Without a yesterday or a to-morrow,
A brightness laid like a blue lake around them,
Or endless field to play or linger in.
They were so gay and innocent, you'd have thought
A god had won a glorious prize for them
In some celestial field, and the odds were gone,
Fate sent on holiday, the earth and heaven
Thenceforth in endless friendly talk together.
They were quite storyless and had clean forgotten
That memory burning in another world;
But they too leaf-light now for any story.
If anyone spoke a word of other guilt
By chance before them, then they stamped their feet
In rage and gnashed their teeth like peevish children.
But then forgot. The road their welcoming home.
They would not stay in a house or let a door
Be shut on them. The surly Spartan farmers
Were kind to them, pitying their happiness.

Last Words ▪ Eleanor Wilner

Blind Oedipus
is old, death sits
at his side, its cold breath
on his hand. If you lean close,
you can hear him speak;

"Cursed with words, yet still
    they are my eyes, and what I say
        I see: old men
who put their sons on distant hills
    to die, and calling it god's will,
those armies of the young are led
        to think the enemy
    is somewhere over there
and so are spared the messenger's
arrival with the news: the twisted root,
        the lame foot—your father's legacy
        to you, your mother dreaming
        the king's dream, the oracle mouthing
        his desires,
                    the rain dark
as we begin, like statues
made of earth, to melt back into mud,
eyes pouring water, faces streaked
and losing shape, returning to earth—
        like the terra-cotta army
        buried in the tomb
        of the Emperor Qin, but this time
        no beautiful figures to dig up,
        no one to comment on the exquisite realism,
        how each face is faithful
        to its original, the way each costume
        shows the rank, how the handsome horses
        flank imperial pride—only
one common mud, earth closing
over its own eyes …

we, who would give dumb matter
voice, and to inherent numbers
bring an intricate and abstract mirror, and span
the distance between stars with the silver
strands of mind, and link all difference
in the shimmering bridge
of imagery, and with blind molecules
grow eyes and hands that, phototropic,
grope their way to light,
pull all creation in our wake

into the brilliant day—and yet
as twins will hatch from the selfsame egg,
awareness split between its joys
and horror at the short term set to them,
the quick return
of dark, the mind fell under
the spell of death, which took
no end of forms:

        a lost shoe, a blighted hope, a misplaced
        name, the slightest hint of disagreement
        from a subordinate, a woman
        out of reach, the sight of a young
            son growing strong
could bring on rage, the blood
wash in the eyes, the red letter
days of war, the bellow
            of a dying animal—
        Mud, I say, and mud, I see,
        all dark, I say, from so much
        light, from such abundant
        vision as I had, such
        abomination, such
        continual night."

If you wish, you may close
his eyes now, and close
the quote, put
the double marks,
like the bite of a small animal,
there, on the white page.

TROY

*… three goddesses, Venus, Pallas and
Juno, set their delicate feet on the turf.
My hair stood on end, I trembled and
lost speech. "Do not fear," said the winged messenger.
"You are the final judge of beauty,
end the contentions of these three goddesses;
decide which of them such beauty has
that will conquer the other two."*
—OVID, HEROIDES, XVI (TR. BY HAROLD ISBELL)

The Judgment of Paris ■ W.S. Merwin

for Anthony Hecht

Long afterwards
the intelligent could deduce what had been offered
and not recognized
and they suggest that bitterness should be confined
to the fact that the gods chose for their arbiter
a mind and character so ordinary
albeit a prince

and brought up as a shepherd
a calling he must have liked
for he had returned to it

when they stood before him
the three
naked feminine deathless
and he realized that he was clothed
in nothing but mortality
the strap of his quiver of arrows crossing
between his nipples
making it seem stranger

and he knew he must choose
and on that day

the one with the gray eyes spoke first
and whatever she said he kept
thinking he remembered
but remembered it woven with confusion and fear
the two faces that he called father
the first sight of the palace
where the brothers were strangers
and the dogs watched him and refused to know him
she made everything clear she was dazzling she
offered it to him

205

to have for his own but what he saw
was the scorn above her eyes
and her words of which he understood few
all said to him *Take wisdom*
take power
you will forget anyway

the one with the dark eyes spoke
and everything she said
he imagined he had once wished for
but in confusion and cowardice
the crown
of his father the crowns the crowns bowing to him
his name everywhere like grass
only he and the sea
triumphant
she made everything sound possible she was
dazzling she offered it to him
to hold high but what he saw
was the cruelty around her mouth
and her words of which he understood more
all said to him *Take pride*
take glory
you will suffer anyway

the third one the color of whose eyes
later he could not remember
spoke last and slowly and
of desire and it was his
though up until then he had been
happy with his river nymph
here was his mind
filled utterly with one girl gathering
yellow flowers
and no one like her
the words
made everything seem present
almost present
present
they said to him *Take*
her
you will lose her anyway

it was only when he reached out to the voice
as though he could take the speaker
herself
that his hand filled with
something to give
but to give to only one of the three

an apple as it is told
discord itself in a single fruit its skin
already carved
To the fairest   ,

then a mason working above the gates of Troy
in the sunlight thought he felt the stone
shiver

in the quiver on Paris's back the head
of the arrow for Achilles' heel
smiled in its sleep

and Helen stepped from the palace to gather
as she would do every day in that season
from the grove the yellow ray flowers tall
as herself

whose roots are said to dispel pain

Paris Reconsiders ■ Norman Iles

I love Venus. No one loves her more.
But I have to hang her big breasts on
The goddess of wisdom. I can't lose them,
Could never not see them. Forever,
Shine like lamps on me! But be hung, golden,
Around the neck of wise Athene!
Comfort my eyes, not blaze and blind them.
If need be, oh goddess of proportion,
Make small seem great, to mortal me!

*"Wishing to gain Cassandra's favors, Apollo promised to teach her the art of prophecy;
she learned the art but refused her favours; hence Apollo deprived her prophecy of power
to persuade."*
—APOLLODORUS, THE LIBRARY, III.xii (TR. BY J.G. FRAZER)

How Cassandra Became Clairvoyant ▪ Nina Kossman

So. You are Apollo. Well, that's a new one.
As good a line as any to get a girl.

A godhead must be like a flowering tree,
open in every pore. But you
are closed in upon yourself.

Devious god, I see right through you.
You guard the image that protects the space
in which you hide, aloof and conscious godhead.

Grant you your desire?
But I'm only an image in your dream,
an inverse reflection of yourself,
a bit of instinct, a bit of soil …

Love you?
Foolish god, I'm a mortal girl,
I cannot love a consciousness,
perfection of a mind that is god.
Besides, I'm not a starry-eyed virgin from a storybook,
although I may look like one to you
as I stand here discoursing with an emptiness,
the disembodied space that claims to be a god.

We trade?…
Lord of the lyre, master of song, lord of prophecy,
king of praise and of timely whispers,
prove now that you are you,
and not an empty cloud begging for a shape.

My wish?
To have the future at my fingertips!
To have the power of your priestesses, Apollo,
but without the laurel-chewing nonsense, if you please:
I'd get a headache from all the chewing.
Measure the price of my body in prophecy:
how many foresights am I worth? Ah! Now!…

Grant you your desire?
Now that I am a goddess as much as you are a god?

Who do you think you are kidding, lover?
The scales of the future are eloquent, delicate, quick.
A kiss, only one, don't ask for more.
I must go. To Troy, to tell them.
I owe you nothing, lord of good manners,
god of frost and diluted dreams.

Back to your void, Apollo.

"Why do I wear these mockeries upon my body,
this staff of prophecy, these flowers at my throat?
At least I will spoil you before I die. Out, down,
break, damn you! This for all that you have done to me.
Make someone else, not me, luxurious in disaster....
Lo now, this is Apollo who has stripped me here
of my prophetic robes. He watched me all the time
wearing this glory, mocked of all, my dearest ones
who hated me with all their hearts, so vain, so wrong;
called like some gypsy wandering from door to door
beggar, corrupt, half-starved and I endured it all."
—AESCHYLUS, AGAMEMNON (TR. BY RICHMOND LATTIMORE)

Even then can Cassandra chant of what will come
with lips the gods had doomed to disbelief
by Trojans.
—THE AENEID OF VIRGIL, II (TR. BY ALLEN MANDELBAUM)

The Real Reason ■ Yannis Ritsos

No, it isn't that Apollo reneged on his promise
and took the conviction out of Cassandra's words
by spitting in her face, thereby making her prophecies
useless both for her and for others—no. It's just that
nobody wants to believe the truth. And when you see
the net in your bath, you think they've gotten it out
for your fishing trip tomorrow, and neither inside you
nor outside you do you hear, on the palace's marble stairs,
the dark tidings coming up with hapless Cassandra's wailing.

Translated from the Greek BY EDMUND KEELEY

Soliloquy for Cassandra ■ Wislawa Szymborska

Here I am, Cassandra.
And this is my city under ashes.
And these are my prophet's staff and ribbons.
And this is my head full of doubts.

It's true, I am triumphant.
My prophetic words burn like fire in the sky.
Only unacknowledged prophets

are privy to such prospects.
Only those who got off on the wrong foot,
whose predictions turned to fact so quickly—
it's as if they'd never lived.

I remember it so clearly—
how people, seeing me, would break off in mid-word.
Laughter died.
Lovers' hands unclasped.
Children ran to their mothers.
I didn't even know their short-lived names.
And that song about a little green leaf—
no one ever finished it near me.

I loved them.
But I loved them haughtily.
From heights beyond life.
From the future. Where it's always empty
and nothing is easier than seeing death.
I am sorry that my voice was hard.
Look down on yourselves from the stars, I cried,
look down on yourselves from the stars.
They heard me and lowered their eyes.

They lived within life,
Pierced by that great wind.
Condemned.
Trapped from birth in departing bodies.
But in them they bore a moist hope,
a flame fueled by its own flickering.
They really knew what a moment means,
oh any moment, any one at all
before—

It turns out I was right.
But nothing has come of it.
And this is my robe, slightly singed.
And this is my prophet's junk.
And this is my twisted face.
A face that didn't know it could be beautiful.

Translated from the Polish BY STANISLAW BARANCZAK AND CLARE CAVANAGH

Cassandra ■ Robinson Jeffers

The mad girl with the staring eyes and long white fingers
Hooked in the stones of the wall,
The storm-wrack hair and the screeching mouth: does it matter, Cassandra,
Whether the people believe
Your bitter fountain? Truly men hate the truth; they'd liefer
Meet a tiger on the road.
Therefore the poets honey their truth with lying; but religion-
Venders and political men
Pour from the barrel new lies on the old and are praised for kindly
Wisdom. Poor bitch, be wise.
No: you'll still mumble in a corner a crust of truth, to men
And gods disgusting—You and I, Cassandra.

Cassandra ■ Stephen Mitchell

Nobody can stand her anymore. She has become obsessed, boring. Her friends
turn the other way. Even her husband no longer listens, as he used to do out of
kindness, with glazed eyes.

So she has taken to selling herself on the street corners. She is attractive enough;
the men buy. Up in a cheap hotel room, in the dark, she writhes with them, whis-
pering *nuclear holocaust, acid rain.*

Cassandra ■ Louise Bogan

To me, one silly task is like another.
I bare the shambling tricks of lust and pride.
This flesh will never give a child its mother,—
Song, like a wing, tears through my breast, my side,
And madness chooses out my voice again,
Again. I am the chosen no hand saves:
The shrieking heaven lifted over men,
Not the dumb earth, wherein they set their graves.

Helen

*"... Helen of Argos, Helen for whom so many Argives
lost their lives in Troy, far from native land!"*
—HOMER, THE ILIAD, II (TR. BY ROBERT FAGLES)

*"Alas, Helen, wild heart,
for the multitude, for the thousand lives
you killed under Troy's shadow,
you alone, to shine in man's memory
as blood flower never to be washed out."*
—AESCHYLUS, AGAMEMNON (TR. BY RICHMOND LATTIMORE)

Helen ■ Paul Valéry

Blue! Here I am, come out of the deadly caves
To hear the thundering surf break on the shores
And see those ships, when sunrise strikes the waves,
Emerge from the dark with banks of golden oars.

My lonely hands summon those majesties
Whose salty beards amused my soft, light fingers.
I cried. They sang of their nebulous victories
And of those bays where the wake of their warships lingers.

I hear the martial trumpets, the profound
Sea shells beat a rhythm for the flying blades;
The clear song of the oarsmen stills the storms,

And the gods on heroic prows where the rollers pound,
Their ancient smiles battered by foam cascades,
Stretch out to me their indulgent, sculptured arms.

Translated from the French BY CHARLES GUENTHER

Helen ■ H.D. (Hilda Doolittle)

All Greece hates
the still eyes in the white face,
the lustre as of olives
where she stands,
and the white hands.

All Greece reviles
the wan face when she smiles,
hating it deeper still
when it grows wan and white,
remembering past enchantments
and past ills.

Greece sees unmoved,
God's daughter, born of love,
the beauty of cool feet
and slenderest knees,
could love indeed the maid,
only if she were laid,
white ash amid funereal cypresses.

■ Marina Tsvetaeva

Thus—only Helen looks past the Trojan
Roofs. In the stupor of her eyes
Four provinces left bloodless
And a hundred centuries forlorn.

Thus—only Helen, towering above the marital strife,
Thinks: my nudity
Has left four Arabias frozen
And five seas drained of pearls.

Thus only Helen—do not expect to see
Her wringing her hands!—wonders at this host
Of crown princes left homeless
And chieftains rushing to fight.

Thus only Helen—do not expect to see
Her pleading lips!—wonders at this ditch
Heaped up with princes:
At the sonlessness of a hundred tribes.

But no, not Helen! Not that bigamous
Thief, the pestilential draught.
What treasury have you squandered
That you now look into our eyes as

Even Helen at the great supper
Did not dare—into the eyes of her slaves:
Gods. "The land left husbandless by an outsider
Still, like a caterpillar, grovelling towards her feet."

Translated from the Russian BY NINA KOSSMAN

■ Marina Tsvetaeva

There are rhymes in this world.
Disjoin them, and it trembles.
You were a blind man, Homer.
Night sat on your eyebrows.

Night, your singer's cloak.
Night, on your eyes, like a shutter.
Would a seeing man not have joined
Achilles to Helen?

Helen. Achilles.
Name a better sounding match.
For, in defiance of chaos
The world thrives on accords.

Yet, disjointed (with accord
At its core) it seeks revenge
In wifely unfaithfulness
And the burning Troy.

You were a blind man, bard.
You littered fortune like trash.
Those rhymes have been forged in *that*
World, and as you draw them apart

This world crumbles. Who needs
An accord! Grow old, Helen!
Achaia's best warrior!
Sparta's sweet beauty!

Nothing but the murmur
Of myrtle, a lyre's dream:
"Helen. Achilles.
The couple kept apart."

Translated from the Russian BY NINA KOSSMAN

Helen's Burning ■ Laura Riding

Her beauty, which we talk of,
Is but half her fate.
All does not come to light
Until the two halves meet
And we are silent
And she speaks,
Her whole fate saying,
She is, she is not, in one breath.

But we tell only half, fear to know all
Lest all should be to tell
And our mouths choke with flame
Of her consuming
And lose the gift of prophecy.

Helen's Faces ■ Laura Riding

Bitterly have I been contested for,
Though never have I counted numbers—
They were too many, less than all.
And kindly have I warded off
Contest and bitterness,
Given each a replica of love,
Beguiled them with fine images.

To their hearts they held them.
Her dear face, its explicitness!
Clearly, of all women, the immediate one
To these immediate men.

But the original woman is mythical,
Lies lonely against no heart.
Her eyes are cold, see love far off,
Read no desertion when love removes,
The images out of fashion.

Undreamed of in her many faces
That each kept off the plunderer:
Contest and bitterness never raged round her.

Helen ■ George Seferis

> Teucer: ... in sea-girt Cyprus, where it was decreed
>   by Apollo that I should live, giving the city
>   the name of Salamis in memory of my island home.
>   * * *
> Helen: I never went to Troy; it was a phantom.
>   * * *
> Servant: What? You mean it was only for a cloud
>   that we struggled so much?
>   —EURIPIDES, HELEN

'The nightingales won't let you sleep in Platres.'

Shy nightingale, in the breathing of the leaves,
you who bestow the forest's musical coolness
on the sundered bodies, on the souls
of those who know they will not return.
Blind voice, you who grope in the darkness of memory
for footsteps and gestures—I wouldn't dare say kisses—
and the bitter raving of the frenzied slave-woman.

'The nightingales won't let you sleep in Platres.'

Platres: where is Platres? And this island: who knows it?
I've lived my life hearing names I've never heard before:
new countries, new idiocies of men
or of the gods;
                    my fate, which wavers
between the last sword of some Ajax
and another Salamis,
brought me here, to this shore.
                    The moon
rose from the sea like Aphrodite,
covered the Archer's stars, now moves to find
the heart of Scorpio, and alters everything.
Truth, where's truth?
I too was an archer in the war;
my fate: that of a man who missed his target.

Lyric nightingale,
on a night like this, by the shore of Proteus,
the Spartan slave-girls heard you and began their lament,
and among them—who would have believed it?—Helen!
She whom we hunted so many years by the banks of the Scamander.
She was there, at the desert's tip; I touched her; she spoke to me:
'It isn't true, it isn't true,' she cried.
'I didn't board the blue-bowed ship.'
I never went to valiant Troy.'

Breasts girded high, the sun in her hair, and that stature
shadows and smiles everywhere,
on shoulders, thighs and knees;
the skin alive, and her eyes
with the large eyelids,
she was there, on the banks of a Delta.
                    And at Troy?
At Troy, nothing: just a phantom image.
That's how the gods wanted it.
And Paris, Paris lay with a shadow as though it were a solid being;
and for ten whole years we slaughtered ourselves for Helen.

Great suffering had desolated Greece.
So many bodies thrown
into the jaws of the sea, the jaws of the earth
so many souls
fed to the millstones like grain.
And the rivers swelling, blood in their silt,
all for a linen undulation, a filmy cloud,
a butterfly's flicker, a wisp of a swan's down,
an empty tunic—all for a Helen.

And my brother?
                    Nightingale nightingale nightingale,
what is a god? What is not a god? And what is there in between them?

'The nightingales won't let you sleep in Platres.'

Tearful bird,
        on sea-kissed Cyprus
consecrated to remind me of my country,
I moored alone with this fable,
if it's true that it is a fable,
if it's true that mortals will not again take up
the old deceit of the gods;
                        if it's true
that in future years some other Teucer,
or some Ajax or Priam or Hecuba,
or someone unknown and nameless who nevertheless saw
a Scamander overflow with corpses,
isn't fated to hear
messengers coming to tell him
that so much suffering, so much life,
went into the abyss
all for an empty tunic, all for a Helen.

Translated from the Greek BY EDMUND KEELEY AND PHILIP SHERRARD

When Helen Lived ■ William Butler Yeats

We have cried in our despair
That men desert,
For some trivial affair
Or noisy, insolent sport,
Beauty that we have won
From bitterest hours;
Yet we, had we walked within
Those topless towers
Where Helen walked with her boy,
Had given but as the rest
Of the men and women of Troy,
A word and a jest.

No Second Troy ■ William Butler Yeats

Why should I blame her that she filled my days
With misery, or that she would of late
Have taught to ignorant men most violent ways,
Or hurled the little streets upon the great,
Had they but courage equal to desire?
What could have made her peaceful with a mind
That nobleness made simple as a fire,

With beauty like a tightened bow, a kind
That is not natural in an age like this,
Being high and solitary and most stern?
Why, what could she have done, being what she is?
Was there another Troy for her to burn?

■ Osip Mandelshtam

Wakefulness. Homer. Taut sails.
I have read half the list of ships:
The outstretched brood, the string of cranes
That once soared over Hellas.

Like a wedge of cranes into alien lands—
Divine foam on the heads of the kings—
Where are you sailing? Were it not for Helen,
What would Troy be to you, Achaean men?

The sea and Homer—both impelled by love.
To whom shall I listen? And now Homer is silent,
And a black sea, with its ornate noise,
Approaches my pillow with a ponderous roar.

Translated from the Russian BY NINA KOSSMAN AND ANDY NEWCOMB

Helen ■ Odysseus Elytis

Summer was slain with the first drop of rain
Soaked were the words that gave birth to starlight
All those words whose single aim was You!
Where will we stretch our hands now that time takes no notice of us
Where will we turn our eyes now that the horizon has shipwrecked in the clouds
Now that your eyelids have closed on our land
And now—as if the mist had taken root inside us—
Alone all alone surrounded by lifeless images of You.

Forehead to the glass we keep watch for the latest grief
It isn't grief that will cast us down so long as you remain
So long as elsewhere there's a wind to bring you full to life
To clothe you nearby as our hope clothes you from afar
So long as elsewhere there's a field
Deep green beyond your smile reaching to the sun
Promising in confidence that we'll meet again
No it isn't death we must face
But a simple drop of autumn rain
A dull emotion
Aroma of damp earth in our souls growing ever more distant

And if it isn't your hand in ours
And if it isn't our blood in the veins of your dreams

The light in the immaculate sky
And the invisible O melancholic music inside us
Passerby of the things that hold us to the earth
Then it's the damp air the fall season the parting
The bitter propping of the elbow to recollection
That comes when the dark begins to cleave us from the light
Behind the square window which opens onto sorrow
And sees nothing
For already it's become invisible music flame in the fireplace
      the chiming of the huge clock on the wall
For already it's become
Poem verse another verse sound like falling rain tears and words
Words not like the others yet these too with that solitary aim: You

   Translated from the Greek BY AVI SHARON

On the Walls ■ Rhina Espaillat

From the first look I knew he was no good.
That perfumed hair, those teeth, those smiling lips
all said, "Come home with me." I knew I would.

Love? Who can say? Daylight withdrew in strips
along those vaulted archways waiting where
the slaves would hear us whisper on the stair.
Not smart, not interesting—no, not the best
at anything, all talk and fingertips.
The best I left behind; they're in those ships
nosing your harbor. You can guess the rest.
The heart does what it does, and done is done.

Regret? What for? The future finds its Troys
in every Sparta, and your fate was spun
not by old crones, but pretty girls and boys.

Iphigenia

He knew an angry virgin like Diana
Would need the solace of a young girl's blood.
When he began to feel that public duty
Was of more consequence than private virtue
(The politician over-ruled the father),
King Agamemnon, while her servants wept,
Took Iphigenia to a blood-stained altar
Where she was well-prepared to give her life.
Even the goddess felt something go wrong:
She wrapped a fog around them, closed their eyes,
And as the scene grew slightly mad with weeping,
She placed a red-haired doe upon the altar—
So someone said—and spared Mycenae's child.

—OVID, THE METAMORPHOSES, XII (TR. BY HORACE GREGORY)

Iphigenia ■ Sophia de Mello Breyner Andresen

Iphigenia, led to sacrifice
Between the piercing cries of those who weep for her,
Serenely marches with the light
And, face turned forward to the wind,
Like victory riding a vessel's prow,
Untouched, annihilates catastrophe.

Translated from the Portuguese BY ALEXIS LEVITIN

The Sacrifice of Iphigenia ■ Zbigniew Herbert

Agamemnon is closest to the pyre. He has thrown a coat
over his head, but hasn't closed his eyes. He thinks that through
the fabric he will perceive the glimmer which melts his daughter
like a hairpin.

Hippias stands in the front row of soldiers. He sees only the
small mouth of Iphigenia which breaks with weeping, as it did
when they had a terrible quarrel because she pinned flowers in
her hair and let unknown men accost her on the street. Again
and again the vision of Hippias grows immeasurably longer, and
the small mouth of Iphigenia occupies the huge space from the
sky to the earth.

Calchas, his eyes glazed with leucoma, sees everything in the
hazy insect-like light. The only thing that really moves him is
the drooping sails of the ships in the bay, which at this moment
make the sadness of old age seem unbearable to him. There-
fore he lifts his hand for the sacrifice to begin.

The chorus placed on the hillside takes in the world with its
correct proportions. The small shining bush of the pyre, white
priests, purple kings, loud copper and the miniature fires of
soldiers' helmets, all this against a background of bright sand

and the immense colour of the sea.
The view is superb, with the help of the proper perspective.

Translated from the Polish BY JOHN CARPENTER AND BOGDANA CARPENTER

Iphigenia ■ Attilio Bertolucci

Doves' wings scatter
the quiet at noon.
Beneath the dusty hawthorns
a timid fruit tree hides between its leaves
the promises that autumn will keep.
Iphigenia imagines her bridegrom and herself
as the wagon carries her deeper
into this still, foreign land.
The moon has already risen, a pure crystal moon,
like a livid pool in the luminous sky;
suddenly it brightens.
Her eyelids burning, the young girl
gazes about with her clear, small eyes.
She lifts brown hands to her streaming hair.
She feels like a new-born child, without a past,
as if her life were only now to begin.
Then, at a start, she grabs a fistful
of a passing acacia's long and tender leaves.

Translated from the Italian BY AVI SHARON

Iphigenia: Politics ■ Thomas Merton

The stairs lead to the room as bleak as glass
Where fancy turns the statues.
The empty chairs are dreaming of a protocol,
The tables, of a treaty;
And the world has become a museum.

(The girl is gone,
Fled from the broken altar by the beach,
From the unholy sacrifice when calms became a trade-wind.)

The palaces stare out from their uncurtained trouble,
And windows weep in the weak sun.
The women fear the empty upper rooms
More than the streets as grey as guns
Or the swordlight of the wide unfriendly esplanade.

Thoughts turn to salt among those shrouded chairs
Where, with knives no crueller than pens, or promises,
Took place the painless slaying of the leader's daughter.

O, humbler than the truth she bowed her head,

And scarcely seemed, to us, to die.
But after she was killed she fled, alive, like a surprise,
Out of the glass world, to Diana's Tauris.

The wind cheered like a hero in the tackle of the standing ships
And hurled them bravely on the swords and lances of the wintry sea—
While wisdom turned to salt upon the broken piers.

This is the way the ministers have killed the truth, our daughter,
Steps lead back into the rooms we fear to enter;
Our minds are bleaker than the hall of mirrors:

And the world has become a museum.

Iphigenia, Setting the Record Straight ■ Eleanor Wilner

The towers waited, shimmering just
beyond the edge of vision.
It was only a question
of wind, of the command of trade routes,
a narrow isthmus between two seas, possession
of the gold that men called Helen.
The oldest of adulteries: trade
and art. We were to wait
for the outcome, to see
if we would be the vassals of a king,
or the slaves of slaves.

They never found my grave, who was supposed
to fill their sails, like the skirts of women,
with her charms. Helen, as the second version
goes, had stayed at home; only the echo
of the rustle of her robes
went with Paris to the high-walled town. I
stayed with her to the end, this aunt of mine,
and friend, whose illness drove her husband out the door,
dull-witted Menelaus. When she died
the swans deserted the palace pool
and the torches flared dark
and fitfully. I did not stay for their return,
like that foolish Electra.

I hid in the shrine of Athena—
hearing her, nights, pace overhead
with an iron step, like the sound
of the bronze age ending. The old blind
singer in the forecourt
must have heard her too, but
unlike me, he had to make his living

from his song. She was often sleepless,
as gods will be, and the nights went slow
under her heel's heavy tread.
When she went to stay the arm of
great Achilles, to save my father
for my mother's knife—
I slipped away.

I have just been living, quiet, in this little village
on goats I keep for cheese, and sell for wine, unknown—
the praise of me on every lip, the me
my father made up in his mind
and sacrificed for wind.

The War

*This is the ninth year come round, the ninth
we've hung on here. Who could blame the Achaeans
for chafing, bridling beside the beaked ships?
Ah but still—what a humiliation it would be
to hold out so long, then sail home empty-handed.*
—HOMER, THE ILIAD, II (TR. BY ROBERT FAGLES)

Reading a Greek Pitcher ■ Yunna Morits

She is walking after him, stretching out her fox-like face,
sighing with her timid soul, rustling her green silk,
while the youth is all in his sensual thoughts of escape,
dreaming of heroic deeds, the claptrap of glory.
Sails are humming in the sea, the fleet is sailing out on Tuesday,
they even bring with them a poet, to embellish the war:
the sight of big blood will inspire the recluse.
She is walking after him, bathing him in her gentleness …
The maiden is filled with foreboding—it'll be long until he is back,
sullied with anguish, with frolics of playful gods,
with sores from slave galleys, escape, beggary, theft—
he will scream in his sleep … with a toothless mouth.
She is walking after him, hiding her vengeful smile.
He is standing still, traveling into his hell.
Only the soul travels, everything else stands still,
which anyone who returns will be able to see for himself.

Translated from the Russian BY NINA KOSSMAN

Troy ■ Edwin Muir

He all that time among the sewers of Troy
Scouring for scraps. A man so venerable
He might have been Priam's self, but Priam was dead,
Troy taken. His arms grew meagre as a boy's,
And all that flourished in that hollow famine
Was his long, white, round beard. Oh, sturdily
He swung his staff and sent the bold rats skipping
Across the scurfy hills and worm-wet valleys,
Crying: 'Achilles, Ajax, turn and fight!
Stop cowards!' Till his cries, dazed and confounded,
Flew back at him with: 'Cowards, turn and fight!'
And the wild Greeks yelled round him.
Yet he withstood them, a brave, mad old man,
And fought the rats for Troy. The light was rat-grey,
The hills and dells, the common drain, his Simois,
Rat-grey. Mysterious shadows fell
Affrighting him whenever a cloud offended
The sun up in the other world. The rat-hordes,

Moving, were grey dust shifting in grey dust.
Proud history has such sackends. He was taken
At last by some chance robber seeking treasure
under Troy's riven roots. Dragged to the surface.
And there he saw Troy like a burial ground
With tumbled walls for tombs, the smooth sward wrinkled
As Time's last wave had long since passed that way,
The sky, the sea, Mount Ida and the islands,
No sail from edge to edge, the Greeks clean gone.
They stretched him on a rock and wrenched his limbs,
Asking: 'Where is the treasure?' till he died.

On Reading a Recent Greek Poet ▦ Bertolt Brecht

After the wailing had already begun
along the walls, their ruin certain,
the Trojans fidgeted with bits of wood
in the three-ply doors, itsy-bitsy
pieces of wood, fussing with them.
And began to get their nerve back and feel hopeful.

So, the Trojans too, then.
   Translated from the German BY JOHN PECK

Trojans ▦ Constantine P. Cavafy

Our efforts are those of men prone to disaster;
our efforts are like those of the Trojans.
We just begin to get somewhere,
gain a little confidence,
grow almost bold and hopeful,

when something always comes up to stop us:
Achilles leaps out of the trench in front of us
and terrifies us with his violent shouting.

Our efforts are like those of the Trojans.
We think we'll change our luck
by being resolute and daring,
so we move outside ready to fight.

But when the great crisis comes,
our boldness and resolution vanish;
our spirit falters, paralysed,
and we scurry around the walls
trying to save ourselves by running away.

Yet we're sure to fail. Up there,
high on the wall, the dirge has already begun.

They're mourning the memory, the aura of our days.
Priam and Hecuba mourn for us bitterly.

Translated from the Greek BY EDMUND KEELEY AND PHILIP SHERRARD

■ Osip Mandelshtam

Since I could not keep hold of your hands,
Since I betrayed your salty tender lips,
I must await the dawn in the dense acropolis.
How I hate these ancient weeping logs.

Achaean men rig up the horse in darkness,
Their toothed saws bite into the walls.
The dry rustle of blood won't settle down;
And there is no name for you, no sound, no mold.

How could I think you would return, how dared I?
Why did I tear myself away from you before it was time?
The dark hasn't lifted and the cock hasn't crowed,
The hot axe has yet to cut into timber.

Like a transparent tear, resin oozes from the walls,
And the city feels its wooden ribs.
But blood has flooded the stairs and stormed in,
And thrice men have dreamed of an enticing form.

Where is dear Troy? Where is its royal, maidenly palace?
It will be a ruin, Priam's tall starling-house.
Arrows fall like dry, wooden rain,
And new arrows grow from the ground like nut-trees.

The sting of the last star dies out painlessly.
Like a gray swallow, morning raps at a window.
And a sluggish day, like an ox waking in straw,
Stirs on rough haystacks from its long sleep.

Translated from the Russian BY NINA KOSSMAN AND ANDY NEWCOMB

My Weariness of Epic Proportions ■ Charles Simic

I like it when
Achilles
Gets killed
And even his buddy Patroclus—
And that hothead Hector—
And the whole Greek and Trojan
Jeunesse doree
Are more or less
Expertly slaughtered
So there's finally
Peace and quiet

(The gods having momentarily
Shut up)
One can hear
A bird sing
And a daughter ask her mother
Whether she can go to the well
And of course she can
By that lovely little path
That winds through
The olive orchard

#39   Lesson in Homer ■ Charles Reznikoff

A god could have brought the body of Hector back,
just as Phoebus kept it from decay,
but Priam had to get it himself;
so Pallas could have killed Hector easily,
but Achilles had to do it.
She would hand him his spear when he missed
but he had to throw it again.

A Moment in Troy ■ Wislawa Szymborska

Little girls—
skinny, resigned
to freckles that won't go away,

not turning any heads
as they walk across the eyelids of the world,

looking just like Mom or Dad,
and sincerely horrified by it—

in the middle of dinner,
in the middle of a book,
while studying the mirror,
may suddenly be taken off to Troy.

In the grand boudoir of a wink
they all turn into beautiful Helens.

They ascend the royal staircase
in the rustling of silk and admiration.
They feel light. They all know
that beauty equals rest,
that lips mold the speech's meaning,
and gestures sculpt themselves
in inspired nonchalance.

Their small faces

worth dismissing envoys for
extend proudly on necks
that merit countless sieges.

Those tall, dark movie stars,
their girlfriends' older brothers,
the teacher from art class,
alas, they must all be slain.

Little girls
observe disaster
from a tower of smiles.

Litttle girls
wring their hands
in intoxicating mock despair.

Little girls
against a backdrop of destruction,
with flaming towns for tiaras,
in earrings of pandemic lamentation.

Pale and tearless.
Triumphant. Sated with view.

Dreading only the inevitable
moment of return.

Little girls
returning.

Translated from the Polish BY STANISLAW BARANCZAK AND CLARE CAVANAGH

Boy, Cat, Canary ■ Stephen Spender

Our whistling son called his canary Hector.
'Why?' I asked. 'Because I had always about me
More of Hector with his glittering helmet than
Achilles with his triple-thewed shield.' He let Hector
Out of his cage, fly up to the ceiling, perch on his chair, hop
On to his table where the sword lay bright among books
While he sat in his yellow jersey, doing his homework.
Once, hearing a shout, I entered his room, saw what carnage:
The Siamese cat had worked his tigerish scene;
Hector lay on the floor of his door-open cage
Wings still fluttering, flattened against the sand.
Parallel, horizontal, on the rug, the boy lay
Mouth biting against it, fists hammering boards.
'Tomorrow let him forget.' I prayed, 'Let him not see
What I see in this room of miniature Iliad—
The golden whistling howled down by the dark.'

Achilles & Patroclus

"Ah son of royal Peleus, what you must hear from me!
What painful news—would to god it had never happened!
Patroclus has fallen. They're fighting over his corpse.
He's stripped, naked—Hector with that flashing helmet,
Hector has your arms!"
                              So the captain reported.
A black cloud of grief came shrouding over Achilles.
—HOMER, THE ILIAD, XVIII (TR. BY ROBERT FAGLES)

Patroclus Putting on the Armour of Achilles ■ Daryl Hine

How clumsy he is putting on the armour of another,
His friend's, perhaps remembering how they used to arm each other,
Fitting the metal tunics to one another's breast
And setting on each other's head the helmet's bristling crest.
Now for himself illicitly he foolishly performs
Secret ceremonial with that other's arms,
Borrowed, I say stolen, for they are not his own,
On the afternoon of battle, late, trembling, and alone.

Night terminal to fighting falls on the playing field
As to his arm he fastens the giant daedal shield.
Awhile the game continues, a little while the host
Lost on the obscure litoral, scattered and almost
Invisible, pursue the endless war with words
Jarring in the darkening air impassable to swords.

But when he steps forth from the tent where Achilles broods
Patroclus finds no foe at hand, surrounded by no gods,
Only the chill of evening strikes him to the bone
Like an arrow piercing where the armour fails to join,
And weakens his knees under the highly polished greaves,
Evening gentle elsewhere is loud on the shore, it grieves
It would seem for the deaths of heroes, their disobedient graves.

The Horses of Achilles ■ Constantine P. Cavafy

Seeing that Patroclos was slaughtered,
who was so manly, strong, and young,
the horses of Achilles began weeping;
their deathless nature leapt in rage
at this accomplishment of death.
They waved their heads, and shook their long manes;
with their hooves they struck the earth, and lamented,
knowing Patroclos was lifeless, ruined,
base flesh now—his mind lost—
undefended, breathless,
returning to the great Nothing out of life.

Zeus saw the deathless horses' tears
and pity moved him. "It was wrong,"
he said, "for me to act so carelessly
at Peleus' wedding feast. Not giving you
would have been better, my poor horses.
What could you have found, degraded there,
with miserable mankind,
the plaything of Fate?
Exempt from death, exempt from age,
time's offending rule still subjects you.
Men have tied you on their racks."
And yet not that, but death's eternal ruin
still forced the tears from these two noble beasts.

Translated from the Greek BY THEOHARIS C. THEOHARIS

> *"Anguish for all that armor—sweep it from your mind.*
> *If only I could hide him away from pain and death,*
> *that day his grim destiny comes to take Achilles,*
> *as surely as glorious armor shall be his, armor*
> *that any man in the world of men will marvel at*
> *through all the years to come—whoever sees his splendor."*
> —HOMER, THE ILIAD, XVIII (TR. BY ROBERT FAGLES)

The Shield of Achilles ■ W.H. Auden

She looked over his shoulder
For vines and olive trees,
Marble well-governed cities
And ships upon untamed seas,
But there on the shining metal
His hands had put instead
An artificial wilderness
And a sky like lead.

A plain without a feature, bare and brown,
No blade of grass, no sign of neighborhood,
Nothing to eat and nowhere to sit down,
Yet, congregated on its blankness, stood
An unintelligible multitude.
A million eyes, a million boots in line,
Without expression, waiting for a sign.

Out of the air a voice without a face
Proved by statistics that some cause was just
In tones as dry and level as the place:
No one was cheered and nothing was discussed;
Column by column in a cloud of dust
They marched away enduring a belief
Whose logic brought them, somewhere else, to grief.

She looked over his shoulder

For ritual pieties,
White flower-garlanded heifers,
Libation and sacrifice,
But there on the shining metal
Where the altar should have been,
She saw by his flickering forge-light
Quite another scene.

Barbed wire enclosed an arbitrary spot
Where bored officials lounged (one cracked a joke)
And sentries sweated for the day was hot:
A crowd of ordinary decent folk
Watched from without and neither moved nor spoke
As three pale figures were led forth and bound
To three posts driven upright in the ground.

The mass and majesty of this world, all
That carries weight and always weighs the same
Lay in the hands of others; they were small
And could not hope for help and no help came:
What their foes liked to do was done, their shame
Was all the worst could wish; they lost their pride
And died as men before their bodies died.

She looked over his shoulder
For athletes at their games.
Men and women in a dance
Moving their sweet limbs
Quick, quick, to music,
But there on the shining shield
His hands had set no dancing-floor
But a weed-choked field.

A ragged urchin, aimless and alone,
Loitered about that vacancy, a bird
Flew up to safety from his well-aimed stone:
That girls are raped, that two boys knife a third,
Were axioms to him, who'd never heard
Of any world where promises were kept,
Or one could weep because another wept.

The thin-lipped armourer,
Hephaestos hobbled away,
Thetis of the shining breasts
Cried out in dismay
At what the god had wrought
To please her son, the strong
Iron-hearted man-slaying Achilles
Who would not live long.

> "… *glorious Hector,*
> *quickly lifting the helmet from his head,*
> *set it down on the ground, fiery in the sunlight,*
> *and raising his son he kissed him, tossed him in his arms,*
> *lifting a prayer to Zeus and the other deathless gods:*
> *"Zeus, all you immortals! Grant this boy, my son,*
> *may be like me, first in glory among the Trojans,*
> *strong and brave like me, and rule all Troy in power*
> *and one day let them say, "He is a better man than his father!"—*
> *when he comes home from battle bearing the bloody gear*
> *of the mortal enemy he has killed in war—*
> *a joy to his mother's heart."*
> —HOMER, THE ILIAD, VI (TR. BY ROBERT FAGLES)

The Helmet ■ Michael Longley

When shiny Hector reached out for his son, the wean
Squimed and buried his head between his nurse's breasts
And howled, terrorised by his father, by flashing bronze
And the nightmarish nodding of the horse-hair crest.

His daddy laughed, his mammy laughed, and his daddy
Took off the helmet and laid it on the ground to gleam,
Then kissed the babbie and dandled him in his arms and
Prayed that his son might grow up bloodier than him.

Priam

The majestic king of Troy slipped past the rest
and kneeling down beside Achilles, clasped his knees
and kissed his hands, those terrible, man-killing hands
that had slaughtered Priam's many sons in battle.
—HOMER, THE ILIAD, XXIV (TR. BY ROBERT FAGLES)

Ceasefire ■ Michael Longley

I
Put in mind of his own father and moved to tears
Achilles took him by the hand and pushed the old king
Gently away, but Priam curled up at his feet and
Wept with him until their sadness filled the building.

II
Taking Hector's corpse into his own hands Achilles
Made sure it was washed and, for the old king's sake,
Laid out in uniform, ready for Priam to carry
Wrapped like a present home to Troy at daybreak.

III
When they had eaten together, it pleased them both
To stare at each other's beauty as lovers might,
Achilles built like a god, Priam good-looking still
And full of conversation, who earlier had sighed:

IV
'I get down on my knees and do what must be done
And kiss Achilles' hand, the killer of my son.'

In the Shadow of Homer ■ Eugénio de Andrade

It is fatal, this August—its heat
climbs all the stairs of night,
it doesn't let me sleep.
I open the book always to the supplicating hand
of Priam—but when
impetuous Achilles tells the aged
King he will torment
his heart no more, I stop reading.
Morning comes slowly. How can one sleep
in the tortured shadow
of an old man on the threshold of death,
or with the tears of Achilles
in one's soul, tears for a friend
buried just a moment ago?
How can one sleep at the gates of old age
with that weight upon one's heart?

Translated from the Portuguese BY ALEXIS LEVITIN

Hecuba

> *... The last to leave—*
> *O what a fearful sight—was Hecuba;*
> *The Greeks had found her crouching in drear tombs,*
> *The very tombs where all her sons lay buried.*
> *And there she clung: she tried to kiss their bones.*
>
> —OVID, THE METAMORPHOSES, XIII (TR. BY HORACE GREGORY)

Hecuba's Testament ■ Rosario Castellanos

A tower, no ivy, I. The wind was powerless,
horns lunging round and round me like a bull's.
It stirred up clouds of dust to north and south
and in quarters I've forgotten or never knew.
But I endured, foundations deep in earth,
walls broad, heart strong
and warm within, defending my own brood.

Sorrow was closer kin than any of those.
Not the favorite, not the eldest. But a kinsman
agreeable in the chores, humble at table,
a shadowy teller of tales beside the fire.
There were times he went off hunting far away
at the masculine call
of his steady pulse, his eye sharp on the target.
He returned with game, consigned it
to a helper shrewd with the knife
and the zealous care of women.

On retiring I'd say: What a fine
piece of work my hands are weaving out of the hours.
From girlhood on I kept before my eyes
a handsome sampler;
was ambitious to copy its figure; wished no more.

Unmarried, I lived chaste while that was right;
later was loyal to one, to my own husband.
Never a dawn that found me still asleep,
never a night that overtook me till
the beehive hum of my home had sunk to rest.
The house of my lord was rich with works of my hand;
his lands stretched out to horizons.

And so that his name would not die
when his body died,
he had sons of me; they were valiant sons; had stamina.
Of me he had virtuous girls
that all made a suitable match

(except for one, a virgin, that held aloof,
as offering, it well may be, to a god himself).

Those who knew me called me fortunate.
Not satisfied with receiving
the happy praise of my equals,
I leaned to the little ones,
to sow in these a harvest of gratitude.

When the lightning bolt came probing
that tree of the conversations,
he who was struck by it raged about injustice.

I said not a word, for my way is
to listen to one thing only: bounden duty.
Disaster spoke; I obeyed:
a widow without reproach, a queen made slave
without loss to her queenly pride,
and mother, ah, and mother
orphaned of all her brood.

I dragged along old age like a tunic
too heavy to wear.
I was blind with years and weeping
and in my blindness saw
the vison that sustained my soul at its post.

Helplessness came, the cold, the cold,
and I had to surrender myself to the charity
of those alive. As before I had
surrendered myself to love, and to misfortune.

Someone cares for me in my final sufferings. Makes me
drink down a harsh docility,
which I more and more learn to accept
so that all be fulfilled in me: those ultimate mysteries.

Translated from the Spanish BY JOHN FREDERICK NIMS

Menelaus

"… Menelaus … led Helen away to the ships."
—APOLLODORUS, EPITOME, V (TR. BY J.G. FRAZER)

The Menelaus ■ Robert Kelly

Be sure to hold the least of it in your cool arms
how do they stay so in this intolerable climate
as if the fever-snake had bitten the whole earth
& the river bleeds.
     I have come for you at last.
You are my possession: or for the sense of you
as my possession it has been fought. Whatever was
now has been burnt down, died down. I came here
in my own shape but lost it on the way.
        Your name
is what I chiefly remembered. Sometimes the spread
of your legs as you leaned back to receive me.
But mostly an image, if an image, of you coming
up out of a sun-infested pool. I dreamed it once,
never saw it so, for all the pools of our kinder
kingdom. Queendom. It was not a place without you.

AFTER TROY

The Homecoming of Agamemnon
The Wanderings of Aeneas

The Homecoming of Agamemnon

"I stand now where I struck him down. The thing is done.
Thus have I wrought, and I will not deny it now.
That he might not escape nor beat aside his death,
as fishermen cast their huge circling nets, I spread
deadly abundance of rich robes, and caught him fast.
I struck him twice. In two great cries of agony
he buckled at the knees and fell.... "

—AESCHYLUS, AGAMEMNON (TR. BY RICHMOND LATTIMORE)

Clytemnestra (1) ■ Robert Lowell

'After my marriage, I found myself in constant
companionship with this almost stranger I found
neither agreeable, interesting, nor admirable,
though he was always kind and irresponsible.
The first years after our first child was born,
his daddy was out at sea; that helped, I could bask
on the couch of inspiration and my dreams.
Our courtship was rough, his disembarkation
unwisely abrupt. I was animal,
healthy, easily tired; I adored luxury,
and should have been an extrovert; I usually
managed to make myself pretty comfortable ...
'Well,' she laughed, 'we both were glad to dazzle.
A genius temperament should be handled with care.'

The Missing Knot ■ Zbigniew Herbert

Clytemnestra opens the window, looks
at herself in the glass to put on her new
hat. Agamemnon stands in the vestibule,
lights a cigarette, and waits for his wife.
Aegisthus comes in at the main door. He
doesn't know that Agamemnon returned
home last night. They meet on the stairs.
Clytemnestra suggests that they go to the
theatre. From now on they will be going
out a lot together.

Electra works in the cooperative.
Orestes studies pharmacology. Soon he'll
marry his careless classmate with the pale
complexion and eyes continually filled
with tears.

Translated from the Polish BY JOHN CARPENTER AND BOGDANA CARPENTER

Agamemnon in Hades ■ Peter Russell

In the three days of Easter
        Lacking bread or wine,
On the feast of Dionysus
        I was human and divine.

I thought of the Pelopidae
        But told of my own sin.
I placed a mask upon me
        And revealed what lay within.

A god spoke through that sounding-box—
        I never broke my fast.
Slow beneath the yoke the ox
        Groaned out his grief at last.

His grief that like a shadow walks
        Beneath the beast at noon,
Makes him like a god, and talks
        Of comfort late or soon.

My own bad faith, betrayals, errors,
        Sorrows that tamed me late,
Were turned to Love that eased my terrors,
        And I embraced my Fate.

Mycenae ■ Salvatore Quasimodo

On the Mycenae road with its eucalyptus
trees you can find resiny
wine and cheese of sheep's milk "À la belle
Hélenè de Ménélas," a tavern
that leads thought away from the blood
of the Atridae. Your palace, Agamemnon,
is a bandits' hide-out under Mount
Zara, of stone unscratched by roots,
perched over twisted ravines.
The poets speak much of you, of the crime
invented in your house of crises,
of Electra's sombre frenzy,
for ten years drawing her distant
brother to matricide with the eye
of her sex; the diabolical speak
of the queen's logic—wife
of the absent soldier Agamemnon,
mind, sword betrayed.
And you alone are lost
Orestes, your face vanished without

a golden mask. To the Lions of the gate,
and skeletons of the scenic harmony
raised by philologists of the stones,
greetings from a Greek Sicilian.

Translated from the Italian BY JACK BEVAN

ELECTRA

"*How shall we be lords*
in our house? We have been sold, and go as wanderers
because our mother bought herself, for us, a man,
Aegisthus, he who helped her hand to cut you down.
Now I am what a slave is, and Orestes lives
outcast from his great properties, while they go proud
in the high style and luxury of what you worked
to win.
* * *
I pray that your avenger come, that they
who killed you shall be killed in turn, as they deserve."

—AESCHYLUS, THE LIBATION BEARERS (TR. BY RICHMOND LATTIMORE)

Electra, Waiting ▪ Laurie Sheck

This is the solace of the soil: wet with slaughter
it still knows no tyranny nor treason;

the smallest flower
finds its place between the rocks,

the shallow-rooted cactus hoards water in its stem,
it lives on what is hidden.

Each night through my window I see how the moon
loves the earth from a great distance,

never drawing near.
Some nights she hides most of her face.

I hide in the smallest chamber of the palace.
I have heard of a tree

which blossoms only once each hundred years.
It keeps its deepest nature

secret; many must believe it barren.
How patient the earth is!—its winter trees,

its mountains diminishing more slowly than can be seen.
Each year I cut my hair

and place it on my father's grave.
The bitter tree which grows there

sways gently in the wind; I rest my hands
between its branches as if between his hands.

Nights I serve his enemies their food.
But each day that tree grows stronger,

its leaves like vultures casting shadows on the land,
vigilant as prophecy, more faithful than kind.

Electra ■ Sophia de Mello Breyner Andresen

for Aspassia Papathanassiou
The sounds of summer torment Electra in her solitude
The sun has thrust its lance into the waterless plains
She lets her hair flow loose like lamentations
And her cry resounds through courtyard after courtyard
Where the heat, in columns, shimmers vertical.
Her cry pierces the cicada's song
And, in the sky, disturbs the bronzed silence
Of eagles slowly crossing its path.
Her cry pursues the Furies' pack of hounds
Who search, in vain, for sleep deep within the sepulchres
Or in forgotten corners of the palace

For Electra's cry is the sleeplessness of all things
Exposed
In the open brightness of the out-of-doors
In the hard courtyard sun

That the justice of the gods be summoned forth
Translated from the Portuguese BY ALEXIS LEVITIN

ORESTES AND THE FURIES

"Neither Apollo nor Athene's strength must win
you free, save you from going down forgotten, without
knowing where joy lies anywhere inside your heart,
blood drained, chewed dry by the powers of death, a wraith, a shell.
You will not speak to answer, spew my challenge away?
You are consecrate to me and fattened for my feast,
and you shall feed me while you live, not cut down first
at the altar. Hear the spell I sing to bind you in."

—AESCHYLUS, THE EUMENIDES (TR. BY RICHMOND LATTIMORE)

Mythistorema (16) ◼ George Seferis

The name is Orestes

On the track, once more on the track, on the track,
how many times around, how many blood-stained laps, how many black
rows; the people who watch me,
who watched me when, in the chariot,
I raised my hand glorious, and they roared triumphantly.

The froth of the horses strikes me, when will the horses tire?
The axle creaks, the axle burns, when will the axle burst into flame?
When will the reins break, when will the hooves
tread flush on the ground
on the soft grass, among the poppies
where, in the spring, you picked a daisy.
They were lovely, your eyes, but you didn't know where to look
nor did I know where to look, I, without a country,
I who go on struggling here, how many times around?
and I feel my knees give way over the axle
over the wheels, over the wild track
knees buckle easily when the gods so will it,
no one can escape, what use is strength, you can't
escape the sea that cradled you and that you search for
at this time of trial, with the horses panting,
with the reeds that used to sing in autumn to the Lydian mode
the sea you cannot find no matter how you run
no matter how you circle past the black, bored Eumenides,
unforgiven.

Translated from the Greek BY EDMUND KEELEY AND PHILIP SHERRARD

Chorus of Furies ◼ Basil Bunting

Guarda, mi disse, le feroce Erine

Let us come upon him first as if in a dream,
anonymous triple presence,
memory made substance and tally of heart's rot:
then in the waking Now be demonstrable, seem
sole aspect of being's essence,
coffin to the living touch, self's Iscariot.

Then he will loath the year's recurrent long caress
without hope of divorce,
envying idiocy's apathy or the stress
of definite remorse.
He will lapse into a halflife lest the taut force
of the mind's eagerness
recall those fiends or new apparitions endorse
his excessive distress.
He will shrink, his manhood leave him, slough selfaware
the last skin of the flayed: despair.
He will nurse his terror carefully, uncertain
even of death's solace,
impotent to outpace
dispersion of the soul, disruption of the brain.

The Furies ■ May Sarton

One is large and lazy;
One is old and crazy;
One is young and witty;
One is a great beauty,
But all feed you the wind,
And each of them is blind.

How then to recognize
The hard unseeing eyes,
Or woman tell from ghost?
Human each is, almost—
That wild and glittering light—
Almost, and yet not quite.

Never look straight at one,
For then your self is gone.
The empty eyes give back
Your own most bitter lack,
And what they have to tell
Is your most secret Hell:

The old, the sad pursuit
Of the corrupting fruit,
The slightly tainted dish
Of the subconscious wish,
Fame, love, or merely pride
Exacerbate, provide.

Wrap you in glamour cold,
Warm you with fairy gold,
Till you grow fond and lazy,
Witty, perverse, and crazy,
And drink their health in wind,
And call the Furies kind.

The Wanderings of Aeneas

DIDO AND AENEAS
She mounts in madness that high pyre, unsheathes
the Dardan sword, a gift not sought for such
an end. And when she saw the Trojan's clothes
and her familiar bed, she checked her thought
and tears a little, lay upon the couch
and spoke her final words: 'O relics, dear
while fate and god allowed, receive my spirit
and free me from these cares; for I have lived
and journeyed through the course assigned by fortune.
* * *

o fortunate, too fortunate—if only
the ships of Troy had never touched our coasts.'
—THE AENEID OF VIRGIL, IV (TR. BY ALLEN MANDELBAUM)

Dido's Farewell to Aeneas ■ Stevie Smith

I have lived and followed my fate without flinching, followed it gladly,
And now, not wholly unknown, I come to the end.
I built this famous city, I saw the walls rise,
As for my abominable brother, I don't think I've been too lenient.
Was I happy? Yes, at a price, I might have been happier
If our Dardanian Sailor had condescended to put in elsewhere.
Now she fell silent, turning her face to the pillow,
Then getting up quickly, the dagger in her hand,
I die unavenged, she cried, but I die as I choose,
Come Death, you know you must come when you're called
Although you're a god. And this way, and this way, I call you.

■ Anna Akhmatova

Do not be frightened—I can portray us
As still more alike than this.
Are you a ghost—or just a passer-by?
I treasure your shadow—I don't know why.

Not for long were you my Aeneas,—
Back then it was easy—just the pyre.
We know how to keep silent about each other.
You've forgotten my damned home

And these arms which, in horror and torment,
Stretched out to you through the fire
For the message of cursed hope.

You don't know how much was forgiven you …
Rome is built, herds of flotillas sail past,
And conquest is glorified by flattery.

Translated from the Russian BY NINA KOSSMAN

Dido's Farewell ■ Linda Pastan

The rain is chronic
at my windows, and candles drown
in their own wax.
Abandoned by light,
even the filaments of stars
go black. This afternoon
I propped your drenched roses
up on sticks,
they look like young girls
on crutches now.

You left
a partial map
of your right hand
on every doorknob,
and I follow from room
to room, nomad
in my own house,
my own heart knocking
at my ribs, demanding
to be let out.

Body Politic ■ Judith Johnson

You think yourself Aeneas, it may be,
and call me Dido: easy to leave. You claim
i hold you with intolerable demands,
say i fast net you whom your gods force free
and fire upon the planet to found Rome,
your Pax Romana bleeding from your hands.
I am no Dido though i am your home,
your vault which, once you join me, justly stands
communitas, the city's network. See:
that room, that arched chain, that linked self, that dome
you'd raise, i am. Not elsewhere. Here. Demands
your flame an honest place built honestly?
Turn from mine, all Rome's roads will take false turns.
The Pax Humana burns as my hearth burns.

AENEAS, EXILE AND FOUNDER

The power of Asia and Priam's guiltless race
are overturned, proud Ilium is fallen,
and all of Neptune's Troy smokes from the ground;
this the Highest Ones were pleased to do.
Then we are driven by divine commands
and signs to sail in search of fields of exile
in distant and deserted lands.

—THE AENEID OF VIRGIL, III (TR. BY ALLEN MANDELBAUM)

The Mediterranean ■ Allen Tate

Quem das finem, rex magne, dolorum?

Where we went in the boat was a long bay
A slingshot wide, walled in by towering stone—
Peaked margin of antiquity's delay,
And we went there out of time's monotone:

Where we went in the black hull no light moved
But a gull white-winged along the feckless wave,
The breeze, unseen but fierce as a body loved,
That boat drove onward like a willing slave:

Where we went in the small ship the seaweed
Parted and gave to us the murmuring shore,
And we made feast and in our secret need
Devoured the very plates Aeneas bore:

Where derelict you see the low twilight
The green coast that you, thunder-tossed, would win,
Drop sail, and hastening to drink all night
Eat dish and bowl to take that sweet land in!

Where we feasted and caroused on the sandless
Pebbles, affecting our day of piracy,
What prophecy of eaten plates could landless
Wanderers fulfill by the ancient sea?

We for that time might taste the famous age
Eternal here yet hidden from our eyes
When lust of power undid its stuffless rage;
They, in a wineskin, bore earth's paradise.

Let us lie down once more by the breathing side
Of Ocean, where our live forefathers sleep
As if the Known Sea still were a month wide—
Atlantis howls but is no longer steep!

What country shall we conquer, what fair land
Unman our conquest and locate our blood?

We've cracked the hemispheres with careless hand!
Now, from the Gates of Hercules we flood

Westward, westward till the barbarous brine
Whelms us to the tired land where tasseling corn,
Fat beans, grapes sweeter than muscadine
Rot on the vine: in that land were we born.

Aeneas at Washington ■ Allen Tate

I myself saw furious with blood
Neoptolemus, at his side the black Atridae,
Hecuba and the hundred daughters, Priam
Cut down, his filth drenching the holy fires.
In that extremity I bore me well,
A true gentleman, valorous in arms,
Disinterested and honourable. Then fled:
That was a time when civilization
Run by the few fell to the many, and
Crashed to the shout of men, the clang of arms:
Cold victualing I seized, I hoisted up
The old man my father upon my back,
In the smoke made by sea for a new world
Saving little—a mind imperishable
If time is, a love of past things tenuous
As the hesitation of receding love.

(To the reduction of uncitied littorals
We brought chiefly the vigor of prophecy,
Our hunger breeding calculation
And fixed triumphs.)

                    I saw the thirsty dove
In the glowing fields of Troy, hemp ripening
And tawny corn, the thickening Blue Grass
All lying rich forever in the green sun.
I see all things apart, the towers that men
Contrive I too contrived long, long ago.
Now I demand little. The singular passion
Abides its object and consumes desire
In the circling shadow of its appetite.

There was a time when the young eyes were slow,
Their flame steady beyond the firstling fire,
I stood in the rain, far from home at nightfall
By the Potomac, the great Dome lit the water,
The city my blood had built I knew no more
While the screech-owl whistled his new delight
Consecutively dark.

Stuck in the wet mire
Four thousand leagues from the ninth buried city
I thought of Troy, what we had built her for.

■ John Peck

He who called blood builder is now memory, sound.
Dear, if we callled blood wrecker we'd not lie,
but how thinly we should hear time's curved cutwater,   ,
and never the full song of the falling pine,
that swish the nets make running through swells gone starry.

The steersman heard nothing, and then felt nothing,
toppling through the salt humus of passage.
And when Aeneas taking the tiller gathered
our woody landfall, the turning belt of worlds
spread out sparks of a brotherly burnishing.

Memory may work for us as did his mother
Venus, sluicing his wound invisibly,
its hurt going as a flood
                          with which he heard
one life wash over and another rise,
but faster than remembering. He fought again,

and so the other thing may not be refused,
stand with me hearing it: from the bushy hill
the sound of fellings as huge nets hauled dripping,
plasma from slaughter clotting into nebular
founding stones, and smoke breathing screens of columns.

> When Aeneas entered
> the high doorway, they beat their breasts and raised
> a great groan of lamentation. When he saw
> the pillowed head of Pallas, his white face,
> and the Ausonian spearhead's yawning wound
> in his smooth chest, Aeneas speaks with tears,
> "Poor boy, when Fortune came with happiness,
> was she so envious as to grudge me this:
> not let you live to see my kingdom...."
> —VIRGIL, THE AENEID, XI (TR. BY ALLEN MANDELBAUM)

Falling Asleep over the Aeneid ■ Robert Lowell

*An old man in Concord forgets to go to morning service. He falls asleep, while
reading Vergil, and dreams that he is Aeneas at the funeral of Pallas, an Italian prince.*
The sun is blue and scarlet on my page,
And *yuck-a, yuck-a, yuck-a, yuck-a,* rage
The yellowhammers mating. Yellow fire
Blankets the captives dancing on their pyre,

And the scorched lictor screams and drops his rod.
Trojans are singing to their dunken God,
Ares. Their helmets catch on fire. Their files
Clank by the body of my comrade—miles
Of filings! Now the scythe-wheeled chariot rolls
Before their lances long as vaulting poles,
And I stand up and heil the thousand men,
Who carry Pallas to the bird-priest. Then
The bird-priest groans, and as his birds foretold,
I greet the body, lip to lip. I hold
The sword that Dido used. It tries to speak,
A bird with Dido's sworded breast. Its beak
Clangs and ejaculates the Punic word
I hear the bird-priest chirping like a bird.
I groan a little. "Who am I, and why?"
It asks, a boy's face, though its arrow-eye
Is working from its socket. "Brother, try,
O Child of Aphrodite, try to die:
To die is life." His harlots hang his bed
With feathers of his long-tailed birds. His head
Is yawning like a person. The plumes blow;
The beard and eyebrows ruffle. Face of snow,
You are the flower that country girls have caught,
A wild-pillaged honey-suckle brought
To the returning bridegroom—the design
Has not yet left it, and the petals shine;
The earth, its mother, has, at last, no help:
It is itself. The broken-winded yelp
Of my Phoenician hounds, that fills the brush
With snapping twigs and flying, cannot flush
The ghost of Pallas. But I take his pall,
Stiff with its gold and purple, and recall
How Dido hugged it to her, while she toiled,
Laughing—her golden threads, a serpent coiled
In cypress. Now I lay it like a sheet;
It clings and settles down upon his feet,
The careless yellow hair that seemed to burn
Beforehand. Left foot, right foot—as they turn,
More pyres are rising: armored horses, bronze,
And gagged Italians, who must file by ones
Across the bitter river, when my thumb
Tightens into their wind-pipes. The beaks drum;
Their headman's cow-horned death's-head bites its tongue,
And stiffens, as it eyes the hero slung
Inside his feathered hammock on the crossed
Staves of the eagles that we winged. Our cost
Is nothing to the lovers, whoring Mars
And Venus, father's lover. Now his car's
Plumage is ready, and my marshals fetch

His squire, Acoetes, white with age, to hitch
Aethon, the hero's charger, and its ears
Prick, and it steps and steps, and stately tears
Lather its teeth; and then the harlots bring
The hero's charms and baton—but the King,
Vain-glorious Turnus, carried off the rest.
"I was myself, but Ares thought it best
The way it happened." At the end of time,
He sets his spear, as my descendants climb
The Knees of Father Time, his beard of scalps,
His scythe, the arc of steel that crowns the Alps.
The elephants of Carthage hold those snows,
Turms of Numidian horse unsling their bows,
The flaming turkey-feathered arrows swarm
Beyond the Alps. "Pallas," I raise my arm
And shout, "Brother, eternal health. Farewell
Forever." Church is over, and its bell
Frightens the yellowhammers, as I wake
And watch the whitecaps wrinkle up the lake.
Mother's great-aunt, who died when I was eight,
Stands by our parlor sabre. "Boy, it's late.
Vergil must keep the Sabbath." Eighty years!
Blue-capped and bird-like. Philip Brooks and Grant
Are frowning at his coffin, and my aunt,
Hearing his colored volunteers parade
Through Concord, laughs, and tells her English maid
To clip his yellow nostril hairs, and fold
His colors on him.... It is I. I hold
His sword to keep from falling, for the dust
On the stuffed birds is breathless, for the bust
Of young Augustus weighs on Vergil's shelf:
It scowls into my glasses at itself.

> *"In Turnus' wavering Aeneas sees*
> *his fortune; he holds high the fatal shift;*
> *he hurls it far with all his body's force.*
> * * *
> *... The giant Turnus,*
> *struck, falls to earth; his knees bend under him."*
> —VIRGIL, THE AENEID, XII (TR. BY ALLEN MANDELBAUM)

Turnus ▦ Rosanna Warren

for Michael Putnam

Not lion, not wind, not fire, not sacrificial
bull, not in strength and sinew god-
like, nor even as stag, Silvia's gentle
one, tame, tower-antlered, awash in the sweet blood

of his groin where the Trojan arrow struck—

no beast, no simile, Turnus, but a man alone
when your knees buckle and you look back
at the ashen city, the girl with her eyes cast down,

away. You've crashed to your side, the spear
has whispered its only message through the air.
And when you speak, and He seems inclined to hear,
it's the woods that reply, the shadowed hilltops near

and farther, and what they speak is a groan
for a lost world, for leaflight, the childhood grove
where the small stream stammered its rhymes in amber and green.
And if He pauses? If His sword hovers above

Your chest? Here's where you tear a hole in the poem,
a hole in the mind, here's where the russet glare
of ships aflame and the pyre and the amethyst gleam
from the boy's swordbelt rise and roil in a blur.

We are trapped in meanings that circulate like blood.
The sword descends. And He who kills you is not
a myth, nor a city. His eyes searching yours could
be a lover's eyes. It was love He fought.

THE WANDERINGS
& THE HOMECOMING
OF ODYSSEUS

Far from Ithaca
At Ithaca

Far from Ithaca

All other Greeks who had been spared the steep
descent to death had reached their homes—released
from war and waves. One man alone was left,
still longing for his home, his wife, his rest.
—THE ODYSSEY OF HOMER, I (TR. BY ALLEN MANDELBAUM)

Odysseus ■ Haim Guri

Returning to his native town he found a sea
with grass and fish above the swelling waves
and the sun fading on the sky's rim.

"Error always returns" said Odysseus to his weary heart
and came to the crossroads of the next town
to find the way home that was not water.

Faint as in a dream and full of longing,
among people who spoke a different Greek;
the words he'd left with, the journey's provisions, had meanwhile expired.

For a moment he thought he'd slept a lifetime
and appeared to a people unmoved by his return;
whose eyes did not gape wide with wonder.

He spoke with his hands; they tried to hear him
across the distance;
purple ripened into violet on the sky's rim.

Parents rose and took the children from round him
and drew them away;
lights were kindled in house after house.

Dew came and settled on his head,
wind came and kissed his lips,
water came and bathed his feet like old Euryclea,
but saw not the scar, and flowed, as water does, down the slope.
    Translated from the Hebrew BY AVI SHARON

Ithaka ■ Constantine P. Cavafy

As you set out for Ithaka
hope the voyage is a long one,
full of adventure, full of discovery.
Laistrygonians and Cyclops,
angry Poseidon—don't be afraid of them:
you'll never find things like that on your way
as long as you keep your thoughts raised high,

as long as a rare excitement
stirs your spirit and your body.
Laistrygonians and Cyclops,
wild Poseidon—you won't encounter them
unless you bring them along inside your soul,
unless your soul sets them up in front of you.

Hope the voyage is a long one.
May there be many a summer morning when,
with what pleasure, what joy,
you come into harbors seen for the first time;
may you stop at Phoenician trading stations
to buy fine things,
mother of pearl and coral, amber and ebony,
sensual perfume of every kind—
as many sensual perfumes as you can;
and may you visit many Egyptian cities
to gather stores of knowledge from their scholars.

Keep Ithaka always on your mind.
Arriving there is what you are destined for.
But do not hurry the journey at all.
Better if it lasts for years,
so you are old by the time you reach the island,
wealthy with all you have gained on the way,
not expecting Ithaka to make you rich.

Ithaka gave you the marvelous journey.
Without her you would not have set out.
She has nothing left to give you now.

And if you find her poor, Ithaka won't have fooled you.
Wise as you will have become, so full of experience,
you will have understood by then what these Ithakas mean.

Translated from the Greek BY EDMUND KEELEY AND PHILIP SHERRARD

Odysseus ■ W.S. Merwin

for George Kirstein

Always the setting forth was the same,
Same sea, same dangers waiting for him
As though he had got nowhere but older.
Behind him on the receding shore
The identical reproaches, and somewhere
Out before him, the unraveling patience
He was wedded to. There were the islands,
Each with its woman and twining welcome
To be navigated, and one to call "home."
The knowledge of all that he betrayed
Grew till it was the same whether he stayed

Or went. Therefore he went. And what wonder
If sometimes he could not remember
Which was the one who wished on his departure
Perils that he could never sail through,
And which, improbable, remote, and true,
Was the one he kept sailing home to?

Ulysses ■ Umberto Saba

O sad Ulysses in decline, seer
of terrible omens, does
no sweetness in your soul foment
Desire
for a
pale dreamer of shipwrecks,
who loves you?

Translated from the Italian BY STEVEN SARTARELLI

Ulysses ■ Umberto Saba

When I was young I sailed along the shores
off the Dalmatian coast. Small islands there
rose from the waves where a solitary bird
intent on seeking prey sometimes would pause;
covered with seaweed, slippery underfoot,
those islands shone like emeralds in the sun;
and when high tide and night shrouded the land,
vessels swerved leeward, listing, and stood clear
to escape the treacherous reefs.
                          My kingdom now
is only that no-man's-land. The harbor lights
are lit for others; and I stand out to sea,
my indomitable spirit still impelled
by melancholy love and love for life.

Translated from the Italian BY CHARLES GUENTHER

The Grave of Odysseus ■ Peter Huchel

No one will find
the grave of Odysseus,
no stab of a spade
the encrusted helmet
in the haze of petrified bones.

Do not look for the cave
where down below the earth
a wafting soot, a mere shadow,
went to its dead companions,
raising weaponless hands,
splattered with blood of slaughtered sheep.

All is mine, said the dust,
the sun's grave behind the desert,
the reefs full of the sea's roar,
unending noon that still warns
the pirate's boy from Ithaca,
the rudder jagged with salt,
the maritime charts and lists
of ancient Homer.

Translated from the German BY MICHAEL HAMBURGER

▨ Pentti Saarikoski

Aft, he sleeps,
untwitching,
he has seen all places
and been made to suffer,
they call him godlike,
the ship rides the wine-dark waves,
he is on his way home,
he sleeps.

Translated from the Finnish BY ANSELM HOLLO

A Second Odyssey ▨ Constantine P. Cavafy

DANTE, *Inferno, Canto XXVI*
TENNYSON, *"Ulysses"*

A second Odyssey, long again,
equal, it may be, to the first. But without
Homer, alas, without hexameters.

The roof where he was father was small,
the city where he was father was small,
and the whole of his Ithaca was small.

The affection of Telemachus, the faith
of Penelope, the father's old age,
his old friends, the devoted
subjects' love,
the providential comfort of home
came like rays of happiness
to the heart of the sea-farer.

And like rays they fastened.

　　　　The thirst
the sea gives woke in him.
He hated dry land's air.
The ghosts of the Hesperides
troubled his sleep at night.

Nostalgia for the voyage hurt
him everywhere, and for morning
arrivals in harbors that you enter,
with such joy, for the first time.

The affection of Telemachus, the faith
of Penelope, the father's old age,
his old friends, the devoted
subjects' love,
and the peace and repose
of home bored him.
   And he left.

Gradually, while the shores of Ithaca
vanished in the way before him
and he set all sails west,
to Iberia, to the Pillars of Hercules—
far from every Achaian sea—
he felt he was alive again, that
he had cast aside the heavy bonds
of known, of household things.
And his adventuring heart
exulted in a cold and vacant love.

  Translated from the Greek BY THEOHARIS C. THEOHARIS

ODYSSEUS AND POLYPHEMUS

… He said that I would be
a victim of Odysseus: he would blind me.
But I was always watching out for one
handsome and grand, a formidable man;
instead one small and insignificant,
a weakling, now has gouged my eye….

  —THE ODYSSEY OF HOMER, IX (TR. BY ALLEN MANDELBAUM)

Mortal Infliction ■ Gregory Corso

I think of Polyphemus bellowing his lowly woe
seated high on a cliff
sun-tight legs dangling into the sea
his fumbling hands grappling his burnt eye
And I think he will remain like that
because it's impossible for him to die—

Ulysses is dead
by now he's dead
And how wise was he
who blinded a thing of immortality?

The Greeks Are Blinding Polyphemus ■ György Rába

Because he is one-eyed
because his dinner his choice morsel are different
because his footpath is not known
because he shepherds it though he is a born blacksmith
because he has not heard cormorants for days
because he perks an ear to the song of the present
because he won't build he camps out in his cave
because he builds his cave adorns it with curtains of bay leaf
shins knee-bends dress and cover
they lift a red-hot pole
like the plug hole on a ship's rib
they poke ream out his eye
because his hovel is a home of death

But news lives in him too
every seeing eye gleams alike like a sun
and in everyone there dwells a death
same as someone rowing with bare hands
he'll flex his cliff-ripping muscle
you can see the present's body
and let it trill as sweetly as it might
the future lets drop flakes of enamel

Many a seafarer will yet set sail here
being taken aback will never be over
how long will you be listening
to the dialogue of because and but
lord of eternal waters

    Translated from the Hungarian BY EMERY GEORGE

ODYSSEUS AND CIRCE

"'Who are you? From what family? What city?
You drank my drugs, but you were not entranced.
No other man has ever passed that test;
for once that potion's passed their teeth, the rest
have fallen prey: you have within your chest
a heart that can defeat my sorcery.
You surely are the man of many wiles,
Odysseus, he whom I was warned against ...'"

—THE ODYSSEY OF HOMER, X (TR. BY ALLEN MANDELBAUM)

Circe ■ Gabriel Zaid

My homeland is in your eyes, my duty on your lips.
Ask anything of me, except to leave you.
Shipwrecked, so, on your beaches, stranded on your sands,

I am a happy pig: I am yours: nothing else matters.
I belong to the sun you are; my demesne is in it.
My glory is in your joy, my home in what you have.
   Translated from the Spanish BY ANDREW ROSING

Pity Ulysses ■ Virginia Hamilton Adair

Pity Ulysses, fondly sure
his men exulted in their pure
recovered forms and burned to think
what shame befell from Circe's drink.

Be glad he never did awaken
nights when heroes, memory-shaken,
sicken with longing for the sty,
the brutal tusk, the leering eye.

Circe's Power ■ Louise Glück

I never turned anyone into a pig.
Some people are pigs; I make them
look like pigs.

I'm sick of your world
that lets the outside disguise the inside.

Your men weren't bad men;
undisciplined life
did that to them. As pigs,

under the care of
me and my ladies, they
sweetened right up.

Then I reversed the spell,
showing you my goodness
as well as my power. I saw

we could be happy here,
as men and women are
when their needs are simple. In the same breath,

I foresaw your departure,
your men with my help braving
the crying and pounding sea. You think

a few tears upset me? My friend,
every sorceress is
a pragmatist at heart; nobody

sees essence who can't
face limitation. If I wanted only to hold you

I could hold you prisoner.

Moly ■ Thom Gunn

Nightmare of beasthood, snorting, how to wake.
I woke. What beasthood skin she made me take?

Leathery toad that ruts for days on end,
Or cringing dribbling dog, man's servile friend,

Or cat that prettily pounces on its meat,
Tortures it hours, then does not care to eat:

Parrot, moth, shark, wolf, crocodile, ass, flea.
What germs, what jostling mobs there were in me.

   These seem like bristles, and the hide is tough.
No claw or web here: each foot ends in hoof.

Into what bulk has method disappeared?
Like ham, streaked. I am gross—grey, gross, flap-eared.

The pale-lashed eyes my only human feature.
My teeth tear, tear. I am the snouted creature

That bites through anything, root, wire, or can.
If I was not afraid I'd eat a man.

Oh a man's flesh already is in mine.
Hand and foot poised for risk. Buried in swine.

   I root and root, you think that it is greed,
It is, but I seek out a plant I need.

Direct me gods, whose changes are all holy,
To where it flickers deep in grass, the moly:

Cool flesh of magic in each leaf and shoot,
From milky flower to the black forked root.

From this fat dungeon I could rise to skin
And human title, putting pig within.

I push my big grey wet snout through the green,
Dreaming the flower I have never seen.

Circe ■ W.H. Auden

Her Telepathic-Station transmits thought-waves
the second-rate, the bored, the disappointed,
and any of us when tired or uneasy,
        are tuned to receive.

So, though unlisted in atlas or phone-book,
Her garden is easy to find. In no time
one reaches the gate over which is written
        large: MAKE LOVE NOT WAR.

Inside it is warm and still like a drowsy
September day, though the leaves show no sign of
turning. All around one notes the usual
        pinks and blues and reds,

a shade over-emphasized. The rose-bushes
have no thorns. An invisible orchestra
plays the Great Masters: the technique is flawless,
        the rendering schmaltz.

Of Herself no sign. But, just as the pilgrim
is starting to wonder 'Have I been hoaxed by
a myth?', he feels Her hand in his and hears Her
        murmuring: *At last!*

With me, mistaught one, you shall learn the answers.
What is conscience but a nattering fish-wife,
the Tree of Knowledge but the splintered main-mast
        of the Ship of Fools?

Consent, you poor alien, to my arms where
sequence is conquered, division abolished:
soon, soon, in the perfect orgasm, you shall, pet,
        be one with the All.

She does not brutalize her victims (beasts could
bite or bolt). She simplifies them to flowers,
sessile fatalists who don't mind and only
        can talk to themselves.

All but a privileged Few, the elite She
guides to Her secret citadel, the Tower
where a laugh is forbidden and DO HARM AS
        THOU WILT is the law.

Dear little not-so-innocents, beware of
Old Grandmother Spider: rump Her endearments.

She's not quite as nice as She looks, nor you quite
as tough as you think.

ODYSSEUS AND THE THE SIRENS

"Whoever, unaware, comes close and hears
the Sirens' voice will nevermore draw near
his wife, his home, his infants ..."
—THE ODYSSEY OF HOMER, XII (TR. BY ALLEN MANDELBAUM)

Odysseus's Temptation ■ Igor Vishnevetsky

"Let's stop our ears with wax. Let them sing.
Their voices will not likely fool us,"
thus spoke Odysseus—a snob and a rogue,
as his companions plied the oars.

But he himself, if only for a few moments,
heard how enticingly the sirens sang.
The strong ropes bound him tightly,
no matter how he tried to break loose.

The way is long and dangerous, Odysseus,
and none of the swift ships
will reach home. Neither Telemach,
nor Penelope will be a joy to see.
What an end, what an instantaneous hell
you have traded for sleepy Ithaca!

Translated from the Russian BY NINA KOSSMAN

The Sirens ■ Linda Pastan

Is there no music now
except the chime
of coins in the pocket
for which a man would go breathlessly
off course, would even drown?
Odysseus tied to his mast
regretted his own foresight.

In ordinary days to come in Ithaca
the song of some distant bird,
the chords of water against
the shore, even Penelope
humming to herself at the loom
would make his head turn, his eyes
stray toward the sea.

Siren Song ■ Margaret Atwood

This is the one song everyone
would like to learn: the song
that is irresistible:

the song that forces men
to leap overboard in squadrons
even though they see the beached skulls

the song nobody knows
because anyone who has heard it
is dead, and the others can't remember.

Shall I tell you the secret
and I if do, will you get me
out of this bird suit?

I don't enjoy it here
squatting on this island
looking picturesque and mythical

with these two feathery maniacs,
I don't enjoy singing
this trio, fatal and valuable.

I will tell the secret to you,
to you, only to you.
Come closer. This song

is a cry for help: Help me!
Only you, only you can,
you are unique

at last. Alas
it is a boring song
but it works every time.

Haven ■ Ronald Bottrall

Ever since the State failed to wither
I have never plugged my ears with wax
To block out the song the Sirens sing,
A song I've waited for years to hear.
Through a pilgrim's progress on its tracks
I hear it now and I am sailing
Happy towards those enchanted rocks
Framed against a setting sun that mocks
The few fading flowers strewn on my bier.

The Sirens ■ Richard Wilbur

I never knew the road
From which the whole earth didn't call away,
With wild birds rounding the hill crowns,
Haling out of the heart an old dismay,
Or the shore somewhere pounding its slow code,
Or low-lighted towns
Seeming to tell me, stay.

Lands I have never seen
And shall not see, loves I will not forget,
All I have missed, or slighted, or foregone
Call to me now. And weaken me. And yet
I would not walk a road without a scene.
I listen going on,
The richer for regret.

ODYSSEUS'S MEN AND THE SUN-GOD'S CATTLE

And if our taking of his tall-horned cows
enrages Hélios, and he would wreck
our ship and has the other gods' consent,
I'd rather have my mouth drink brine and let
the waves kill me at once than meet slow death …
—THE ODYSSEY OF HOMER, xii (TR. BY ALLEN MANDELBAUM)

The Companions in Hades ■ George Seferis

fools, who ate the cattle of Helios Hyperion;
but he deprived them of the day of their return.
—*Odyssey*
Since we still had some hardtack
how stupid of us
to go ashore and eat
the Sun's slow cattle,

for each was a castle
you'd have to battle
forty years, till you'd become
a hero and a star!

On the earth's back we hungered,
but when we'd eaten well
we fell to these lower regions
mindless and satisfied.

Translated from the Greek BY EDMUND KEELEY AND PHILIP SHERRARD

ODYSSEUS AND CALYPSO

... And now, against his will,
Calypso keeps him captive in her grotto,
her island home, where he can only sorrow.
And he cannot return to his own land:
he has no ships at hand, no oars, no friends
to carry him across the sea's broad back.
—THE ODYSSEY OF HOMER, V (TR. BY ALLEN MANDELBAUM)

Calypso ■ Peter Davison

She found him facing out into the fog
At the edge of the sea, stooping, winnowing
Stones with all the care of the demented,
Hurling them into the murk, low along
The surface, skipping them like petrels.
He wandered by the shore, halting and stooping,
Leaning abruptly for additional
Hates to send spinning out to sea.
She watched from the cliff over his restlessness
And ached to hold him in her arms—held
Herself away from him, for an embrace
Would only remind his body of its bruises.
Hobbling a step, stooping, sorting the stones,
Hurling them again, as though he hoped
To force them, slippery beneath the sea,
To draw him after them, he threw and threw.
The shore wind whipped the bracken by the path,
Pressed out against the fog which yielded to it
And took it and closed and gave no ground.
A woman could do nothing for him now,
Though she had known for months that this was coming—
Long before he guessed, even before
She herself could have put it into words—
His occupation gone, his enterprise swallowed.
The tide was out, the stones lay high and dry.
Terns chirruped in the fog along the shore.
The fog pressed on the land a little closer
And she could scarcely see him now, while he
Would never look back to where she stood behind him,
Just as he would never know that she
Had watched him strive, delude himself, and fail,
Had known all his evasions and deceits,
His minor infidelities, his hopes
That this time shabbiness would go unnoticed.
The only way to show her love for him
Was learning how to stand unseen
Until he chose to notice her—to laugh
Or storm or touch her breast or ask for food
And, though she was invisible, to smile for her.

Now in the fog he'd wandered farther off
Than she had ever lost him, yet she still
Was more aware of him and his despair
Than fog and sea and wind and stones together.
And so she turned, knowing herself helpless,
Leaving her man to men's devices, and the wind
Struck at her face as she walked weeping home.

The Island ■ Anselm Hollo

*

nice place ya got here
the messenger said
to her whose island
it was

      but the boss
give an order
let the guy sail
back to his own
*

there he sat
by the shore
broken nose   missing teeth
balding

     old dog
thinking of elsewhere   as always
traveling hard in his head
*

came up from the cave
patted him told him
time now   to go

"who said I wanted to go?"

■ Gunnar Ekelöf

"Give me poison to die or dreams to live"—Just now
more than dreams to live I want poison to die
Captain without crew, for they all
have eaten of the lotus, turned to swine I refuse to command—
Alone, exhausted steersman, I too was driven ashore
on a beach strange to me, with these corpses as cargo
Give me water! I have had nothing but brine
Give me water from some stream or spring
Give me the magic water that will wash away the blood
Give me back the island where I was sunk in dreams
There I walked under freedom's yoke, in golden reins
He who has once been stranded in its sucking cleft
doesn't struggle with the rudder, hasn't hands to sail
What he must do is teach them to caress—

Like the prince who once dipped his head in a spring
for one moment felt the vertiginous welling of time
back in Time, 1001 years back, I see you mirror
yourself in your glance that is mine. So have I been stranded
with the Nymph who gives poison to die or dreams to live
With no chart, with no stars, with and against currents
I have once been stranded on the island of the red-blonde nymph.

Translated from the Swedish BY RIKA LESSER

ODYSSEUS AND NAUSICAÄ

... seeing Odysseus, she was struck with wonder,
and these were the winged words he heard from her:

"I greet you, guest, as you take leave, so that—
when you've gone back to your homeland—you may
remember me and keep in mind how I,
more than all others, worked to save your life."

—THE ODYSSEY OF HOMER, VIII (TR. BY ALLEN MANDELBAUM)

Nausicaä ■ Judita Vaičiunaitė

"Hail, traveler, when you return
to your own country, see that you
do not forget me."

I've never kissed a man yet. My voice is like a wave.
        And my flesh has not been touched by male hands.
Yet I have hungered for one such as you.
        We were both dazed from exertion and surprise.
Both cursed and blessed be the ball we tossed around,
        having spread the linen out to dry,
that ancient golden morning when two funny mules had drawn my little cart ...
* * *
I am Nausicaä. I am descended from sea-faring ancestors.
        There's something in me of a sinking ship fortuitously met.
My mother spins a thread of merriment, of purple wool.
        And my father's open house is tall and generous.
So under ancient skies we're raising toasts both royally and humbly
        in honor of a lost and unexpected guest ...
Why do you hide your tears under the mantle,
        we are not trying to interrogate you—who are mighty, mysterious and free
...

I melt into the column against which I lean ...
        Let it remain a secret how I stood alone in the great hall,
for none will ever know what I was feeling then,
        as I will not confess it even to myself:
                                I love you, Odysseus.

Translated from the Lithuanian BY IRENE POGOŽELSKYTĖ SUBOSZEWSKI

PENELOPE

"… my heart is sunk in sorrow as I think
of my Odysseus. While the suitors seek
a wedding, I weave schemes. At the beginning,
within my room I set a spacious loom.
The web was wide, the threads were fine, and I
assured us all—unhesitatingly:
'Young men, since bright Odysseus now is dead,
be patient; though you're keen to marry me,
wait till this cloth is done, so that no thread
unravels.

* * *

… So I would weave
that mighty web by day—but then, by night,
by torchlight, I undid what I had done."

—THE ODYSSEY OF HOMER, XIX (TR. BY ALLEN MANDELBAUM)

Ithaca ■ Louise Glück

The beloved doesn't
need to live. The beloved
lives in the head. The loom
is for the suitors, strung up
like a harp with white shroud-thread.

He was two people.
He was the body and voice, the easy
magnetism of a living man, and then
the unfolding dream or image
shaped by the woman working the loom,
sitting there in a hall filled
with literal-minded men.

As you pity
the deceived sea that tried
to take him away forever
and took only the first,
the actual husband, you must
pity these men: they don't know
what they're looking at;
they don't know that when one loves this way
the shroud becomes a wedding dress.

The World as Meditation ■ Wallace Stevens

Is it Ulysses that approaches from the east,
The interminable adventurer? The trees are mended.
That winter is washed away. Someone is moving

On the horizon and lifting himself up above it.
A form of fire approaches the cretonnes of Penelope,
Whose mere savage presence awakens the world in which she dwells.

She has composed, so long, a self with which to welcome him,
Companion to his self for her, which she imagined,
Two in a deep-founded sheltering, friend and dear friend.

The trees had been mended, as an essential exercise
In an inhuman meditation, larger than her own.
No winds like dogs watched over her at night.

She wanted nothing he could not bring her by coming alone.
She wanted no fetchings. His arms would be her necklace
And her belt, the final fortune of their desire.

But was it Ulysses? Or was it only the warmth of the sun
On her pillow? The thought kept beating in her like her heart.
The two kept beating together. It was only day.

It was Ulysses and it was not. Yet they had met,
Friend and dear friend and a planet's encouragement.
The barbarous strength within her would never fail.

She would talk a little to herself as she combed her hair,
Repeating his name with its patient syllables,
Never forgetting him that kept coming constantly so near.

An Ancient Gesture ■ Edna St. Vincent Millay

I thought, as I wiped my eyes on the corner of my apron:
Penelope did this too.
And more than once: you can't keep weaving all day
And undoing it all through the night;
Your arms get tired, and the back of your neck gets tight;
And along towards morning, when you think it will never be light,
And your husband has been gone, and you don't know where, for years,
Suddenly you burst into tears;
There is simply nothing else to do.

And I thought, as I wiped my eyes on the corner of my apron:
This is an ancient gesture, authentic, antique,
In the very best tradition, classic, Greek;

Ulysses did this too.
But only as a gesture,—a gesture which implied
To the assembled throng that he was much too moved to speak.
He learned it from Penelope …
Penelope, who really cried.

You Are Odysseus ■ Linda Pastan

You are Odysseus
returning home each evening
tentative, a little angry.
And I who thought to be
one of the Sirens (cast up
on strewn sheets
at dawn)
hide my song
under my tongue—
merely Penelope after all.
Meanwhile the old wars
go on, their dim music
can be heard even at night.
You leave each morning,
soon our son will follow.
Only my weaving is real.

Penelope's Despair ■ Yannis Ritsos

It wasn't that she didn't recognize him in the light from the hearth; it wasn't
the beggar's rags, the disguise—no. The signs were clear:
the scar on his knee, the pluck, the cunning in his eye. Frightened,
her back against the wall, she searched for an excuse,
a little time, so she wouldn't have to answer,
give herself away. Was it for him, then, that she'd used up twenty years,
twenty years of waiting and dreaming, for this miserable
blood-soaked, white-bearded man? She collapsed voiceless into a chair,
slowly studied the slaughtered suitors on the floor as though seeing
her own desires dead there. And she said "Welcome,"
hearing her own voice sound foreign, distant. In the corner, her loom
covered the ceiling with a trellis of shadows; and all the birds she'd woven
with bright red thread in green foliage, now,
this night of the return, suddenly turned ashen and black,
flying low on the flat sky of her final enduring.
  Translated from the Greek BY EDMUND KEELEY

Fiery Water ■ Pia Tafdrup

  and he looked like a god as he came from the bath (HOMER)
A bath I will give you, as Circe's maids bathe Odysseus,
like those daughters of the groves and the fountains

and of the holy rivers that run down to the sea,
I fill the bath with water and pour you wine.

I mix in a jet hot water with some that is cooling,
while the mirrors mist over, and silence comes creeping;
a long bath you shall have, the wine will illumine your blood
and loosen those muscles I rinse with water from a jug.

As the fourth maid drove the weariness out of Odysseus's limbs, I shall
bathe you, so that the world for a time narrows down to this room, where
mild vapours are yielded ever more densely, and your skin's fragrances
expand in the room as warmth fills you, both from outside and in.

I move closer, wash your neck and your chest,
caress your face, your nape and your shoulders,
notice delight trickle forth as I see you forget your weapons,
see you let all your limbs relax and sink further down in the bath.

There must be water so that there is life,
and men need long baths ...
I soap you and rinse you again, your body acquires gravity,
you are not just one man, but many men.

And when you stand up in the bath to emerge,
you are no less charming than Telemachus,
who was bathed by the lovely maiden Polycaste,
before he was anointed with glistening oil and covered with shirt and mantle.

Whose is the love that shines through the world like a running river,
and why does it flow as a soul
that comes towards me, so different from anything I have met
in the maze of the palace I long on my own strayed about in.
          Translated from the Danish BY DAVID McDUFF

Odyssey, Book Twenty-three ■ Jorge Luis Borges

Now has the rapier of iron wrought
The work of justice, and revenge is done.
Now spear and arrows, pitiless every one,
Have made the blood of insolence run out.
For all a god and all his seas could do
Ulysses has returned to realm and queen.
For all a god could do, and the grey-green
Gales and Ares' murderous hullabaloo.
Now in the love of their own bridal bed
The shining queen has fallen asleep, her head
Upon her king's breast. Where is that man now
Who in his exile wandered night and day
Over the world like a wild dog, and would say

His name was No One, No One, anyhow?
    Translated from the Spanish BY ROBERT FITZGERALD

TELEMACHUS
"Forget the pastimes of a child: you are
a boy no longer."
—THE ODYSSEY OF HOMER, BOOK I (TR. BY ALLEN MANDELBAUM)

Ulysses ◼ Cesare Pavese

This old man feels cheated and bitter. His son was born
too late. Now and then they look each other in the eyes,
but a slap in the face stops all that. (The old man goes outside,
comes back with the boy holding his cheek in his hand,
his eyes lowered). Now the old man
sits waiting until it's dark in front of the big window,
but the road is empty, nobody's coming.

This morning the boy took off, he'll be back home
tonight. A smile of contempt on his face. And he won't tell
anyone whether he's had his supper or not. No,
his eyes will look tired, he'll go to bed without a word:
a pair of boots spattered with mud. After a month of rain
the morning was blue.

                    A sharp smell of leaves
flows through the cool of the window. But the old man doesn't
budge in the darkness, he isn't sleepy at night.
And he would love to sleep and forget it all,
the way he used to once, coming home after a long walk.
Once, he kept warm by shouting and slapping himself.

The boy comes home before long. Too big to be beaten,
the boy is turning into a young man, every day
discovering something, and not talking, not to anyone.

There's nothing on that road that can't be seen
by standing at the window. But the boy is walking the road
all day long. Not out looking for women, not yet,
he's done with playing in the mud. He always comes back.
The boy has a way of leaving the house that
tells the man inside he's finished with home, and him, it's over.
    Translated from the Italian BY WILLIAM ARROWSMITH

GLOSSARY

Achilles Son of Peleus and the sea deity Thetis. The greatest Greek hero of the Trojan War.

Actaeon A hunter who accidentally saw Artemis and her nymphs bathing. Artemis punished him by turning him into a stag, and he was devoured by his own hounds.

Aeneas A Trojan who carried his father, Anchises, on his shoulders out of the wreck of Troy. In his quest for a new country, Aeneas came to Carthage where Dido (q.v.), the queen, fell in love with him. The gods ordered him to leave Carthage and sail forth to Italy where he founded the Roman line.

Agamemnon King of Mycenae and commander of the Greek army in the Trojan war. In the victory over Troy he took as his captive Priam's daughter Cassandra (q.v.). On his arrival at Mycenae he was murdered by his wife Clytemnestra and her lover Aegisthus.

Alcestis Wife of Admetus, king of Pherae. When it was foretold that Admetus would not live unless someone close to him died in his place, Alcestis volunteered to die for her husband.

Alcmene Wife of Amphitryon. While her husband was away, Zeus made love to Alcmena, and she gave birth to twins. One of them, Heracles (q.v.), was the son of Alcmene by Zeus, and the other, Iphicles, was the son of Amphitryon.

Aphrodite (Rom. Venus) Goddess of love and beauty, arisen from the sea's foam.

Apollo Son of Zeus and Latona; brother of Artemis. God of music, light, and balance; also of archery and prophecy. Identical with the sun god known as Phoebus.

Ares Son of Zeus and Hera. God of war.

Arachne An accomplished weaver who boasted that her skill was superior to that of Athene, the goddess of the craft. Athene took revenge by turning the girl into a spider, in which form Arachne continued her work.

Argonauts Fifty-four heroes who accompanied Jason (q.v.) in his voyage to Colchis, aboard the ship Argo, in quest of the Golden Fleece.

Ariadne Daughter of Minos, king of Crete. She fell in love with Theseus (q.v.) and gave him a ball of thread to help him find his way out of the Labyrinth. At first, Theseus kept his promise to take her away with him but then he abandoned her on the island of Naxos. Later, according to some versions of the myth, Dionysus married her and gave her a crown which, upon her death, became the constellation Corona Borealis.

Artemis (Rom. Diana) Goddess of childbirth, hunting, and wild animals. Also the moon goddess. Apollo's sister, Artemis was the daughter of Zeus and Leto.

Athene Also Athena, Pallas Athena. (Rom. Minerva). Goddess of wisdom, war, learning, and crafts. Athene was born from Zeus's head, without a mother.

Atlas One of the Titans, Atlas held the sky on his shoulders for hundreds of years. Eventually Perseus (q.v.), by showing Medusa's (q.v.) head to Atlas, caused him to be transformed into a mountain.

Bacchae (Also Bacchantes, maenads). Female followers of Dionysus.

Calypso Nymph or goddess who lived on the island of Ogygia. Calypso cared for Odysseus (q.v.) when he was shipwrecked on her coast. She offered to make him immortal if he would stay with her.

Cassandra One of the daughters of Priam

(q.v.) and Hecuba (q.v.). Cassandra was loved by Apollo who promised to grant her the power to see the future if she would submit to his passion. She received his gift but rejected his love; for revenge Apollo made sure that no one would ever believe her predictions. She warned that Paris' abduction of Helen would result in the destruction of Troy but she was ignored.

Centaurs Half-horse, half-human creatures.

Cerberus The three-headed dog of Hades (q.v.).

Charon The ferryman who conducted souls of the dead in a boat across the Styx (q.v.). Each soul had to pay him a fee of one obol for his work.

Chiron A wise Centaur who educated many heroes, among them Jason (q.v.) and Achilles (q.v.).

Circe Sorceress on the island of Aeaea who transformed Odysseus's (q.v.) companions into pigs. Fortified against her spells, Odysseus forced her to restore his companions to their human form; afterwards, he stayed with her for a year.

Clytemnestra Daughter of Leda and Tyndareus; wife of Agamemnon (q.v.); mother of Orestes (q.v.), Electra (q.v.), and Iphigenia (q.v.). Clytemnestra and her paramour Aegisthus killed Agamemnon when he returned to Mycenae after the Trojan War.

Daedalus An ingenious craftsman, father of Icarus. To escape from Crete, he made wings for himself and Icarus. Icarus soared too high, the sun melted the wax on his wings, and he fell into the sea.

Daphne A nymph who was changed into a laurel tree so that she could escape from Apollo.

Demeter (Rom. Ceres) Goddess of fertility and of crops, especially corn. After the disappearance of her daughter Persephone (q.v.), Demeter searched the earth until she found out that her daughter had been carried off by Hades.

Dido Queen of Carthage According to Virgil, Dido fell in love with Aeneas (q.v.) and was so distraught when he sailed away that she committed suicide by stabbing herself on a funeral pyre.

Dionysus (Rom. Bacchus) God of wine.

Dryads Tree-nymphs whose life ended with the death of the tree whose spirit they were connected to.

Echo A nymph who was deprived of speech by Hera and allowed only to repeat others' words. When Narcissus (q.v.) rejected her love, her body wasted away and only her voice remained.

Electra Daughter of Agamemnon and Clytemnestra; saved her brother Orestes' life and waited for him to avenge their father.

Endymion Son of Aëthlius (or of Zeus) and Calyce who asked Zeus to grant him eternal youth and the choice to sleep forever. The moon goddess saw him while he was sleeping and fell in love with him.

Eros (Rom. Amor, Cupid) God of love.

Europa Daughter of Agenor, king of Phoenicia. Zeus fell in love with her, transformed himself into a bull and, with Europa on his back, crossed the sea to Crete.

Eurydice Orpheus's wife. Bitten by a snake, Eurydice died, but Orpheus (q.v.) was allowed to bring her back from Hades on the condition that he not look behind him before he was out of Hades; yet he turned to look at his wife and lost her forever.

Furies (Erinyes, Euminides) Avenging female spirits.

Galatea A statue transformed into a woman by Aphrodite in response to Pygmalion's (q.v.) prayers.

Ganymede A beautiful youth carried away by Zeus to serve as cupbearer at Olympus.

Hades (Rom. Pluto) God of the underworld, brother of Zeus and Poseidon; also, the name of his underworld kingdom.

Hecate Goddess of witchcraft and underworld, represented as a three-headed woman, and in one of her aspects often identified with Artemis.

Hector Son of Priam and Hecuba, husband of Andromache. Led the Trojan forces when Troy was attacked by the Greeks. The bravest Trojan; killed by Achilles (q.v.).

Hecuba Queen of Troy at the time of its destruction; Priam's (q.v.) wife.

Helen Daughter of Leda (q.v.) and Zeus, hatched from an egg of Leda's. Most of the Greek princes vied for her hand.

Helen's elopement from Sparta with Paris (q.v.)—while she was married to Menelaus—is regarded as the cause of the Trojan War.

Hephaestus (Rom.Vulcan) Son of Zeus and Hera. God of metals, fire, and the forge.

Hera (Rom. Juno) Daughter of Chronus and Rhea. Goddess of marriage and childbirth; queen of heaven, wife of Zeus.

Heracles (Rom. Hercules) The most famous of all Greek heroes; celebrated especially for the Twelve Labors.

Hermes (Rom. Mercury) Son of Zeus and Maia. God of travelers, orators, thieves, and liars; messenger of the gods; also a psychopomp, a conductor of souls of the dead to Hades.

Icarus See Daedalus.

Io Daughter of the river god Inachus. Io was changed by Zeus into a heifer when jealous Hera learned of Zeus's affair with her.

Iphigenia Daughter of Agamemnon and Clytemnestra. To appease the gods who detained the Greeks on their way to Troy with unfavorable winds, Agamemnon (q.v.) agreed to have his daughter sacrificed. Before the fatal blow could land the goddess, Artemis placed a stag in Iphigenia's place.

Jason Leader of the Argonauts (q.v.) who sailed to Colchis in quest of the Golden Fleece.

Jocasta (Also Epicasta) Wife of Laius, king of Thebes; mother of Oedipus. Jocasta killed herself upon learning that her second husband was her own son Oedipus (q.v.).

Lethe River of oblivion in Hades (q.v.).

Marpessa Wife of Idas. When she was given a choice between her mortal husband and Apollo, Marpessa chose her husband.

Marsyas A remarkable flute player, Marsyas challenged Apollo to a music contest. Apollo won; as punishment, he hung Marsyas from a pine tree and flayed him.

Medea Powerful witch, niece of Circe (q.v.) and daughter of Aeetes, king of Colchis. Medea fell in love with Jason (q.v.) and helped him steal the golden fleece. When Jason later tried to divorce her, Medea killed their two sons and fled to Athens.

Medusa A monster, one of the three Gorgons. Her eyes had the power to turn men into stone. Perseus (q.v.) cut off her head and placed it on Athena's shield where it retained its deadly power.

Menelaus Brother of Agamemnon (q.v.), husband of Helen (q.v.), king of Sparta. He fought bravely in the Trojan War, at the end of which he took Helen home to Sparta.

Minotaur A monster, half bull, half man, born of Pasiphae (q.v.) and a bull. Until Theseus killed it, the Minotaur was kept in the labyrinth and fed the flesh of young Athenean men and women.

Narcissus A beautiful young man who fell in love with his own reflection in a pool of water and died of the inability to fulfill this love.

Nausicaä Daughter of Alcinous, king of the Phaeacians. She was friendly to the shipwrecked Odysseus (q.v.) and asked her father to receive him with kindness.

Niobe Mother of ten sons and ten daughters. Niobe boasted of having more children than Leto. Outraged, Leto appealed to her son Apollo and daughter Artemis, and they avenged the insult to their mother by killing all of Niobe's children. Niobe was so overwhelmed with grief that even after being turned to stone she could not stop weeping.

Odysseus (Rom. Ulysses) King of Ithaca, famous for his sagacity and courage in the Trojan War, and for his misadventures on his way back from Troy.

Oedipus Son of Laius and Jocasta. After having unwittingly killed his father, Oedipus solved the riddle of the Sphinx and became a ruler of Thebes where he unknowingly married his own mother. When he learned of his crimes, Oedipus put out his own eyes and left Thebes, accompanied only by his daughter Antigone.

Olympus, Mount A high mountain in Thessaly; the home of the gods.

Orestes Son of Agamemnon (q.v.) and Clytemnestra (q.v.); brother of Electra (q.v.). Orestes avenged the murder of Agamemnon by killing Clytemnestra and her lover Aegisthus.

Orpheus A celebrated singer and player of the lyre. His music was so enchanting that mountains moved to listen to it, and trees,

animals, and birds followed him. Soon
after he came out of the underworld, hav-
ing lost Eurydice (q.v.) forever, he
returned to Thrace where he was torn
apart by the maenads (see Bacchae).

Pallas 1. Young son of Evander who fought
on the side of Aeneas and was killed by
Turnus (q.v.), king of the Rutulians. 2.
Another name for Athene.

Pan God of shepherds and forests, part
man, part goat.

Pandora The first mortal woman, made
from clay by Hephaestus at the request of
Zeus, Pandora was offered to Prometheus
(q.v.) who refused to marry her;
Prometheus's brother Epimetheus gladly
married her instead. Zeus gave Pandora a
box which she opened; out of the box
issued innumerable sorrows which from
then on afflicted mankind; only Hope
remained in the box.

Paris Trojan prince, the second son of
Priam and Hecuba. After he judged
Aphrodite the most beautiful goddess and
awarded her the golden apple, Paris jour-
neyed to Sparta and abducted Helen
(q.v.), the wife of Spartan king Menelaus,
precipitating the Trojan War.

Pasiphae Wife of Minos, mother of Ari-
adne (q.v.), Phaedra (q.v.), and the Mino-
taur (q.v.).

Patroclus Friend and companion of Achilles
(q.v.). When Patroclus was killed by Hec-
tor (q.v.), Achilles's grief and anger at the
loss of his friend caused him to re-enter
the war in order to avenge Patroclus's
death on the Trojans by killing Hector.

Penelope Queen of Ithaca, wife of
Odysseus (q.v.), celebrated for her faith-
fulness to Odysseus during the years of his
absence.

Pentheus King of Thebes who denied the
divinity of Dionysus; torn apart by Bac-
chantes (see Bacchae).

Persephone (Rom. Proserpina) Daughter
of Demeter and Zeus; wife of Hades;
queen of the underworld. Persephone was
carried off by Hades while she was gather-
ing flowers in Sicily. Demeter demanded
that Zeus order Hades to let her daughter
go, or else she would plunge the earth
into a nightmare of infertility. Zeus
agreed to set Persephone free on condi-
tion that she had eaten nothing while she

was the underworld. But Persephone had
already eaten a pomegranate, and there-
fore was allowed to spend only six months
of each year with her mother, while the
rest of the year, as Hades' wife, she
presided over the dead.

Perseus Son of Zeus and Danae, husband
of Andromeda whom he rescued from a
monster. Among Perseus' many heroic
deeds the most renowned is his slaying of
Medusa (q.v.).

Phaedra Daughter of Minos and Pasiphae
(q.v.); wife of Theseus. Phaedra fell in
love with her stepson Hippolytos.
Rejected by him, she accused him of try-
ing to seduce her. According to some ver-
sions of the myth, Phaedra hanged herself
in despair when she learned of Hippoly-
tos's death.

Phaethon (Also Phaeton) Son of Phoebus
(see Apollo), Phaethon made his father
swear that he would grant him any wish,
then wished to drive the chariot of the sun
for one day. Phaethon was unable to con-
trol the horses, and when his ride threat-
ened to set the world on fire, Zeus struck
him with a thunderbolt.

Philemon & Baucis Aged husband and
wife who received Zeus and Hermes with
such hospitality that in return for it Zeus
changed their poor cottage into a beauti-
ful temple. The couple were granted their
wish to die together, so that neither one
would grieve for the other. Their bodies
were changed into two trees in front of
their temple.

Philomela Princess of Athens; sister of
Procne. Tereus, Procne's husband, raped
Philomela and cut out her tongue to keep
his crime secret. Philomela wove the story
of her misfortune into a tapestry which
she sent to Procne. In revenge, the sisters
killed Procne's son Itylus, cooked his
body, and served him as food to Teresus.
Philomela was turned by the gods into a
nightingale, Procne into a swallow, Tereus
into a hoopoe. According to another ver-
sion, Philomela was turned into a swallow,
and Procne into a nightingale.

Polyphemus Son of Poseidon. The one-
eyed giant king of the island of Cyclopes.
His eye was put out by Odysseus (q.v.)
when Odysseus and his men stopped
there on their way back from Troy.

Poseidon (Rom. Neptune) Son of Chronus and Rhea. God of the sea.

Priam King of Troy before and during the Trojan War. Husband of Hecuba; father of fifty sons, among them Paris (q.v.) and Hector (q.v.), and fifty daughters, among them Cassandra (q.v.) and Polyxena.

Prometheus A Titan, brother of Atlas, Epimetheus, and Menoetius; according to Apollodorus, created mankind from clay. Prometheus ridiculed Zeus and stole fire from the gods to give to men. Zeus punished him by chaining him to a rock at Caucasus where an eagle daily devoured his liver.

Proteus A sea deity capable of assuming various shapes, Proteus was granted the power of prophecy.

Psyche A nymph who was married to Eros (q.v.). Psyche was depicted with the wings of a butterfly signifying the lightness of the human soul which she personified.

Pygmalion A famous sculptor who fell in love with a statue he had made. Aphrodite heard his prayers and turned the statue into a woman (Galatea, q.v.) whom he married.

Satyrs (Rom. fauns) Attendants of Dionysus, with human torsos but legs, ears, tail, and horns of goats.

Sibyl Famous prophetess who lived for a thousand years in her cave at Cumae. Knowledge of the future and a thousand-year lifespan were gifts to her from Apollo whose advances she rejected and whom she forgot to ask for perpetual youth.

Sirens Sea nymphs, part bird, part woman, who lured sailors to death with their singing.

Sisyphus King of Corinth who, for his many crimes, was condemned to roll a large stone up the hill in Hades; every time he reached the top, the stone rolled down again.

Styx The river which flowed around Hades (q.v.) and across which Charon (q.v.) ferried the dead.

Tantalus Condemned by the gods to an eternal torment in Hades, Tantalus was placed up to his chin in water, yet as soon as he tried to quench his thirst, the water dried up; whenever he tried to reach for fruit on a nearby bough, the wind carried it away; and a large stone was hung over his head, threatening to crush him.

Telemachus Son of Odysseus and Penelope. Helped his father kill his mother's suitors.

Theseus One of the most renowned heroes in Greek mythology. Among his exploits were the killing of the Minotaur and the conquest of the Amazons.

Titans Sons of Uranus (sky) and Gaea (earth), the Titans were imprisoned in the bowels of the earth by their father. Chief among them was Chronus (Lat. Saturn) who castrated Uranus and ruled in his place, until he in turn was overthrown by his son Zeus.

Trojan War See Troy.

Troy (Also Ilium) Ancient city in northwestern Asia Minor, famous for being the site of the Trojan War (c.1194–1184 B.C.).

Turnus King of the Rutulians. Turnus waged war against Aeneas (q.v.) to prevent him from marrying the daughter of Latinus and to drive Aeneas from Italy. Aeneas killed Turnus in single combat.

Zeus (Rom. Jupiter, Jove) The youngest son of Chronus (Rom. Saturn), Zeus was the principal god of the Olympian pantheon, the ruler of heaven and earth, famous for his philandering. He assumed many shapes to pursue mortal women and to hide his affairs from Hera.

INDEX OF POETS

INDEX OF TRANSLATORS

ACKNOWLEDGMENTS AND PERMISSIONS

Grateful acknowledgment is made to the Foundation for Hellenic Culture and the Alexander S. Onassis Public Benefit Foundation for grants to help cover publishers' permissions fees.

Thanks to Andy Newcomb, for sound advice and help, as always; to Dina Koutsoukou of the Greek Press & Information Center for her enthusiasm for my project; Charles Guenther and John Peck for translations and valuable suggestions; Judith Zupnick of the Dorot Jewish Division of the New York Public Library; the editorial and production staff at Oxford University Press; and, most of all, to the Greek gods who inspired this book.

Virginia Adair: "Pity Ulysses" from *Ants on the Mellon*. Copyright © 1996 by Virginia Hamilton Adair. (Random House, 1996). Reprinted by permission of Random House, Inc.

Anna Akhmatova: "Do not be frightened." Translated by Nina Kossman. First published in *Metamorphoses*. Used by permission of the translator.

Claribel Alegría: "Hecate" from *Fugues* (Curbstone Press, 1993). Translated by D. J. Flakoll. Reprinted by permission of Curbstone Press.

Eugénio Andrade: "In the Shadow of Homer." Translated by Alexis Levitin. Original translation. Used by permission of the translator.

Sophia de Mello Breyner Andresen: "Iphigenia" and "Electra." Translated by Alexis Levitin. "Iphigenia" was first published in *Helion Nine*, and "Electra" in *Women's Studies Quarterly* (International Supplement). Reprinted by permission of the translator.

Margaret Atwood: "Eurydice" and "Orpheus (2)" from *Selected Poems 1966–1987*. Copyright © 1990 by Margaret Atwood. From *Interlunar, Selected Poems II: 1976–1986*. Copyright © 1987 by Margaret Atwood. Reprinted by permission of Oxford University Press Canada, Virago Press, and Houghton Mifflin Co. "Siren Song" from *Selected Poems 1966–1984*. Copyright © 1990 by Margaret Atwood. From *You Are Happy, Selected Poems 1965-1975*. Copyright © 1976 by Margaret Atwood. Reprinted by permission of Oxford University Press, Virago Press, and Houghton Mifflin Co.

W. H. Auden: "Ganymede," "The Shield of Achilles," Circe," "Musée des Beaux Arts" from The *Collected Poems*. Copyright © 1969 by W. H. Auden. Reprinted by permission of Random House, Inc. and Faber & Faber Ltd.

Ingeborg Bachmann: "Darkness Spoken" from *Songs in Flight*. Translated by Peter Filkins. Translation copyright © 1994 by Peter Filkins. Reprinted by permission of Marsilio Publishers.

Ion Barbu: "The Last Centaur." Translated by John Peck. First published in *Pequod* #40 (1996). Used by permission of the translator.

Barbara Bentley: "Living Next to Leda" from *Living Next to Leda*. Reprinted by permission of Seren Books.

Attilio Bertolucci: "Iphigenia." Translated by Avi Sharon. First published in *Arion*. Used by permission of the translator.

Michael Blumenthal: "Icarus Descended" (first published in *Prairie Schooner*) and

285

"Oedipus II." (Rochester: Boa Editions, 1999). Used by permission of the poet.

Johannes Bobrowski: "Dryad" from *Shadow Lands: Selected Poems*. Translated by Ruth and Mathew Mead. Copyright © 1984 by Matthew Mead. Reprinted by permission of New Directions Publishing Corp. and Anvil Press Poetry.

Louise Bogan: "Cassandra" from *The Blue Estuaries: Poems 1923–1968*. Copyright © 1968 by Louise Bogan. Copyright © renewed 1996 by Ruth Limmer. Reprinted by permission of Farrar, Straus & Giroux, Inc.

Eavan Boland: "Athene's Song" and "Daphne with Her Thighs in Bark" from *An Origin Like Water: Collected Poems 1967–1987*. Copyright © 1996 by Eavan Boland. Reprinted by permission of W.W. Norton & Co. and Carcanet Press Ltd.

Jorge Luis Borges: "Oedipus and the Riddle," translated by John Hollander. "The Labyrinth," translated by John Updike, "Odyssey, Book Twenty-Three," translated by Robert Fitzgerald. From *Selected Poems 1923-1967* by Jorge Luis Borges. Copyright © 1968, 1969, 1970, 1971, 1972 by Jorge Luis Borges, Emece Editores, S. A. and Norman Thomas Di Giovanni. Used by permission of Delacorte Press / Seymour Lawrence, a division of Random House, Inc. "Proteus" from *The Gold of the Tigers*. Translated by Alastair Reid. Translation copyright © 1972, 1975 by Emece Editores, S.A., Buenos Aires. Used by permission of the translator.

Ronald Bottrall: "Haven" and "Hermes" from *Against the Setting Sun*. Copyright © 1984 by Ronald Bottrall. Reproduced courtesy of Allison & Busby Ltd.

Bertold Brecht: "On Reading a Recent Greek Poet." Translated by John Peck. Originally published in *World Poetry*, ed. Katharine Washburn, W.W. Norton, 1998. Used by permission of the translator.

Joseph Brodsky: "Galatea Encore" from *To Urania: Selected Poems 1965-1985* (Viking, 1988). Copyright © Joseph Brodsky 1977, 1981, 1982, 1983, 1984, 1985, 1987, 1988. "Epitaph for a Centaur" from *So Forth: Poems*. Copyright © by The Estate of Joseph Brodsky, 1996. Both poems are reproduced by permission of Penguin Books Ltd. and Farrar, Straus & Giroux, Inc.

William Bronk: "The Look Back" and "Abnegation" from *Selected Poems*. Copyright © 1995 by William Bronk. Reprinted by permission of New Directions Publishing Corp.

Olga Broumas: "Aphrodite" from *Beginning with O*. Copyright © 1977 by Olga Broumas. Reprinted by permission of Yale University Press.

Leonid Bulanov: "Icarus." Translated by Nina Kossman. Original translation. Used by permission of the author.

Basil Bunting: "Chorus of Furies" from *The Complete Poems of Basil Bunting*. Copyright © 1994 by the Estate of Basil Bunting. Reprinted by permission of Oxford University Press (U.K.).

Hayden Carruth: "Niobe, your tears..." from *Collected Shorter Poems 1946–1991*. Copyright © 1992 by Hayden Carruth. Reprinted by permission of Copper Canyon Press, P.O. Box 271, Port Townsend, WA 98368.

Rosario Castellanos: "Hecuba's Testament." Translated by John Frederick Nims. Copyright © 1990 by John Frederick Nims. Reprinted by permission of the University of Arkansas Press.

Constantine P. Cavafy: "Athena's Vote," "Oedipus," "The Horses of Achilles" (first published in *Persephone*), and "A Second Odyssey" translated by Theoharis C. Theoharis. Used by permission of the translator. "Ithaka" and "Trojans" from *C. P. Cavafy. Collected Poems*. Translated by Edmund Keeley and Philip Sherrard. Copyright © 1975, 1992 by Edmund Keeley and Philip Sherrard. Reprinted by permission of Princeton University Press.

Nicholas Christopher: "Ariadne Auf Naxos" from *In the Year of the Comet*. (Viking Penguin, 1992). Copyright © 1992 by Nicholas Christopher. Reprinted by permission of the author.

Lucille Clifton: "Atlas," "Leda 3," "nothing is told about the moment..." from *The Book of Light*. Copyright © 1993 by Lucille Clifton. Reprinted by permission of Copper Canyon Press, P.O. Box 271, Port Townsend, WA 98368.

Gregory Corso: "Mortal Affliction" from *The Happy Birthday of Death*. Copyright ©

1960 by New Directions Publishing Corp. Reprinted by permission of New Directions Publishing Corp.

Robert Creeley: "The Death of Venus" from *Collected Poems by Robert Creeley, 1945–1975*. Copyright © 1982 by the Regents of the University of California. Reprinted by permission of University of Califiornia Press.

Kate Daniels: "Alcestis" from *The White Wave*. Copyright © 1984 by Kate Daniels. Copyright © 1988 by Kate Daniels. Reprinted by permission of the University of Pittsburgh Press.

Ann Deagon: "Sphinx Ludens," "Daphne on Woodbrook Drive,' and "Icarus by Night" from *Carbon 14*. (Amherst: University of Massachusetts Press, 1974). Copyright © 1974 by the University of Massachusetts Press.

Peter Davison: "Calypso" and "Eurydice in Darkness" from *The Poems of Peter Davison*. Copyright © 1995 by Peter Davison. Reprinted by permission of Alfred Knopf, Inc.

John Dickson: "Pygmalion." Used by permission of the poet.

H.D.: "Eurydice," "Helen," and "Lethe" from *Collected Poems, 1912–1944*. Copyright © 1982 by The Estate of Hilda Doolittle. Reprinted by permission of New Directions Publishing Corp. and Carcanet Press.

Rita Dove: "The Search" and "Demeter's Prayer to Hades" from *Mother Love*. Copyright © 1995 by Rita Dove. Reprinted by permission of the author and W.W. Norton & Company, Inc.

Alan Dugan: "Orpheus" from *New and Collected Poems 1961-1983* by Alan Dugan. Copyright © 1961–1962, 1968, 1972–74, 1983 by Alan Dugan. Reprinted by permission of The Ecco Press.

Gunnar Ekelöf: "Give me poison to die or dreams to live" from *Guide to the Underworld*. Translated by Rika Lesser. (Amherst: The University of Massachusetts Press, 1980). Copyright © 1980 by Rika Lesser.

Odysseus Elytis: "Helen." Translated by Avi Sharon. Original translation. Used by permission of the translator.

Hans Magnus Enzenberger: "instructions for sisyphus" from *Contemporary German*

Poetry. Translated by Gertrude Clorius Schwebel. Copyright © 1964 by Gertrude Clorius Schwebel. (New York: New Directions Publishing Corp., 1964).

Rhina Espaillat: "Arachne" and "On the Walls." "Arachne" was originally published in *Voices International*. Used by permission of the author.

Rosario Ferré: "Requiem" from The Massachusetts Review. Copyright © 1996 The Massachusetts Review, Inc. Reprinted by permission.

Jerzy Ficowski: "New Prometheus." Translated by Yala Korwin. Original translation. Used by permission of the translator and the author.

Boris Filipoff: "After abducting Europa..." Translated by Nina Kossman. First published in *Metamorphoses*. Used by permission of the translator.

Lars Forssell: "Canto 26" from *Sånger* (Stockholm: Bonniers, 1986). Translation copyright © 2000 by Roger Greenwald. Used by permission of the translator.

Erich Fried: "Philomela with a Melody." Translated by Leonid Kossman. Original translation. Used by permission of the translator.

Robert Frost: "Pan With Us" from *The Poetry of Robert Frost*, ed. by Edward Connery Lathem. Copyright © 1962 by Robert Frost. Copyright © 1934, c 1969 by Henry Holt & Co. Reprinted by permission of Henry Holt and Co. and Jonathan Cape.

John Fuller: "A Footnote to Ovid" and "The Labours of Hercules (13)" from *Poems and Epistles*. Copyright © 1974 by John Fuller. Reprinted by permission of David R. Godine, Publisher, Inc.

Emery George: "Prometheus" from *The Boy and the Monarch* (Ann Arbor: Ardis, 1987). Copyright © 1987 by Emery E. George. Reprinted by permission of the poet.

Jack Gilbert: "Finding Eurydice" from *The Great Fires* by Jack Gilbert. Copyright © 1994 by Jack Gilbert. Reprinted by permission of Alfred A. Knopf, Inc.

Louise Glück: "Circe's Power" and "Ithaca" from *Meadowlands* by Louise Glück. Copyright © 1996 by Louise Glück. Reprinted by permission of The Ecco Press.

Alfred Gong: "Mars" from *Contemporary*

German Poetry. Translated by Gertrude Clorius Schwebel. Copyright © 1964 by Gertrude Clorius Schwebell. (New York: New Directions Publishing Corp., 1964). Reprinted by permission.

Jorie Graham: "Orpheus and Eurydice" by Jorie Graham from *The Dream of the Unified Field* by Jorie Graham. Copyright © 1980, 1983, 1987, 1991, 1993, 1995 by Jorie Graham. Reprinted by permission of The Ecco Press and Carcanet Press.

Günter Grass: "Diana—or the Objects" from *The Egg and Other Poems*. Translated by Christopher Middleton. Copyright © 1977 by Günter Grass. Reprinted by permission of Harcourt Brace & Co.

Michael Graves: "Apollo to Daphne." First published in *Rattapallax*. Used by permission of the author.

Robert Graves: "Prometheus," "Leda," "Apollo of Physiologists," "Hercules at Nemea," "Lament for Pasiphae," "Theseus and Ariadne" from *Collected Poems*. Reprinted by permission of Carcanet Press Ltd.

Allen Grossman: "Alcestis, or Autumn: A Hymn" from *The Woman Over the Chicago River*. Copyright © 1979 by Allen Grossman. Reprinted by permission of New Directions Publishing Corp.

Thom Gunn: "Moly," "Philemon and Baucis," "Phaedra in the Farm House." Reprinted from *Collected Poems*, copyright © 1994 by Thom Gunn, by permission of Farrar, Straus & Giroux, Inc., and from *Selected Poems 1950–1975*, *The Man with Night Sweats*, and *Moly*, by permission of Faber & Faber Ltd.

Haim Guri: "Odysseus" translated by Avi Sharon. First published in *Dialogos*. Used by permission of the translator.

Ramon Guthrie: "Dialogue with the Sphinx," "The Clown's Report on Satyrs," "Icarus to Eve" from *Maximum Security Ward and Other Poems*. Copyright © 1970 by Ramon Guthrie. Reprinted by permission of Persea Books, Inc.

Seamus Heaney: "Hercules and Antaeus." Copyright © 1998 by Seamus Heaney. Reprinted from *Opened Ground: Selected Poems 1966–1996* by permission of Farrar, Straus & Giroux, Inc. and from *New Selected Poems 1966–1987* by permission of Faber & Faber Ltd.

John Heath-Stubbs: "The Theban Sphinx" from *Chimaeras*. (Hearing Eye, 1994). Copyright © 1994 by John Heath-Stubbs. Reprinted by permission of David Higham Associates.

Zbigniew Herbert: "The Sacrifice of Iphigenia," "Shore," "The Missing Knot," "Hermes, Dog, and Star" from *Zbigniew Herbert: Selected Poems* (1977). Copyright © 1977 John & Bogdana Carpenter. Reprinted by permission of Oxford University Press. "Old Prometheus" from *Mr. Cogito*. Translated by John and Bogdana Carpenter. Copyright © 1974 by Zbigniew Herbert. Translation copyright © 1993 by John and Bogdana Carpenter. Reprinted by permission of The Ecco Press.

Geoffrey Hill: "Orpheus and Eurydice," "The Re-Birth of Venus," from *Geoffrey Hill: Collected Poems*. First published in *For the Unfallen*, 1959 (Penguin Books Ltd, 1985). Copyright © Geoffrey Hill, 1959, 1985. Reproduced by permission of Penguin Books Ltd. From *New & Collected Poms 1952–1992* by Geoffrey Hill. Copyright © 1994 by Geoffrey Hill. Previously published in *Somewhere is Such a Kingdom* (1975). Reprinted by permission of Houghton Mifflin Co.

Daryl Hine: "Tableau Vivant" from *Minutes*. Copyright © 1968 by Daryl Hine. "Patroclus Putting on the Armour of Achilles" from *The Wooden Horse*. Copyright © 1965 by Daryl Hine. "Linear A" from *Resident Alien*. Copyright © 1975 by Daryl Hine. "Aftermath I-IV" from *Daylight Saving*. Copyright © 1978 by Daryl Hine. All of the above are reprinted with the permission of Scribner, a div. of Simon & Schuster.

John Hollander: "Powers of Thirteen, #44" ("This whole business of outliving..."), from *Selected Poetry*. Copyright © 1993 by John Hollander. Reprinted by permission of Alfred A. Knopf, Inc. "Arachne's Story." Copyright © 1999. Used by permission.

Anselm Hollo: "The Island." Copyright © 1999 by Anselm Hollo. Used by permission of the poet.

A.D. Hope: "Jupiter on Juno" and "Pasiphae" from *Selected Poems* (HarperCollins Australia, 1992). Copyright ©

1992 by A. D. Hope. Reprinted by permission of Curtis Brown (Aust.).

Peter Huchel: "Persephone" and "The Grave of Odysseus" from *The Garden of Theophrastus*, translated by Michael Hamburger. (Manchester: Carcanet, 1983). Used by permission of the translator.

Ted Hughes: "Prometheus on his Crag" from *Moortown* by Ted Hughes. Reprinted by permission of Faber & Faber Ltd.

Norman Iles: "Paris Reconsiders" from *The Green Man* by Norman Iles, 1968. Reprinted by permission of the author.

Max Jacob: "Centaur" translated by Armand Schwerner, from *Random House Book of Twentieth-Century French Poetry* by Paul Auster. Copyright © 1943 by Editions Gallimard. Reprinted by permission of Random House.

Randall Jarrell: "The Sphinx's Riddle to Oedipus" from *The Complete Poems*. Copyright © 1969 and copyright © renewed © 1997 by Mary von S. Jarrell. Reprinted by permission of Farrar, Straus & Giroux, Inc. and Faber & Faber Ltd.

Robinson Jeffers: "Cassandra" from *The Selected Poems of Robinson Jeffers*. Copyright © 1941 by Yardstick Press. Copyright © 1944 by Oscar Williams. Reprinted by permission of Vintage Books, a div. of Random House, Inc.

Judith Johnson: "Body Politic" from *The Ice Lizard* (New York: The Sheep Meadow Press, 1992). Copyright © 1992 by Judith Johnson. Used by permission of the author.

Donald Justice: "Orpheus Opens His Morning Mail" from *Selected Poems*. (New York: Atheneum, 1985). Reprinted by permission of the author.

Margaret Kaufman: "Waking." Used by permission of the author.

Robert Kelly: "The Head of Orpheus" from *Red Actions: Selected Poems 1960–1993*. Copyright © 1995 by Robert Kelly. "The Menelaus" from *Kill the Messenger*. Copyright © 1979 by Robert Kelly. Both poems are reprinted with the permission of Black Sparrow Press.

Thomas Kinsella: "Endymion" from *Poems 1956–1975*. Copyright © 1980 by Thomas Kinsella. Reprinted by permission of the author.

Nina Kossman: "Daphne Herself" and

"Leda" from *Po Pravuyu Ruku Sna: Selected Poems in Russian and English*. Copyright © 1996 by Nina Kossman. "Phaethon's Dream" and "How Cassandra Became Clairvoyant." Used by permission of the author.

Mikhail Kreps: "Philomela." Translated by Nina Kossman. Original translation. Used by permission of the translator.

Len Krisak: "Tantalus." Used by permission of the poet.

Stanley Kunitz: "The Approach to Thebes," copyright © 1957 by Stanley Kunitz, and "Among the Gods," copyright © 1958 by Stanley Kunitz. From *The Poems of Stanley Kunitz 1928–1978*. Reprinted by permission of W.W. Norton & Co.

James Laughlin: "The Fate of Actaeon" from *The Owl of Minerva* © 1984 by James Laughlin. Reprinted by permission of Copper Canyon Press, P.O. Box 271, Port Townsend, WA 98368.

D. H. Lawrence: "The Argonauts," "Leda," "Bavarian Gentians," "Purple Anemones" from *The Complete Poems* of D.H. Lawrence, edited by V. de Sola Pinto and F.W. Roberts. Copyright © 1964, 1971 by Angelo Ravagli and C.M. Weekley, Executors of the Estate of Frieda Lawrence Ravagli. Used by permission of Viking Penguin, a division of Penguin Putnam, Inc., and Laurence Pollinger Ltd.

Denise Levertov: "Eros" and "Hymn to Eros" from *Poems 1960–1967*. Copyright © 1966 by Denise Levertov. Reprinted by permission of New Directions Corp. and Laurence Pollinger Ltd. "A Tree Telling of Orpheus" from *Poems 1968–1972*. Copyright © 1970 by Denise Levertov. Published by New Directions Corp. *Selected Poems*, published by Bloodaxe Books. Reprinted by permission of New Directions Publishing Co. and Laurence Pollinger Ltd.

Xiaoyun Lin: "Marsyas and the Flute." Translated by the author. Used by permission of the author.

Erik Lindegren: "Icarus." Translated by John Matthias and Göran Printz-Påhlson. Original translation. Used by permission of the translators.

Michael Longley: "The Helmet" and "Ceasefire" from *The Ghost Child*. Copy-

right © 1995 by Michael Longley.
Reprinted by permission of Wake Forest
University Press and Jonathan Cape.

Robert Lowell: "Falling Asleep over the
Aeneid" from *The Mills of the Cavanaughs*.
Copyright © 1948 and renewed 1976 by
Robert Lowell. Reprinted by permission
of Harcourt Brace & Co. and Faber &
Faber Ltd. "Clytemnestra (I)" reprinted
from *History* by Robert Lowell by permis-
sion of Faber & Faber Ltd., and from
Robert Lowell's *Poems / A Selection* by per-
mission of Farrar Straus & Giroux, Inc.

Archibald MacLeish: "Birth of Eventually
Venus," "Psyche with the Candle," "What
Riddle Asked the Sphinx" from *Collected
Poems 1917–1982*. Copyright © 1985 by
the Estate of Archibald MacLeish.
Reprinted by permission of Houghton
Mifflin Co. All rights reserved.

Louise MacNeice: "Charon" and "Perseus"
from *Collected Poems* (London: Faber &
Faber, 1979). Copyright © 1966, 1979 by
The Estate of Louis MacNeice. Reprinted
by permission of David Higham Associates.

Osip Mandelshtam: "Since I could not keep
hold of your hands" and "Wakefulness.
Homer. Taut Sails," translated by Nina
Kossman and Andy Newcomb. "Pink
foam of exhaustion," "Zeus fired Hep-
haestus," and "When Psyche—life—goes
down to the shades" translated by Nina
Kossman. With the exception of "Zeus
fired Hephaestus" which was first pub-
lished in *Metamorphoses*, all of the above
are original translations. Used by permis-
sion of the translators.

Thomas Merton: "Ariadne," "Iphigenia:
Politics," and "Eurydice" from *Collected
Poems of Thomas Merton*. Copyright ©
1948 by New Directions Publishing
Corp. Reprinted by permission of New
Directions Publishing Corp. and Lau-
rence Pollinger Ltd.

W.S. Merwin: "Ode: The Medusa Face" and
"Proteus" from *A Mask For Janus*. Copy-
right © 1952 by Yale University Press.
"Odysseus" from *The Drunk in the Fur-
nace* (New York: The Macmillan Co.,
1960). Copyright © 1956, 1957, 1958,
1959, 1960 by W. S. Merwin. All of the
above are reprinted by permission of
George Borchadt, Inc. for the author.
"The Judgment of Paris" from *The Car-

rier of Ladders*. Copyright © 1970 by
W. S. Merwin. Reprinted by permission
of The Wylie Agency.

Edna St. Vincent Millay: "Daphne,"
"Lethe," and "An Ancient Gesture" from
Collected Poems, HarperCollins, Inc. Copy-
right © 1922, 1928, 1950, 1954, 1955,
1982 by Edna St. Vincent Millay and
Norma Millay Ellis. All rights reserved.
Reprinted by permission of Elizabeth
Barnett, literary executor.

Stephen Mitchell: "Orpheus," "Narcissus,"
"The Myth of Sisyphus," "Cassandra,"
"Cerberus" from *Parables and Portraits*.
Copyright © 1990 by Stephen Mitchell.
HarperPerennial, 1994. Reprinted by per-
mission of HarperCollins Publishers, Inc.
and Michael Katz.

Yunna Morits: "Reading a Greek Pitcher."
Translated by Nina Kossman.
"Prometheus and "Episode with
Aphrodite." Translated by Nina Kossman
and Andy Newcomb. "Reading a Greek
Pitcher" and "Episode with Aphrodite"
were published in *Metamorphoses*. Used by
permission of the author and translators.

Edwin Muir: "Orpheus' Dream," "Troy" and
"The Other Oedipus" from *Collected
Poems* by Edwin Muir. Copyright © 1960
by Willa Muir. Used by permission of
Oxford University Press, Inc. and Faber
& Faber Ltd.

John Frederick Nims: "Minotaur" from *John
Frederick Nims. Selected Poems*. Reprinted
by permission of The University of
Chicago Press.

Joyce Carol Oates: "Wooded Forms," origi-
nally a greeting card by Wm. Ferguson
for Albodocani Press. Copyright © 1973
by Joyce Carol Oates. Reprinted by per-
mission of the author.

Frank O'Hara: "The Satyr" and "Jove" from
Collected Poems of Frank O'Hara. Copy-
right © 1971 by Maureen Granville-
Smith, Administratrix of the Estate of
Frank O'Hara. Reprinted by permission
of Alfred A. Knopf, Inc.

Charles Olson: "There is No River Which is
Called Lethe," "Hymn to Proserpine"
from *The Collected Poems of Charles Olson*.
Copyright © 1987 Estate of Charles
Olson. Reprinted by permission of Uni-
versity of California Press on behalf of
Estate.

George Oppen: "Daedalus: The Dirge" and "Vulcan" from *Collected Poems*. Copyright © 1975 by George Oppen. Reprinted by permission of New Directions Publishing Corp.

Joel Oppenheimer: "Orpheus" from *Names & Local Habitations*. Copyright © 1988 by Joel Oppenheimer. Reprinted by permission of The Jargon Society.

Gregory Orr: "Betrayals / Hades, Eurydice, Orpheus" from *City of Salt*. Copyright © 1995. Reprinted by permission of the University of Pittsburgh Press.

Vincent O'Sullivan: "Medusa" from *An Anthology of Twentieth-Century New Zealand Poetry*. (Wellington: Oxford University Press, 1970). Reprinted by permission of the author.

José Emilio Pacheco: "New Sisyphus" from *Selected Poems*. Translated by George McWhirter. Copyright © 1975, 1987 by George McWhirter. Reprinted by New Directions Publishing Corp.

Dan Pagis: "Jason's Grave in Jerusalem" from *The Selected Poetry of Dan Pagis*. Translated by Stephen Mitchell. Reprinted by permission of University of California Press.

Linda Pastan: "Dido's Farewell." Copyright © 1982 by Linda Pastan. "You are Odysseus." Copyright © 1975 by Linda Pastan. From *PM/AM: New and Selected Poems*. "The Sirens" from *Imperfect Paradise*. Copyright © 1988 by Linda Pastan. "Narcissus at Sixty" from *An Early Afterlife*. Copyright © 1995 by Linda Pastan. All of the above are reprinted by permission of W.W. Norton & Co, Inc.

Cesare Pavese: "Ulysses" from *Hard Labor* by Cesare Pavese. Translated by Wm. Arrowsmith. Translation copyright © 1976 by Wm. Arrowsmith. *Lavorare Stanca*. Copyright © 1943 by Guilio Einaudi Editore, Torino. Reprinted by permission of Guilio Einaudi Editore and Penguin Putnam, Inc.

John Peck: "He who called blood builder..." from *Argura*. Copyright © 1993 by John Peck. Reprinted by permission of Carcanet Press Ltd.

Valentine Penrose: "Demeter" from *Poems and Narrations*. Translated by Roy Edwards. (Manchester: Carcanet Press Ltd. & Elephant Trust, 1977). Copyright © 1976 by Valentine Penrose. Used by permission.

Sylvia Plath: "Virgin in a Tree" from *Collected Poems of Sylvia Plath*, edited by Ted Hughes. Copyright © 1960, 1965, 1971, 1981 by The Estate of Sylvia Plath. Editorial material copyright © 1981 by Ted Hughes. Reprinted by permission of HarperCollins Publishers, Inc. and Faber & Faber Ltd.

Ezra Pound, "Pan Is Dead" and "The Return" from *Personae*. Copyright © 1926 by Ezra Pound. Reprinted by permission of New Directions Publishing Corp. From *Collected Shorter Poems*, reprinted by permission of Faber & Faber Ltd..

Salvatore Quasimodo: "Mycenae" from *Salvatore Quasimodo: Complete Poems*. Translated by Jack Bevan. Reprinted by permission of Anvil Press Poetry Ltd.

György Rába: "The Greeks Are Blinding Polyphemus." Translated by Emery George. Originally published in *The Age of Koestler*, an anthology, ed. Nicolaus P. Kogon (Kalamazoo, Michigan: Practices of the Wind, 1994). Used by permission of the translator.

Kathleen Raine: "Daphne," "Playing Dionysos in The Bacchae," "Go Loudly, Pentheus," "Phaeton," "Medea" from *Selected Poems*. Copyright © Golgonooza Press, 1988. Reprinted by permission of Golgonooza Press.

Alastair Reid: "Daedalus" from *An Alastair Reid Reader*. (Hanover: Middlebury College Press / University Press of New England, 1994). Reprinted by permission of the author.

Charles Reznikoff: "#39, Lesson in Homer." Copyright © 1977 by Marie Syrkin Reznikoff. Reprinted from *Poems 1918–1975: The Complete Poems of Charles Reznikoff* with the permission of Black Sparrow Press.

Laura Riding: "Helen's Burning" and "Helen's Faces" from *Poems of Laura Riding*. Copyright © 1980 by Laura (Riding) Jackson. Reprinted by permission of Persea Books, Inc. and The Board of Literary Management of the late Laura (Riding) Jackson. In conformity with the late author's wish, her Board of Literary Management asks us to record that, in 1941, Laura (Riding) Jackson renounced, on grounds of linguistic principle, the writing of poetry: she had come to hold that "poetry obstructs general attainment to something better in our linguistic way-of-life than we have."

Rainer Maria Rilke: "Leda," "Cretan Artemis," "A Sibyl," and "Narcissus (I)," translated by John Peck. Original translations. Used by permission of the translator. "Sonnet XXVI" and "Sonnet XIII" from *From Ahead of All Parting: The Selected Poetry and Prose of Rainer Maria Rilke*, edited and translated by Stephen Mitchell, *The Modern Library*, 1995. Used by permission of the translator. "Orpheus. Eurydice. Hermes" and "Alcestis" from *Between Roots*, translated by Rika Lesser. Copyright © 1986 by Rika Lesser. Reprinted by permission of Princeton University Press.

Yannis Ritsos: "Descent" from *Subterranean Horses*, translated by Minas Savvas. Copyright © 1980 by Pittsburgh International Poetry Forum. Reprinted by permission of Samuel Hazo, Byblos Editions. "Penelope's Despair," Alcmene," "Marpessa's Choice," Expiation," "Philomela," "The Decline of the Argo," "The Real Reason" from *Repetition, Testimonies, and Parenthesis*, translated by Edmund Keeley. Copyright © 1991 by Princeton University Press. Reprinted by permission of Princeton University Press.

Theodore Roethke: "The Centaur" from *The Collected Poems*. Copyright © 1957 by Beatrice Roethke, administratrix of the Estate of Theodore Roethke. Used by permission of Doubleday, a div. of Random House, Inc. and Faber & Faber Ltd.

Muriel Rukeyser: "The Poem as a Mask" from *A Muriel Rukeyser Reader*, first published by W.W. Norton & Co., Inc. Copyright © 1994 by Wm. L. Rukeyser. "Niobe Now" from *Out of Silence*, first published in *Triquarterly*. Copyright © 1992 by Wm. L. Rukeyser. "Waiting for Icarus," "The Minotaur," "Myth" from The *Collected Poems of Muriel Rukeyser*, first published by McGraw-Hill. Copyright © 1978 by Muriel Rukeyser. All of the above are reprinted by permission of International Creative Management.

Peter Russell: "Agamemnon in Hades" and "Hephaestus" from Berlin-Tegel 1964, Univ. of Salzburg, 1994. Reprinted by permission of the publisher.

Pentti Saarikoski: "Aft, he sleeps..." Translated by Anselm Hollo. From *Poems 1958–1980* (West Branch, Iowa: Toothpaste Press, 1983). Translation copyright © 1999 by Anselm Hollo.

Umberto Saba: "Ulysses" (7 lines) and "The Rape of Ganymede" from *Songbook* (New York: The Sheep Meadow Press, 1998). Translated by Stephen Sartarelli. Reprinted by permission of the translator. "Ulysses" (13 lines). Translated by Charles Guenther. Original translation. Used by permission of the translator.

May Sarton: "Narcissus." Copyright © 1978 by May Sarton. "The Muse as Medusa." Copyright © 1971 by May Sarton. "The Furies." Copyright © 1978 by May Sarton. From *Selected Poems of May Sarton* by Serena Sue Hilsinger and Lois Brynes, editors. Reprinted by permission of W.W. Norton and A M Heath & Co. Ltd. on behalf of the Estate of the late May Sarton.

Delmore Schwartz: "Psyche Pleads with Cupid," "Cupid's Chant," and "Once and for All" from *Selected Poems: Summer Knowledge*. Copyright © 1959 by Delmore Schwartz. Reprinted by permission of New Directions Publishing Corp. and Laurence Pollinger Ltd. "The Maxims of Sisyphus" from *Last and Lost Poems*. Copyright © 1979, 1989 by Kenneth Schwartz. Reprinted by permission of New Directions Publishing Corp.

George Seferis: "Pentheus," "Mythistorema (4)," "Mythistorema (16)," "Helen," and "The Companions in Hades." From *George Seferis. Collected Poems*. Translated by Edmund Keeley and Philip Sherrard. Copyright © 1995 by Princeton University Press. Reprinted by permission of Princeton University Press.

Sidhveswar Sen: "For Pandora, Again." Translated by Ron D.K. Banerjee. (London: Forest Books, 1989). Used by permission of the translator.

Anne Sexton: "Where I Live in This Honorable House of the Laurel Tree" and "To a Friend Whose Work Has Come to Triumph" from *The Complete Poems* by Anne Sexton. Copyright © 1981 by Linda Gray Sexton and Loring Conant, Jr., executors of the will of Anne Sexton. Reprinted by permission of Houghton Mifflin Co. and Sterling Lord Literistic, Inc.

Laurie Sheck: "Niobe, Also of the Beautiful Hair Thought of Eating" and "To Io, Afterwards" from *Io at Night*. Copyright © 1990 by Laurie Sheck. Both of the above are reprinted by permission of Alfred A. Knopf, Inc. "Electra, Waiting" from *Amaranth*. Copyright © 1981 by Laurie Sheck. Reprinted by permission of The University of Georgia Press.

Charles Simic: "In the fourth year..." from *The World Doesn't End: Prose Poems*. Copyright © 1987 by Charles Simic, reprinted by permission of Harcourt Brace & Co. "Charon's Cosmology" and "My Weariness of Epic Proportions" from *Selected Poems 1963–1983*. Reprinted by permission of George Braziller, Inc.

Louis Simpson: "Orpheus in the Underworld" from *Collected Poems*. Copyright © 1988 by Paragon Publishers. Used by permission of the author.

Stevie Smith: "Dido's Farewell to Aeneas" from *Collected Poems of Stevie Smith*. Copyright © 1972 by Stevie Smith. Reprinted by permission of New Directions Publishing Corp. and the Stevie Smith Estate.

Martin Sorescu: "Inhabited Liver." Translated by Adam J. Sorkin and Lidia Vianu. Original translation. Used by permission.

Stephen Spender: "Boy, Cat, Canary" from *Collected Poems 1928–1985*. Copyright © 1986 by Stephen Spender. Reprinted by permission of Random House, Inc. and Faber & Faber Ltd.

Maura Stanton: "Proteus's Tale" from *Snow on Snow*. Copyright © 1975 by Yale University Press. Reprinted by permission of Yale University Press. "Alcestis" from *Cries of Swimmers*. Copyright © 1984 by Maura Stanton. Reprinted by permission of Carnegie University Press.

Stephen Stepanchev: "Medusa" from *Sparrow 36*. Used by permission of the author.

Wallace Stevens: "The World as Meditation" from *Collected Poems*. Copyright © 1952 by Wallace Stevens. Reprinted by permission of Alfred A. Knopf, Inc. and Faber & Faber Ltd.

Samn Stockwell: "Aphrodite at Solstice" from *Theater of Animals*. Copyright © 1995 by Samn Stockwell. Used by permission of the poet and the University of Illinois Press.

Mark Strand: "Orpheus Alone" from *The Continuous Life*. Copyright © 1990 by Mark Strand. Reprinted by permission of Alfred A. Knopf.

Larissa Szporluk: "Io Remembers" from *Dark Sky Question*. Copyright © 1998 by Larissa Szporluk. Reprinted by permission of Beacon Press, Boston.

Wislawa Szymborska: "Soliloquy for Cassandra," "A Moment in Troy," and "On the Banks of the Styx" from *View with a Grain of Sand*. Translated by Stanislaw Baranczak and Clare Cavanagh. Copyright © 1993 by Harcourt Brace & Co. Reprinted by permission of the publisher.

Pia Tafdrup: "Fiery Water." Translated by David McDuff. Used by permission of the author and the translator.

Allen Tate: "The Mediterranean" and "Aeneas at Washington" from *Collected Poems 1919–1976*. Copyright © 1977 by Allen Tate. Reprinted by permission of Farrar, Straus & Giroux, Inc.

Veno Taufer: "Orpheus." Translated by Judita Mia Dintinjana. Originally published in *The Fire under the Moon*, an anthology, ed. Richard Jackson & Rachel Morgan. Used by permission of the translator.

D.M. Thomas: "Persephone," "Pomegranate," and "Orpheus in Hell" from *The Puberty Tree. New and Selected Poems*. Reprinted by permission of Bloodaxe Books.

Miguel Torga: "Sisyphus." Translated by Ivana Rangel Carlsen. Original translation. Used by permission of the translator.

Georg Trakl: "Passion" from *Autumn Sonata. Selected Poems of Georg Trakl*. Translated by Daniel Simko. Copyright © 1989 by Daniel Simko. Reprinted by permission of Moyer Bell Ltd.

Marina Tsvetaeva: "Praise to Aphrodite," "The Sibyl," "Thus—only Helen looks past," and "There are rhymes in this world" from *In the Inmost Hour of the Soul: Poems of Marina Tsvetayeva*. Copyright © 1989 by Humana Press. (Totowa, NJ: Humana Press, 1989). "So they drifted: the lyre and the head" from *Poem of the End: Selected Lyrical and Narrative Poems of Marina Tsvetaeva* (Ardis, 1998). "Eurydice to Orpheus." All of the above are translated by Nina Kossman and used by permission of the translator.

Judita Vaičiunaitė: "Nausicaä." Translated by Irene Pogozelskyte Suboczewski. From *Contemporary East European Poetry*, edited by Emery George (Ann Arbor: Ardis, 1983). Used by permission.

Paul Valéry: "Helen." Translated by Charles Guenther. First published in *The Formalist*, 1991. Used by permission of the translator.

Mona Van Duyn: "Leda Reconsidered" from *If It Be Not I*. Copyright © 1971 by Mona Van Duyn. Reprinted by permission of Alfred A. Knopf, Inc.

Igor Vishnevetsky: "Odysseus's Temptation." Translated by Nina Kossman. First published in *The Literary Review* , 1991. Used by permission of the translator.

Mihai Ursachi: "The Rape of Narcissus." Translated by Adam J. Sorkin. Original translation. Used by permission of the translator.

Derek Walcott: "Europa" from *Collected Poems 1948–1984*. Copyright © 1986 by Derek Walcott. Reprinted by permission of Farrar, Straus & Giroux, Inc. and Faber & Faber Ltd.

Rosanna Warren: "Turnus." First published in *Arion* (Fall '95–Winter '96). Used by permission of the author.

Vernon Watkins: "Atlas on Grass" and "The Sibyl" from *The Collected Poems of Vernon Watkins*. (Ipswich: Golgonooza Press, 1986). Copyright © 1986 by Golgonooza Press.

Sándor Weöres: "Proteus." Translated by Gábor G. Gyukics and Michael Castro. Original translation. Used by permission of the translators.

Richard Wilbur: "The Sirens" from *Ceremony and Other Poems*. Copyright © 1950 and renewed 1978 by Richard Wilbur. Reprinted by permission of Harcourt Brace & Co.

C.K. Williams: "Heracles" from *Flesh and Blood*. Copyright © 1987 by C.K. Williams. Reprinted by permission of Farrar, Straus & Giroux, Inc. and Bloodaxe Books.

William Carlos Williams: "Venus over the Desert," "Narcissus in the Desert" from *Collected Poems*, vol. II. Copyright © 1953 by William Carlos Williams. Reprinted by permission of New Directions Publishing Corp. and Carcanet Press Ltd.

Clive Wilmer: "Narcissus, Echo" from *Devotions*. Copyright © 1982 by Clive Wilmer. Used by permission of the poet.

Eleanor Wilner: "Last Words" from *Otherwise*. Copyright © 1993 by The University of Chicago Press. Used by permission of the author. "Iphigenia, Setting the Record Straight" from *Maya* (University of Massachusetts, 1979). Copyright © 1979 by Eleanor Wilner.

Yvor Winters: "Apollo and Daphne" from *Collected Poems*. Copyright © 1978 by Janet Lewis Winters. Reprinted with the permission of Ohio University Press / Swallow Press. "Chiron" from *Collected Poems*. Used by permission of Carcanet Press Ltd. and New Directions Publishing Corp.

Rod Wooden: "Orpheus." Reprinted with the permission of the poet.

William Butler Yeats: "No Second Troy," "When Helen Lived," Leda and the Swan" from *The Poems of W.B. Yeats: A New Edition*, ed. by Richard J. Finneran. Copyright © 1928 by Macmillan Publishing Co., renewed 1956 by Bertha Georgie Yeats. Reprinted with the permission of Simon & Schuster.

Adam Zagajewski: "Persephone" from *Mysticism for Beginners*. Translated by Claire Cavanaugh. Copyright © 1998 by Adam Zagajewski. Reprinted with the permission of Farrar, Straus & Giroux and Faber & Faber Ltd.

Gabriel Zaid: "Circe" from *Twentieth-Century Latin American Poetry*, a bilingual anthology, ed. Stephen Tapscott. Translated by Andrew Rosing. Copyright © 1997 by Andrew Rosing. Reprinted by permission of Stephen Tapscott.

Excerpts from Apuleuis, *The Golden Ass*. Translated by Robert Graves. Reprinted by permission of A.P. Watt Ltd. on behalf of The Trustees of The Robert Graves Copyright Trust.

Excerpts from Apollodorus. Reprinted by permission of the publishers and the Loeb Classical Library from *Apollodorus*. Translated by J.G. Frazer. Cambridge, Mass.: Harvard University Press, 1921.

Excerpt from Euripides, *Helen*. Translated by Robert Emmet Meagher. Copyright © 1986 by Robert Emmet Meagher.

Reprinted by permission of The University of Massachusetts Press.

Excerpt from Euripides, "The Bacchae," *Euripides: Helen. The Trojan Women. The Bacchae*. Translated by Neil Curry. Copyright © 1981 by Cambridge University Press. Reprinted by permission of the translator.

Excerpts from Aeschylus, "Oresteia," *The Complete Greek Tragedies*. Translated by R. Lattimore. Copyright © 1953 by The University of Chicago Press. Reprinted by permission of The University of Chicago Press.

Excerpt from Euripides, "Alcestis," *The Complete Greek Tragedies*. Translated by R. Lattimore. Copyright © 1955 by The University of Chicago Press. Reprinted by permission of The University of Chicago Press.

Excerpts from Athanassakis, *Homeric Hymns*. Copyright © 1976 by The John Hopkins University Press. Reprinted by permission of The John Hopkins University Press.

Excerpts from Athanassakis, Hesiod, *Theogony, Works and Days, Shield*. Copyright © 1983 by The John Hopkins University Press. Reprinted by permission of The John Hopkins University Press.

Excerpts from *The Odyssey of Homer* by Allen Mandelbaum. Translation copyright © 1990 by Allen Mandelbaum. Used by permission of Bantam Books, a div. of Random House, Inc.

Excerpts from *The Aeneid of Virgil* by Allen Mandelbaum. Translation copyright © 1971 by Allen Mandelbaum. Used by permission of Bantam Books, a division of Random House, Inc.

Excerpts from *The Metamorphoses* by Publius Ovidius Naso. Translated by Horace Gregory. Translation copyright © 1958 by The Viking Press, Inc., renewed c 1986 by Patrick Bolton Gregory. Used by permission of Viking Penguin, a division of Penguin Putnam, Inc.

Excerpts from *The Iliad* by Homer. Translated by Robert Fagles. Translation copyright © 1990 by Robert Fagles. Introduction and Notes copyright © 1990 by Bernard Knox. Used by permission of Viking Penguin, a division of Penguin Putnam, Inc.

Excerpts from *Heroides* by Ovid. Translated by Harold Isbell. (Penguin Classics, 1990) Translation © Harold Isbell, 1990. Reproduced by permission of Penguin Books Ltd.

Excerpt from *Sophocles: Three Tragedies*. Translated by H.D.F. Kitto (1962). Copyright © Oxford University Press, 1962. Reprinted by permission of Oxford University Press.